QUEER VOICES FROM JAPAN

Photo courtesy of Mitsuhashi Junko.

QUEER VOICES FROM JAPAN

First-Person Narratives from Japan's Sexual Minorities

Edited by Mark McLelland,
Katsuhiko Suganuma, and James Welker

With a Foreword
by Donald Richie

LEXINGTON BOOKS

A division of
ROWMAN & LITTLEFIELD PUBLISHERS, INC.
Lanham • Boulder • New York • Toronto • Plymouth, UK

LEXINGTON BOOKS

A division of Rowman & Littlefield Publishers, Inc.
A wholly owned subsidiary of The Rowman & Littlefield Publishing Group, Inc.
4501 Forbes Boulevard, Suite 200
Lanham, MD 20706

Estover Road
Plymouth PL6 7PY
United Kingdom

British Library Cataloguing in Publication Information Available

Library of Congress Cataloging-in-Publication Data

McLelland, Mark.
 Queer voices from Japan : first person narratives from Japan's sexual minorities /
Mark McLelland, Katsuhiko Suganuma, and James Welker.
  p. cm.—(Studies in modern Japan)
 Includes bibliographical references.
 ISBN-13: 978-0-7391-2159-7 (pbk. : alk. paper)
 ISBN-10: 0-7391-2159-6 (pbk. : alk. paper)
 ISBN-13: 978-0-7391-0865-9 (cloth : alk. paper)
 ISBN-10: 0-7391-0865-4 (cloth : alk. paper)
 1. Gays—Japan—Biography. 2. Sexual minorities—Japan. I. Suganuma,
Katsuhiko. II. Welker, James. III. Title.
 HQ76.3.J3M37 2007
 306.76'6092252—dc22
 [B]   2006038565

Printed in the United States of America

CONTENTS

FOREWORD

Recorded history fails to hear quite a number of voices, mostly those of the many minorities, including the queer ones. This is because the interests of history are, like most interests, vested. It is the majority that acts and speaks, almost always to its own advantage. As the English historian E. A. Freeman observed as early as 1886: "History is past politics and politics is present history."

Nonetheless, minority voices can be resuscitated. In our own times a number of such retrievals are occurring. The voices of submerged ethnic populations (Native American, Ainu, etc.) are becoming audible, those of the marginalized (black, female, etc.) now speak clearly, and many a minority has found a platform from which to speak.

That this platform is, perforce, political is to be expected. Without the power that goes with politics, the interested party would risk being again forced into the soundless dark. Those who complain that the long suppressed voices are strident fail to understand the pressure of silence.

In Japan there remain in the political arena a number of largely unheard voices—the proscribed *burakumin* "class," those of "mixed blood" descent, the sexual minorities. At the same time, a number of minority articulations do exist—it is just that they are paid no political attention. Drawing them to our notice is the act that enables audibility.

In the case of the queer voices, which form the content of this collection, these have been available in marginalized Japanese publications but have never been disseminated, never been translated. This indeed is the first international outing of the postwar Japanese queer experience.

The majority of these interviews, essays, memoirs, and roundtable discussions come from the back issues of specialized publications that the Japanese know as *hentai zasshi*—perverted publications—which have long had a minority readership. Originally purchased only in specialized venues, thought somehow allied to the printed-porno trade, these were regarded as hobby magazines, as though they were akin to afghan-making or fly-fishing. At the same time their reputation as perverted kept them off the wider bookstore shelves.

Now the term *hentai* has been made recently respectable through wider nonpejorative use. Indeed, it is now so commonly heard that the editors of this translated collection feel that an English translation of the term would be "queer," another pejorative term recently defanged. (Not entirely, however. A newspaper for which I write recently edited an article of mine to remove the word "queer," which I was using in its homosexual sense. When I complained, the editor asked if I didn't know that it was pejorative and that I was encouraging prejudice. At which I could only ask if he did not know that it is no longer pejorative but academic.)

Of course, such word play would not have been necessary had not Japan been so swayed by foreign influences. When the country was still its traditional self, many were the differences from its present state. Among these was that few thought it politically expedient to mess with the sex lives of citizens. Homosexuality was not necessarily thought problematic. No official connection was made between gender and sexual preference. There were codes of ethics for those preferring males just as there were for those preferring females.

Probably there were political reasons for what we can now see only as liberality. Certainly, interest in other, younger warriors made for better warriors all round; certainly, priests who had acolytes made for more occupied priests. In general, however, same-sex love was socially approved (or ignored) to a degree regarded as unthinkable after 1868, the Meiji period, when Japan elected to imitate the West.

One of the results of this imitation was the incorporation of a Judeo-Christian bias that stigmatized homosexuality. There were no enduring laws promulgated against the practice in Japan as there had been almost everywhere else, but an imported prejudice became apparent, and still is. One of those quoted in this volume refers to "the disease of fellowship with the same sex." This phrase would certainly never have occurred to an author in Japan prior to the Meiji Era.

Of all the damage done by prejudice against homosexuals, perhaps the most grievous has been the internalization of homophobia. The practitioner becomes the sufferer, and his already apparent alienation is rendered double by his distaste for what prejudice has done. This tone is clearly audible in these postwar voices.

At the same time, however, Japan has also had those who speak out clearly, who question, and who complain. One of the most articulate even ran for the House of Councilors. He ran in 1971 and was still running in 1995. He wanted to know why there were no representatives from "oppressed" groups in the Diet. "Liberty and equality for whom?" he asked.

This takes an amount of bravery in Japan, where oppressed groups are even more closeted than those in other countries. And in making more audible those queer voices, both male and female, who have articulated their postwar experiences, the editors of this volume have contributed to a more sophisticated understanding of not only this segment but all of Japanese society, what it is like, and how it works.

Donald Richie

ACKNOWLEDGMENTS

This book would not have been possible were it not for a generous grant made to Mark McLelland by the Australian Research Council in 2003 when he was a research fellow in the University of Queensland's Centre for Critical and Cultural Studies. The grant made possible several trips to Japan in search of the archival material that comprises seven of the early chapters in this collection. A smaller grant from the University of Queensland was invaluable in commissioning both a research assistant and professional translators when the body of work and its complexity seemed about to overwhelm the editors and their small band of volunteers.

We would like to thank all the translators. Takashi Fujita and particularly Wim Lunsing deserve thanks for putting up with our short deadlines and limited budgets. We are also especially indebted to Micah Auerback, Todd Henry, and Joseph Hawkins, who lent their valuable expertise free of charge. We would also like to thank David d'Heilly for allowing us to reproduce his existing translation. Ishida Hitoshi, Murakami Takanori, and others connected with Chūō University's Postwar Japan Transgender Study Association must also be thanked for their assistance in tracking down hard-to-find records of queer life from the early postwar period, for making their own archives available, and for assisting with introductions to helpful persons.

The editors are also extremely grateful to the all of the individuals who generously allowed us to translate and reproduce their words and experiences here without financial reward, trusting that our intentions were good and this project worthwhile. If it were not for their willingness to share their stories, *Queer Voices from Japan* would not have been possible. While their names are also in the table of contents, they bear repeating here. We would like to thank Sawabe Hitomi, Toyama Hitomi, Hisada Megumi, Izumo Marou, Tsuzura Yoshiko, Hara Minako, Ikeda Kumiko, Hirano Hiroaki, Ōtsuka Takashi, Oikawa Kenji, and Akira the Hustler.

For some of these individuals, this generosity required revisiting words they penned or spoke as many as two decades ago, and recalling experiences even further back. Several of the chapters were written especially for this volume, and we are most grateful that the authors were willing to share both painful and pleasant experiences—a grand thank you to Noriko Kohashi (who wrote her contribution in English), Sunagawa Hideki, Mitsuhashi Junko, and Takafumi Fujio. Many of these individuals carefully answered sometimes numerous requests for clarification as the translators worked and the editors reviewed the translations. In some cases these individuals painstakingly reviewed the English translations, offering suggestions for improvement and pointing out errors. The responsibility for any remaining errors, however, naturally remains with the editors and translators.

It was at Hara Minako's suggestion (*insistence* is perhaps a better word) that we even considered that it might be possible to get permission to include selections from the priceless *Onna wo ai suru onnatachi no monogatari* (Stories of women who love women). Her supportive introduction of James Welker to Sawabe Hitomi, the driving force behind the book, made this happen and enriched this volume's coverage of lesbian lives of the 1970s and 1980s. While the editors are aware that there are many other texts and voices that could just as well have been presented here, it was not always possible to gain introductions to copyright holders or to negotiate permission to translate existing work, and we remain deeply indebted to all those who gave us permission to make their thoughts, their words, and their experiences available to an English-reading audience.

Regarding the early postwar material reproduced in chapters 2 through 8, the earliest of these narratives was published in 1949 and the latest in 1955. The magazines that first published these stories as well as the publishing houses that they were affiliated with no longer exist. Furthermore, the majority of the authors and participants are identified by pseudonyms only. After making some initial inquiries it became apparent that it would be impossible to track down copyright holders for these texts. However, given the extreme importance of these stories and the fact that this material has largely been overlooked by both Japanese and Western historians of Japan's postwar culture, we decided to go ahead and make this material available in English. In so doing we were heartened by Kabiya Kazuhiko's statement in his 1955 description of contemporary "gay bars" (chapter 7) that "I wanted to leave an accurate record of the particular manners and customs (*fūzoku*) of the postwar gay bars for future historians." Kabiya was clearly writing for posterity, and we are extremely grateful for his efforts which have made available to us a rare glimpse of postwar gay life. Likewise, we are also respectful of and grateful for the other life experiences contained in these early narratives and would hope that any participants still living would understand our motivation in helping preserve these records of valuable human experience. If anyone reading this volume has information as to the whereabouts of the copyright holders of the original texts, kindly contact the editors.

Finally, Jotaro Arimori was of invaluable assistance to James Welker in clarifying the meanings of Japanese texts and offering astute translations and rephrasings of his own, both as Welker translated the articles he was responsible for and as he worked on the editing of the volume as a whole.

A NOTE ON JAPANESE TERMINOLOGY

Throughout the text we have reproduced Japanese names in the traditional Japanese order: that is, surname first. In the case of Japanese people who either live in the West or who write in English, we have followed their wishes in representing their names in Western order, that is, given name first—these individuals are Jotaro Arimori, Takashi

Fujita, Noriko Kohashi, and Katsuhiko Suganuma. Japanese text uses neither capitalization nor italicization and the use of these features in Romanized Japanese is always complex. We have tended to limit the use of initial capitalization to Japanese personal and place names and to the names of organizations. Japanese terms that occur in the translations, as well as book and journal titles, have been italicized. Macrons designating long vowels have been employed in all Romanization, except in names and terms commonly rendered in English without them, such as city names and historical period titles.

INTRODUCTION: RE(CLAIMING) JAPAN'S QUEER PAST

Mark McLelland, Katsuhiko Suganuma, and James Welker

WHY "QUEER" VOICES?

Recently there has been much debate about a process sometimes referred to as "global queering," the idea that originally Western (that is,
North American) sexual identity categories such as lesbian, gay, bisexual,
and transgender are now circulating globally and being taken up by sexual
minority populations in locations as diverse and distinct as Bangkok, Bom-
bay, and Tokyo. Theorists associated with this position argue that the result
is a "gay world"—an emerging global subculture in which a transnational
class of homosexuals have more in common across national and continental
boundaries than they do with others in their own geographically defined
locations. Other researchers have been more tentative in their analysis of
this global spread of originally American identity categories. William Leap
and Tom Boellstorff, for instance, argue that the term "gay" should always
be treated as "polyvalent and contingent," and although they find use for
the term "as a referential shorthand for a broad range of same-sex desires,
practices, and subjectivities," they do so "without presuming that this usage establishes a universal ethnographic referent" (2003: 4).

In this collection, we recognize that Japan has, since opening to the
West in the Meiji period (1868–1912), been a part of this ongoing pro-

cess of globalization, in the sexual realm as much as in the economic. However, as will become apparent through the course of this introduction, Japan was by no means a passive recipient of influences from the West, and Western sexological discourse, like much else, was only ever selectively borrowed and strategically deployed to enunciate very nuanced Japanese understandings of sexual diversity. The purpose of this collection, which introduces a wide range of texts discussing events taking place from as early as the 1920s until the present, is to give some sense of this long history of development and at least gesture toward the wide variety of subject positions and experiences that have been given voice by members of "nonstandard" sexual minorities in Japan. Accordingly, throughout the collection we have sometimes left untranslated (and generally include reference to) the specific, local Japanese terminology that the original writers used to describe themselves and their interactions in order to underline the fact that homophones such as the Japanese *gei* and the English "gay" do not always have the same referent or nuance.

Despite having emphasized the necessity of paying close attention to local usages, we have, as a matter of convenience, settled upon the term "queer" as a useful rubric for discussing together a wide range of Japanese same-sex desiring and transgender roles, practices, and identities. We do use the term cautiously, aware that the connections we are making between the communities and individuals represented in this book may not be made by members of those communities themselves. However, there is good reason to use a term like "queer" since it is a very apt translation for an indigenous Japanese term, *hentai*, which has long been in circulation in Japanese popular culture, grouping together a wide range of sexually variant practices or identities that are considered "queer" or "perverse" from a so-called mainstream or "normal" perspective. As discussed in detail below, as early as the 1920s in Japan, there had already developed a genre of journals and magazines that took as their focus *hentai seiyoku* or "queer desire." This genre was to burst once more onto the publishing scene with renewed vigor in the immediate postwar period, and we are able to present several examples translated into English for the first time here.

Although *hentai*, meaning (sexually) perverse, queer, or strange, has historically had a largely pejorative nuance (McLelland 2006), there are examples of it being deployed in a more playful sense since at least 1970. For instance, in 1970 author Akiyama Masami published his *Hentaigaku nyūmon*, which can be nicely translated as "Introduction to queer studies." While Akiyama was mainly interested in heterosexual "perversions" such as S/M, he does include discussions of lesbianism and cross-dressing and playfully offers readers a *hentai* test aimed at gauging their own level of perversity. More recently, in 1991, as part of the popular *Bessatsu takarajima* series put out by the magazine *Takarajima*, a special collection of interviews and investigative reports on Japanese sexual subcultures entitled *Hentai-san ga iku* (There goes Mr. or Ms. Queer; *Bessatsu takarajima* 1991) was published, which again was primarily heterosexual in focus. In 2000, the term was appropriated by Fushimi Noriaki, one of Japan's leading gay writers and critics, for the title of a special feature on gay salarymen—*Hentai suru sarariiman* (Salarymen doing queer)—contained in a magazine he created, *Queer Japan*. Indeed, Fushimi himself has pointed out how close both queer and *hentai* are in meaning, and in 2003 he released a collection of interviews with a wide range of sex and gender nonconformists entitled *Hentai (kuia) nyūmon* (An introduction to *hentai* [queer]) where he uses the terms interchangeably. It is with an awareness, then, of the long history of the Japanese term *hentai* to describe sexually variant identities and practices that we use the English term "queer" as an approximation for a range of sexual and gender-variant identities, practices, and communities that have come into being in Japan over the course of the last century.

However, despite the comparative freedom with which the Japanese media have discussed sexual diversity, until very recently there has been little sustained academic or community work undertaken into what might be termed queer history. Despite the fact that written records are plentiful, as will become clear throughout the course of this book, prior to the 1990s, little coordinated effort was made by academic institutions or gay, lesbian, bisexual, or transgender individuals and groups to gather this material together, found archives, and begin to construct and publicize this history. This lack of a history is not a problem facing Japanese queers alone; Michael Warner points out that even in the relatively privileged context of the United States, lesbians, gays, and other queer people lack "the institutions for common memory and generational transmission around which straight culture is built" (Warner 1999:

51). Unlike mainstream communities whose histories constitute official narratives that are passed on via families, churches, schools, and community organizations, new generations of queers often have to reinvent themselves. Because of the stigma and shame that queer people face, official bodies cannot be relied upon to record the history of these communities, and the result is that they are simply "hidden from history."[1] All too often, what historical materials do exist are in the form of police records, trial documents, and medical reports—evidence created by those outside and hostile to queer lifestyles and which offer one-sided, distorted accounts. It is no surprise that young queers in Japan and elsewhere still come of age wondering if they are the "only ones" with these transgressive desires.

Having said this, uncovering material relating to the experience and history of queer people in Japan is not difficult since Japan is an immensely literate society with a great love of (and industry supporting) the print media, and both the popular and niche press have long interested themselves in issues to do with queer sexuality. Also, while not enjoying the widespread institutional support that is possible for queer research in some Anglophone institutions, the situation facing queer researchers in Japan is, in comparison with other parts of Asia, not unfavorable. Tokyo's Chūō University, in particular, through its Research Institute for the Social History of Japanese Transgender in Postwar Japan (Sengo Nihon Toransujendā Shakai Rekishi Kenkyūkai), has begun to archive, research, and publish on material related to the history of cross-dressing and transgender in Japan (as well as closely related topics such as male and female homosexuality). So far this work has mainly appeared in their in-house journal and other university-sponsored publications, but it has been of great benefit to us in bringing together the current collection. We hope that by making these translations available to English readers for the first time, students of Japan worldwide will be encouraged to devote more time and resources to elaborating Japanese queer history and making their own findings widely available.

In making our selections from the enormous archive of material available we have been guided by a number of factors. Firstly, we felt it important that the memoirs, interviews, and roundtables we translated should, as far as we can ascertain, present *first-person* narratives, that is, represent the voices of individuals speaking from direct experience of queer desire. We wanted to represent the viewpoints of what in Japanese are referred to as *tōjisha*, that is, "persons (directly) concerned," and not the opinions or reflections of individuals outside their respective communities. While this was relatively unproblematic with more recent material written by individuals that are known to us personally or who were recommended to us by members of Japan's contemporary queer community, the veracity of the early postwar material was more difficult to evaluate. We have, however, tried to represent a flavor of the diversity of surviving narratives and have selected those accounts that seem to us to cast light not just upon the individual circumstances of the authors or participants but to offer insights into the manner in which queer desire was comprehended and institutionalized in the wider society.

We have also attempted to be as comprehensive as possible and to ensure that space is given to the voices of transgenders and women as well as to those of men. It has not always been possible to achieve the right balance since far less has been written about the experience of women and we were unable to receive permission to translate some important lesbian sources. Again, our motivation in bringing together this collection is not to provide any kind of definitive statement about Japanese queer history, but rather to draw attention to the vast and so-far underutilized body of material that exists in the hope that others will be inspired to make more of this history available.

In the remaining pages of the introduction, we will outline the changing paradigms that have structured how a range of queer sexualities came to be constituted and understood as distinct categories of sexual experience so as to situate the texts chosen in their broader cultural and historical context.

HISTORICAL BACKGROUND TO JAPAN'S QUEER CULTURES

When reflecting on the history of sexuality in the Japanese context, it is enlightening to consider that same-sex sexuality, particularly as practiced between men, has only comparatively recently come to be considered problematic and been consigned to the "queer" side of a "normal"/"abnormal" division. During the Edo period (1603–1868), for instance, there was no necessary connection made between gender and sexual preference because men, samurai in particular, were able to engage in both same- and opposite-sex affairs. Same-sex relationships were governed by a code of ethics described as *nanshoku* (male eroticism) or *shudō* (the way of youths) in the context of which elite men were able to pursue boys and young men who had not yet undergone their coming-of-age ceremonies, as well as transgender males of all ages from the lower classes who worked as actors and prostitutes.

The codes governing male homosexual practice during the Edo era were already of ancient heritage and were imported (according to received opinion) from China, where, like much else adapted from this ancient empire, male homosexuality was understood as part of a civilizing process. The main paradigm within which male homosexual relationships took place was age related, tracing its origins back to Buddhist monasteries in the Heian period (794–1185), where adult monks could establish sexual relationships with young child acolytes known as *chigo*—a term that has lived on well into the modern era as a referent for a young boy lover.[2]

Perhaps surprisingly, given the prominence that "lesbian love" was to achieve in male pornography in the post–Pacific War years in Japan, there is little representation of women's same-sex desire in Edo-period culture (and scant mention of it in earlier times). Although a few instances of same-sex sexual acts between women are recorded in literary, artistic, and other sources, such acts were not codified into a *dō* or "way" of loving, and there is little discussion of (or terminology for) specific roles adopted by women (Leupp 1998). Significantly, while *nanshoku*, made up of the characters for "man" and "eroticism," was a general term covering a variety of forms of love practiced between men, *joshoku*, made up of the characters for "woman" and "eroticism," actually referred to love relationships between *men* and women. No concept existed at this time to refer in a general sense to women's same-sex love, and there was no way of cognitively linking both male and female "homosexuality." As a consequence, in lieu of referencing Japanese history, some prewar attempts by men to historicize female same-sex love turned to the story of Sappho because "female same-sex love is simply not visible in the [Japanese] historical record" (Yasuda 1935: 147).

THE DEVELOPMENT OF EARLY-MODERN SEXOLOGY

The closing decades of the nineteenth century, a period in which the new field of sexology was being widely elaborated in European medical circles, was also a time in which Japanese intellectuals were traveling to and borrowing extensively from the West. One of the most important intellectuals who facilitated the spread of foreign ideas about sexuality via his writing was the novelist Mori Ōgai, a military doctor who had spent four years as a student in Berlin. He published a wide range of articles on sexual issues, and these became one of the main conduits through which the categories devised by German sexologists such as Richard von Krafft-Ebing[3] were disseminated into Japanese.

Ōgai was writing at precisely the time that *seiyoku* (sexual appetite or desire) was beginning to be elucidated as a factor behind character development in Japanese fiction, and his novel, *Vita Sexualis*, published in 1909, is one of the first instances to take the "sexuality" of its protagonist as its central theme (Reichert 2006).

The elaboration of a realm of sexuality led to the designation of normal (*seijō*) and perverse (*ijō*) forms of sexuality and, accordingly, people. Indeed, from the end of the Meiji period, drawing upon theorists such as Sigmund Freud, discussions of "perverse" or "queer" desire (*hentai seiyoku*) began to circulate in popular magazines that advocated the improvement of public morals in pursuit of "civilization and enlightenment"—a popular slogan of the period. In particular, the previous discourse of *nanshoku* and the transgender practices associated with male prostitution were portrayed as feudal, incompatible with "civilized morality," and something that ought to be eradicated.

Although the exact date of the introduction of the concept remains unclear, during the Taisho period (1912–1926) *dōseiai* (same-sex love) emerged as the most popular of a handful of terms approximating a translation of the European concept of "homosexuality." For the first time in Japanese a category became available within which a variety of female-female same-sex romantic and physical relationships could be grouped and through which it became possible to speak of both male and female same-sex desire as dimensions of the same phenomenon. Both male-male and female-female same-sex practices were considered perverse, the pathologization of the latter most likely due to a combination of several prominent love suicides in 1911 of female couples that occasioned widespread public discussion on female-female relationships and the pathological tenor of imported discourse on homosexuality. Yet, there was a qualitative difference between them in that same-sex love between women was considered to be more psychological, emotional, and spiritual, whereas men's desires were considered more carnal. As a consequence, *dōseiai* tended to be used more in relation to female same-sex love. In part, this was an accident of the translation of "homosexual" as *dōseiai*, since *ai*, the character chosen to represent love, was more emotional in tone than *koi*, an alternative character that had a stronger erotic charge (Furukawa 1994). This "love" between members of the same sex seemed to describe well the widely reported schoolgirl crushes that occurred in the dormitories of Japan's new educational establishments for girls. Spoken of as "S" relationships in which the "S" stood for *shōjo* (girl), sister, or even sex, these crushes, albeit considered morbid, were not taken too seriously since they were widely regarded as asexual and temporary aberrations, something that the girls would outgrow. Although the association of female same-sex love with the poet Sappho and the island of Lesbos was widely recognized (*Hentai shiryō* 1928: 73; Curran and Welker 2005: 67–68), the *katakana* version of the noun "lesbian" (*resubian* or *rezubian*)[4] did not become current until the early 1960s, making it difficult to speak of "lesbian" identities in the first half of the twentieth century.

In spite of social pathologization, some women did indeed have same-sex relationships beyond adolescence. While most records of these relationships, as noted above, are limited to often-scandalous newspaper accounts, several writers wrote publicly about their relationships with women in coded and not-so-coded terms. Some of these women who first became prominent in the prewar era have been reclaimed as "lesbian foresisters" (*senpai rezubian-tachi*) by contemporary *rezubian* activists looking for their cultural roots. In recent decades, probably the most frequently written about female couples in this context are feminist activist Hiratsuka Raichō and artist Otake Kōkichi, "girls' novel" (*shōjo shōsetsu*) writer Yoshiya Nobuko and her secretary Monma Chiyo, and translator of Russian literature Yuasa Yoshiko and writer Miyamoto Yuriko. Of the three couples, only Yoshiya and Monma spent their lives together. While Yuasa was among a number of women who at one time or another had a romantic relationship with writer and Seitōsha member Tamura Toshiko, it was Miyamoto (née Chūjo) who was the great love of Yuasa's life. Yuasa and Miyamoto lived together for seven years both in Tokyo and Moscow until Miyamoto met and married writer Miyamoto Kenji, leaving Yuasa to spend the rest of her life largely alone. Although the word *rezubian* may not have been available to her while she was involved with Miyamoto, in an interview late in her life, introduced in the opening chapter of this collection as "A Visit with Yuasa Yoshiko," she concurred that she was indeed a *rezubian*.

Although the sexological journals were working within a medical framework that pathologized "abnormal" sexual desires, they did offer readers the opportunity to write in and describe their experiences in the hope that expert advice might shed light on their condition. One unforeseen side effect of this process was that the perverse themselves were given a voice. Also, the experts who wrote these articles and analyzed the perverse desires of their correspondents did so in a popular medium that appealed to a readership far wider than the medical community. Although Meiji-period sexology had been the province of the elite, the Taisho period saw what Matsuzawa Goichi describes as a *"hentai* boom" (1997: 55), the first of several explosions of interest in perverse sexuality that were to sweep the Japanese media over the next half century. Indeed, the perverse press is best understood in relation to the wider cultural phenomenon known as *ero-guro nansensu*, or "erotic grotesque nonsense," which was prominent in the popular culture of the late 1920s (Roden 1990).

However, in contrast to the relatively open discussion of sexual matters in the 1920s, Japan's descent into militarism in the early 1930s saw the government tighten its hold on sexual discourse and practice. Japan's escalating conflict with China beginning in 1931, and its withdrawal from the League of Nations in 1933, ushered in a period of government repression that sought to mobilize the nation as a whole to support the war effort. One result was an increasing didacticism on the part of the nation's leaders and attempts to bring the media under direct state control. Japan's fifteen-year war, as it is sometimes referred to by historians, was characterized by increasing state surveillance of and interference in the personal lives of the Japanese population. At this time, Japan shared with European nations, particularly Nazi Germany, an interest in "race improvement," and both the state and the media were proactively engaged in promulgating eugenicist policies.[5]

One result of this discourse was an increased polarity in gender roles that resulted in women being cast as mothers whose purpose was to breed sons for the empire, and men being regarded as fighting machines, part of the national body. Women, who lacked political agency, were particularly constrained by this system. The most important role for women—that of "good wife, wise mother" (*ryōsai kenbo*)—was actively promoted by government policies, media reports, and social pressure. Indeed, the government went so far as to introduce eugenic policies to ensure maximum reproduction: Women were encouraged to *umeyo fuyaseyo* (bear children and multiply). Feminist group Seitōsha founder Hiratsuka Raichō was among the more prominent early twentieth-century feminists who later married, had children, and, in her own public and private life, ultimately "upheld the dominant gender ideology of her time" (Tamanoi 1999: 289), much to the disappointment of Yuasa Yoshiko, who saw this as capitulation to the system (Sawabe [1990] 1996: 156).

However, despite the fact that the ideology of the period was relentlessly heterosexual and pronatal, actual social organization became increasingly homosocial as the war progressed. Throughout the 1930s, greater numbers of men were drafted into the military, thus delaying the marriage of bachelors and separating married men from their wives, thereby encouraging the development of greater intimacy between men. At the same time unmarried women moved to take the place of these men in the factories and other industries. One of the results of this separation between the sexes was what Isolde Standish has, in relation to films of the period, referred to as "the death of romance" (2000: 51)—since romantic love between a man and a woman was seen as incompatible with the "heroic masculinity" demanded by the war effort. Standish points out how in Japanese films of the early 1940s, "women were marginalized if not deleted from the narrative completely" (2000: 53). The result was that "the underlying text inherent in the images of masculinity dominating Japanese films of the late 1930s and early 1940s was a discourse of sexual repression" in which men's romantic love for women was displaced by a "homosocial brotherhood" (2000: 51).

There is a great deal of evidence pointing to the pivotal role that the Second World War played in the Allied (particularly the United States) context in facilitating and promoting the development of same-sex intimacy and identity among homosocial groups of men and women. However, this process did not take place to the same extent in Japan since, as the selections presented in this volume dealing with wartime homosexual activity illustrate, the category "the homosexual" was not yet clearly cognized in Japanese popular culture.[6] Rather, homosexual behavior was still seen as a potential shared by men in general and an understandable consequence of sex segregation. While Japan's militarism did not in itself contribute toward the development of fixed homosexual identities, there is considerable circumstantial evidence suggesting that homoeroticism and, in certain contexts, explicit homosexual interaction was encouraged by the process of sex segregation that accelerated as Japan's position in the war gradually worsened. There were, for instance, many media accounts of "love between comrades" (sen'yūai) where male homosocial bonding was shown to have encouraged feats of great chivalry, self-sacrifice, and valor on the battlefield. Of course, these official narratives contained no mention of more physical relationships since, due to the severe censorship exercised, among other ways, via the government's control over paper rations, there were few opportunities to discuss sexuality outside of the eugenicist paradigms endorsed by the state.

However, accounts published in the early postwar years do suggest that relationships between senior soldiers and young recruits sometimes had a sexual element. One text dating from 1952 and entitled "Homosexuality on the battlefront" points out that "veteran officers choose for their orderlies soldiers who are beautiful youths [bishōnen]" and that these boys were used as a "substitute for women" and an "outlet for sexual desire" (seiyoku no hakeguchi) on the front line (McLelland 2005: 46). Ōgiya Afu, a prolific postwar commentator on male homosexuality, went so far as to draw a parallel between the apparent "need" for prostitutes, known euphemistically as "comfort women,"[7] and the "unavoidable attraction" that older soldiers felt for the increasingly young "beautiful male youths" who were being drafted at the war's end. He speaks of these relationships being accorded a certain degree of visibility.

One account offered in full translation in chapter 2 of this volume is entitled "My Career in *Danshoku*" and was published in *Fūzoku kurabu* in 1954. It details the author's homosexual career from age nine when he was seduced by a clerk in his father's store. It was not, however, until he was drafted into the infantry and sent to China that he discovered what he describes as his first "homosexual partner" (*homo no aite*), a corporal named Suda, who made him his sleeping partner. This account tends to confirm other reports that mention the propensity for more senior officers to use their position to make sexual demands upon their juniors, but of particular interest here is the manner in which the corporal "responded brazenly" to rumors about his sexual entreaties, and other men began to respond in a similar manner to the extent to that *danshoku* reportedly "became all the rage" throughout the squadron. The use of the term *danshoku* here reflects how the borrowing and adapting of terms and concepts to name queer sexual practices and desires was not limited to Western languages. Gregory Pflugfelder notes that during the Meiji period the Chinese characters that had been used in the preceding centuries to describe male-male love and pronounced *nanshoku* "came increasingly to be read as *danshoku*, a reflection not only of broader phonetic and orthographic changes but also of the growing obsolescence of Edo-period erotic culture" (1999: 184n114).[8] Hence, the Meiji period introduction of new (imported) understandings of sexuality did not preclude the reclamation of more traditional terms and concepts such as *nanshoku/danshoku* and *chigo*; rather, these newly interpreted "traditional" terms were often deployed alongside Western sexological terminology.

While the relationship described in this narrative may have initially been coerced, the author does seem to maintain positive feelings toward his time in the army and he narrates these events with some nostalgia. In contrast, an account published in rival magazine *Kitan kurabu* in 1953 offers a more disturbing description of male homosexual relations during wartime in which coercion played a greater role. Entitled "Nostalgia for My Time in the Army," reproduced in chapter 3, the author of this account details how, in the closing months of the war, he chose as his orderly a mild-mannered, attractive youth who had been a student at Tokyo University. However, there was something about the passive young man that provoked a sadistic response in the officer, who began to physically torment him and take photographs as mementoes of the abuse. The author's motivation in publishing the essay is the hope that his former orderly will read it and "come racing" back to him so that they might reestablish a relationship on more "democratic" terms.

While both the accounts of wartime homosexuality introduced above tend to confirm traditional paradigms of senior/junior, active/passive roles, and in so doing reinforce rather than challenge the predominant gender ideology at work in imperial Japan, there is one account, also offered here in full, which seriously disrupts this gender system. Entitled *"Minyak Kelapa—A* Fragrant Breeze of Homosexuality," published in *Fūzoku kagaku* in 1954 and contained here in chapter 4, the essay details the sexual relationship that developed between a young bed-ridden Japanese soldier and the sixteen-year-old Indonesian recruit whose job it was to tend him while he was stationed in the jungles of Sumatra. The narrator, who was himself only nineteen at the time, speaks of the debilitating effect that malaria had had upon his muscles and how Tora, the young Javanese boy, would come to massage him every day with coconut oil. While these massage sessions were at first purely recuperative, they quickly became "half play" and Tora would entwine himself around the author's body like a snake. The author soon finds himself responding to the lithe body of the boy, which reminds him of a female panther. Although this relationship might have been viewed, as were other accounts, as simply a "release valve" for sexual desire, the author explicitly disavows this explanation, going so far as to confess the central role that Tora's daily visits came to occupy in his life, replacing both his love for his family and his commitment to Japan's imperial project.

Given the extreme indoctrination that recruits underwent upon induction into the Japanese army and the strength of the ideology underpinning the *ie,* or family system, itself a microcosm of the nation in imperial Japan, the author's lack of interest in the war effort and his apparent lack of regard for his biological family in favor of his relationship with the Javanese boy is quite stunning. Of particular interest, too, is the racial crossing in this relationship. While the senior/junior, Japanese/colonial dualities could so easily have played themselves out in a story of coercion and abuse (as they did so horrifically in the "comfort women" system), this story offers us an account of mutual love between men based on equality—a comparatively rare occurrence in prewar (and early postwar) narratives in which so much male homosexual interaction was still hierarchically structured and role based.

The homosocial environment of the military clearly provided opportunities for the development of intense emotional and physical bonds between men, and a similar situation might be expected to have developed between the women in Japan's factory dormitories and other all-female spaces. One commentator, for example, even suggested in 1927 that same-sex desire often occurred when two females were together in the same room (Akatsu 1927: 173), and indeed there had been many reports in the prewar press of "unnatural" occurrences taking place in such locations, although same-sex love between schoolgirls at times attracted the most interest (Hiruma 2003: 16–18). The mid-1930s saw suicide again generate a surge in public interest in female same-sex love, this time with a particular focus on masculine women sometimes referred to as "dandy beauties" (*dansō no reijin*) (Yasuda 1935: 146; see also Robertson 1999). Yet, while writer Yoshiya Nobuko and Monma Chiyo's relationship, which began in 1923 and lasted until Yoshiya's death in 1973 and thus spanned the war years, is well known, other accounts detailing same-sex love between less public women during the height of the wartime era, if any exist, have not yet surfaced.

THE RAPID DEVELOPMENT OF POSTWAR QUEER CULTURE

After the repression of the war years, a new sexual culture arose surprisingly quickly after Japan's defeat and occupation by U.S. forces. The immediate postwar period witnessed a loosening of traditional sex and gender ideologies, resulting in an endorsement of "curiosity seeking" (*ryōki*) in sexual matters and a less judgmental attitude taken in the popular press toward homosexuality and other nonprocreative acts.

One example of this loosening up was the development of a *kasutori* (low-grade, pulp)[9] culture characterized by "a commercial world dominated by sexually oriented entertainments and a veritable cascade of pulp literature" (Dower 2000: 148). For instance, a great deal of information about sexual practices, framed as "sex education" for married couples, was disseminated via magazines entitled *Modern Couple*

(*Shin fūfu*) and *Perfecting Coupledom* (*Kanzen naru fūfu*). What was new about this popular discourse about sex was that it discredited the previous eugenicist model which had reduced sex to procreation, describing it as a patriotic duty to breed new citizens, and instead situated sexual pleasure at the heart of the marital relationship. Practices such as kissing, necking, and petting were given detailed coverage and pamphlets describing these terms newly transliterated into the *katakana* script were often included as free inserts in these magazines.[10] Another important innovation in these magazines is what Akita Masami (2005) describes as a turn toward psychology. While previous sexual education (such as it existed) had all been about establishing "correct" positions for intercourse, the new magazines stressed that there was more to sex than proper technique—there was also a world of fantasy.

Various *kasutori* magazines contained many sex-themed articles dealing with sexual practices other than those considered "normal," which had much in common with the prewar fad for publications specializing in "erotic, grotesque nonsense" (*Bessatsu taiyō* 1997: 198–99; Fukushima 1987: 92–93). Developing out of these fly-by-night publications, from the early 1950s, a range of more high-brow magazines appeared that allowed readers to indulge their interest in "queer" or perverse desires (*hentai seiyoku*). Of particular interest is the freedom with which these magazines discussed people who, in English, were politely spoken of as "sex deviants" or "sex variants," but in common parlance were more usually referred to as "queers" or "perverts."

In fact, the Japanese popular press of the 1950s offers a remarkable resource for the study of postwar minority sexualities. These "perverse" (*hentai*), "abnormal" (*abu*), or "mania" (*mania*) magazines, as they were variously described, had an extremely wide range of interests and, purporting to offer true accounts, drew upon anecdotes from Japan's feudal past as well as stories from European and Asian societies, often relying on anthropological reports. Significantly, these early magazines did not segregate the material into heterosexual or homosexual-themed publications, as became standard in the 1970s, but featured a wide range of perverse acts and queer desires, including practically any type of sexual activity other than "ordinary sex (*futsū no sekkusu*) between a man and a woman" (Ishida, McLelland, and Murakami 2005; Shimokawa 1995: 53).

The "experts" who wrote for the perverse magazines of the 1950s were different from those writing in the prewar sexological publications in that fewer claimed any kind of medical or psychiatric training. Referred to as *sensei* (teacher), many writers were more literary in bent, and their authority derived from their extensive reading about both Japanese and foreign *fūzoku*[11] or "sexual customs" that included psychoanalytic and sexological works such as Kinsey's (1948) *Sexual Behavior in the Human Male*, which had been translated into Japanese in 1950, as well as anthropological, historical, and literary treatises.

The breadth of reference in these magazines and the fact that readers often wrote letters and contributed longer descriptive pieces about their own "perverse desires" meant that pathologizing medical, criminal, and psychoanalytic theories did not establish such a firm hold on popular discourse about transgenderism and homosexuality in Japan as was the case in Anglophone, particularly American, popular writings at this time. The voice of the experts was often muted, given that the magazines relied on contributions from readers for a substantial percentage of their copy and actively solicited confessional stories. Some contributions to the postwar magazines, however, transcended the paradigm of confession and appeal to expert advice, instead advocating the right of individuals to express sexual and gender diversity.

In order to give some sense of how those who understood themselves to be subjects of "queer" or perverse desire at this time were able to gain some sense of agency and visibility through engaging with the perverse press, we have included three "roundtable" discussions in which several cross-dressing male prostitutes (*danshō*), homosexual (*homo*) bargoers, and female homosexuals (*josei no homo*) talk about their lives.

The earliest of the reports, and in many ways the least encouraging, is that concerning the life of Tokyo's cross-dressing male prostitutes published in the *kasutori* magazine *Ōkē* in August 1949. Entitled "Confessions of a Problem," chapter 5, three prostitutes take part in this discussion, and, although the questions of the chairman (who identifies himself as a friend of one of the participants) are supportive and well meaning, the picture given of early postwar male prostitution is very bleak. The cross-dressers involved would probably, in today's terminology, identify as transsexuals, in that, psychologically speaking, they consider themselves to have been born women and they live their lives entirely as women, even to the extent of convincing their customers that they are biological females. While they hope to move on from a life of prostitution and set up their own small business such as a noodle stand, their ultimate wish is to live in a husband-wife relationship with a man in which they perform the conventional duties of a wife. However, as they acknowledge, this is unlikely to eventuate and they fear they have little future to look forward to once their looks have faded.

A much more upbeat account of male homosexual life is given in a "Grand *Sodomia* Conference" that took part in the Tokyo "*homo* bar" Yakyoku (Nocturne) in 1953 and appears in chapter 6. This discussion took place between the bar owner, three "*homo*" customers, and two representatives of the magazine and reveals that by 1953 Tokyo was developing both print media and an extensive social scene for male homosexuals. The role that magazines such as *Fūzoku zōshi* played in introducing this subculture is highlighted, as is the manner in which the personals columns enabled men, particularly those outside metropolitan areas, to make assignations.

A more detailed description of Tokyo's developing bar scene is given in a series of articles entitled "Lifestyles in the Gay Bars" published in *Amatoria* in three installments throughout 1955. The account given here in chapter 7 is an edited version of all three accounts. Written by Kabiya Kazuhiko, a prolific writer about male homosexuality whose career lasted from the 1930s through to the 1960s, these are valuable eyewitness accounts describing the layout, staff, clientele, and mode of interaction in Japan's earliest *gei bā* (gay bars).

This account is particularly significant since it is one of the earliest texts to use the terms *gei bā* and *gei bōi* (gay boy) to describe homosexual nightspots and their staff. In the immediate postwar period, the first homosexual drinking places had been referred to as *danshoku kis-saten*, that is, "male eroticism coffee shops," and those meeting there had been referred to with a wide range of terms, both modern and more traditional, including *sodomia* (from Sodom/sodomite), *homo* (from homosexual), and *danshokuka* (conjoining the nominalizing suffix "ka" or -ist to the Edo-period term for male-male eroticism). However, by the mid-1950s the newly imported term *gei*, which had been introduced during the U.S. Occupation, was being deployed as a trendy term to refer to homosexual nightspots and the professional young men who worked there (but not the customers). Since many of the "boys" working in these establishments exhibited transgender characteristics, *gei* came to represent a group of professional bar workers who engaged in transgender and other performances to entertain a clientele of more gender-normative customers referred to as *homo*—an important distinction within the subculture that was to remain in place until the early 1980s.

While in the early 1950s the main focus of "curiosity seeking" was on male desire, with a large number of articles dedicated to male homosexuality and cross-dressing, women's same-sex sexuality was not entirely overlooked. As mentioned, "female same-sex love" (*joshi dōseiai*) had been regularly featured in the perverse press of the 1920s, and although the term "lesbian" was not itself used, there was some discussion of "Lesbos love" (*resubosu ai*) in the early postwar press. Quite why this term rose to prominence in the early 1950s is difficult to know with any certainty, but since it was often paired in discussions with references to *sodomia* (Sodom/sodomite), it is possible that since both terms derive from place names, they were somehow regarded as equivalent.

Just as there was far less written about female homosexuality, there were far fewer descriptors referring to female homosexuals, and they were in some texts simply referred to as *josei no homo* or "female homos." In the early 1950s, discussion of female homosexuality seems to have been included very much as an afterthought. Given the fact that the magazines' editors were all male, as were the majority of the contributors, the perverse press had a strong masculinist bias wherein sexuality was invariably understood from a male perspective. Many of the discussions of "Lesbos love," even those featuring female names, seem to have been aimed at a male audience and to have presented women-loving women in a manner so as to appeal to male desire. However, while this material obviously needs to be read with caution, occasionally women's voices are discernable, not least in the number of letters written by women readers complaining about the lack of discussion of "Lesbos" issues. Other letter writers asked if the editors could help them to contact other women-loving women or even organize "an association for female homos" where women with an interest in other women could arrange to go to the cinema, jazz clubs, or hiking (McLelland 2004).

There is good reason to believe these letters to be genuine and that the editors of *Fūzoku kagaku*, for instance, were acting in good faith when they organized and then published the results of a roundtable discussion between women-loving women entitled "Female Homos Here We Go," chapter 8, in the March 1955 edition of the magazine. This discussion gives us some idea of the kind of lives that were possible for same-sex-desiring women in Tokyo at the end of the first postwar decade. The three female participants in this discussion point out that in comparison with the rapidly developing male homosexual social world, women who loved women had a much more difficult time seeking each other out. However, there were some bars where same-sex-desiring women were welcome, and, defying popular stereotypes, not all these bars were structured according to masculine and feminine roles. This discussion is particularly important for underlining the agency with which some queer-identified people could use the perverse press to resist and counter popular stereotypes. Despite the masculinist bias of the chairman who constantly uses male homosexual paradigms as the basis for his questions, the women present reject these analogies and give their own account of their desires, practices, and lifestyles. In many ways this is the most upbeat (and perhaps most unexpected) of the three discussions offered from the early postwar period and should encourage us to do more work to uncover the parameters of the lives of women-loving women in 1950s Japan.

Although there does seem to have been a genuine attempt to engage with same-sex-desiring women readers, at least in the perverse magazines of the early 1950s, later in the decade the treatment of "Lesbos love" became increasingly pornographic, and by the 1960s the figure of "the lesbian" (*resubian*) had emerged as a locus of male fantasy and desire. Hence, from the end of the 1950s and throughout the 1960s, there were few resources in the media for women with an interest in other women, and this meant that the bar world remained their main source of contact and community formation. The importance of the bar world is underlined by the account of a female-to-male transgender in chapter 9, Mizuno Makiyo, who reminisces about "his" time as a "host" in the early 1960s at a bar featuring *dansō no reijin* (dandy beauties).[12]

The original bar Yume no shiro (Castle of Dreams) had been founded in 1961 to take advantage of the popularity of the all-female SKD (Shōchiku Kagekidan), an acting troupe that featured many beautiful actresses in "trouser roles," and it attracted a clientele of women hoping to run into some of the cross-dressing stars of the revue or interested in making assignations with the bar's cross-dressing staff. Other similar bars soon developed and it became possible for some women with the money and the leisure (who were themselves often employed in the entertainment trade) to socialize in a world organized according to butch (*tachi*) and femme (*neko*) gender roles—a testament to the enduring popularity of transgender performance within Japanese culture.

Although the figure of "the lesbian" had been colonized by male desire in the perverse press of the 1960s, the fate of male homosexuals was somewhat different. Unlike "lesbianism," male homosexuality was not a fantasy trope for the magazine's general male readership, and so while discussion of "lesbianism" increased in these magazines, articles dealing with male homosexual desire gradually declined in number. However, such articles did not entirely disappear, largely because key writers from the early postwar magazines continued to research and write about the topic. Although the space given to male homosexual issues was much reduced, later magazines such as *Ura mado* and *Kitan kurabu* did continue to publish the occasional article aimed at same-sex-desiring men, and these magazines continued to be a valuable source of information for the male homosexual community until the arrival of dedicated *homo* magazines in the early 1970s.[13]

THE DEVELOPMENT OF QUEER ACTIVISM IN JAPAN

Although the term *gei*/gay did not begin to be deployed in a political sense in the Japanese media until the late 1970s, it would be wrong to assume that there was no activism in Japan prior to this date. In fact, in part a reflection of borrowing from American lesbian feminist discourse, it was the term *rezubian*, not *gei*, that first began to be deployed with political connotations and Japanese lesbians, not gay men, who began to build community ties based on politics and not just sexual attraction.[14]

The 1971 founding of the lesbian group Wakakusa no Kai (Young grass club) in Tokyo, the history of which appears in chapter 10, marked a turning point in terms of lesbian community building in Japan. While some women who went to its meetings were looking for partners rather than a community, other participants just wanted to engage in "completely ordinary" (*goku futsū*) chat in a space where it was acceptable to be a lesbian (Suzuki 1983: 340), echoing the oft-repeated need for a space where one can withdraw, however briefly, from the heterosexual world. The 1970s were also a watershed for lesbian feminism and lesbian organizing, through which many other women developed a sense of lesbian community. Tsuruga Minako (1995: 46), member of lesbian organization Regumi Studio (Regumi Sutajio)—the founding of which is recounted in "They've Got Their Happy Faces On," chapter 11—describes the Japanese lesbian movement itself as having begun within the broader feminist movement. Long-time lesbian activist Wakabayashi Naeko, for instance, was involved in women's liberation both in Japan and the United States before becoming active in the lesbian liberation movement (See *Aniisu* 2001: 39–40; Summerhawk et al. 1998: 184–86). Like feminists in other countries, the almost invariably all-women environments of feminist spaces created a fertile, though not necessarily welcoming, space for women to discover or develop same-sex attraction. While, however, "[lesbian] women have been among the most radical feminist women in Japan" (Lunsing 2001: 294), lesbian activist Kakefuda Hiroko has argued that in fact "feminism in Japan is a very heterosexual oriented movement, and a lot of the time it doesn't consider lesbians" (quoted in Chalmers 2002: 34). And Sharon Chalmers (2002: 36) believes that it was the frustration caused by being denied acknowledgment and support in the feminist movement that led to the creation of the lesbian weekend retreats.[15]

Tension was not exclusive to lesbian-heterosexual relations, however. As recalled in "Wakakusa no Kai" in this volume, the group was criticized by "lesbian liberationists" (*ribu-kei rezubian*) for, among other things, not working to improve the rights of lesbians and for helping to perpetuate the patriarchal paradigm through the butch/femme dynamic that was prevalent at its gatherings (see chapters 10 and 12 in this volume). Women who chose lesbianism as a rejection of men and the patriarchal system were not always welcome in spaces created by those women who writer and activist Izumo Marou describes as "native lesbians" (*nētivu rezubian*).[16] She notes that it was around the time of Wakakusa no Kai creating the *mini-komi* (zine) *Wonderful Women* (*Subarashii onnatachi*) that Japan saw its first "lesbians by political choice" (*seijiteki sentaku toshite no rezubian*). Conflicts between the "natives" and the "lesbians by choice" led to *Wonderful Women* disappearing after just one issue and the appearance of two new *mini-komi*, neither of which lasted long (Miki, Saeki, and Mizoguchi 1995: 239–42). Lesbian translator Hara Minako, who participates in the panel discussion "Japan's Lesbian Movement," an abridged translation of which appears in chapter 12 of this volume, with Izumo and activists Tsuzura Yoshiko and Ochiya Kumiko, indicates that this politicization put undue pressure on some women to declare their sexuality. While not all women have felt welcome at all times, these lesbian weekend retreats have played a fundamental role in the establishment of the community.

Yet, not all women-loving women in the later decades of the twentieth century were actively involved in the metropolitan lesbian communities, whether by choice or opportunity. Ōsaki Harumi, who talks about her life in "Lesbians Living in the Mountains" in chapter 13 of this volume, prefers rural living and, having chosen a life in the mountains, went to the city and found a partner who was interested in moving out there with her. Some women who were unaware of the existence of or had no access to lesbian organizations and bars wrote letters to *homo* magazines in the 1970s and 1980s. Others found each other through personals columns in magazines such as *Allan* and *Luna* (*Gekkō*) in the 1980s, prompting groups like Wakakusa no Kai to advertise in their pages (Welker in press). Perhaps the best connection women living too far away to directly participate in the lesbian community had was through the pages of the *mini-komi* produced by lesbian organizations. Women like Wakabayashi (above) chose to move to the United States for various reasons and when they returned brought back ideas about how the Japanese lesbian community might look. On the other hand, Noriko Kohashi moved to the United States because she was uncomfortable with certain aspects of Japanese society and decided to stay, as she explains in "Breaking Gender Rules without Remorse," chapter 14, although she maintains strong connections with members of the lesbian community in the Osaka-Kyoto area.

As the above account of lesbian networking in 1970s Japan illustrates, it was lesbians and not gay men who were the first to develop a community consciousness outside of the paradigms offered by the bar world. The bar world remained an important locus of male homosexual community throughout the 1960s and 1970s as is described in the reminiscences of Ōtsuka Takashi, now himself a bar owner and a prominent personality on Tokyo's gay scene, reproduced in chapter 15 as "True Tales from Ni-chōme." Ōtsuka points out that despite the relatively high profile that male homosexuality had in the Japanese media of the late 1960s, it was still difficult for young people, in particular, to get accurate information about male homosexual meeting places or to make friends. His touching story about how, in 1968, his first gay friend made his proclivities clear by admitting to a liking for *homo* (that is homogenized) milk, is an example of how tentative the coming-out process could be at this time. Despite the fact that Ōtsuka's first visit to a *"homo* bar" was far from encouraging, he does stress the important role that the bars of Shinjuku ni-chōme (that is the second block of the Shinjuku district in Tokyo) have played not just in gay community formation but also in local gay politics. Indeed, Ōtsuka himself was one of the first Japanese to begin to use the loanword *gei* in a political sense when he appeared on the radical *Snake Man* radio show in 1977. However, as Ōtsuka's account emphasizes, in the absence of the overt oppression such as police raids, antisodomy laws, and homophobic violence that galvanized the gay communities in many Western nations, it was difficult to get Japanese gay men to organize around issues of sexual identity.

Ōtsuka was not, however, the first activist to attempt to get Japanese people to think more critically about the nature of homosexual desire and its relationship to society. The most explicit connection between Japan's heteronormative social system and the oppression of sexual minorities was made by Tōgō Ken, who founded the political party Zatsumin no Kai (Miscellaneous People's Party), which brought together a wide range of individuals who were socially disenfranchised on account of their "failure" to live in accordance with received notions about family life and relationships. Tōgō's story is recounted in chapter 16, "The Legendary *Okama*." Starting in 1971, Tōgō ran many times for a seat in Japan's parliament, the National Diet, and although unsuccessful he continued his campaigning over the next twenty years. It would be incorrect, however, to identify Tōgō as Japan's first "gay" activist since he deliberately used the indigenous term *okama* to describe himself. Technically a term for a large pot for cooking rice, *okama* has been used since at least the Edo Era as a slang reference to the buttocks and by association for effeminate homosexual men (who are assumed to engage in passive anal sex). It is hence a troubling term for many homosexuals who dislike the associations of effeminacy and passivity that it carries. Tōgō, however, insisted on recuperating the term, much as some activists within the lesbian and gay movement in the United States were to do with "queer"—a similarly controversial reclamation—two decades later. Tōgō insisted that to counter homophobia in the Japanese context it was necessary to engage with local Japanese terms for sexual difference no matter how confrontational they might be to mainstream society or to some homosexual men themselves.

Indeed, as the essay by Hirano Hiroaki—chapter 17, "Who Should Be Ashamed of Whom?"—illustrates, the issue of terminology has been a controversial one for many men with homosexual orientations. As detailed in chapters 10, 11, and 12, while same-sex desiring women have at times engaged in heated debate about who should be able to apply to herself the label "lesbian," the label itself has been somewhat less complicated than the multiple terms that have been deployed in the postwar period to describe homosexual men.

On the whole, lesbian and gay activism in Japan developed independently of each other. Homosexual men and women socialized in different environments; there was never any organized police persecution; and, given the absence of sodomy and unequal age-of-consent laws, there were no issues of common concern that might have brought gay men and lesbians together. It was not until the 1980s when the influence of Western lesbian and gay culture began to be felt more strongly in Japan that lesbian and gay collaborations began. This is nowhere more visible than in the lesbian and gay film festivals and pride (*puraido*) events. Takashi Toshiko, producer of the first and second Tokyo International Lesbian and Gay Film Festivals (in 1992 and 1993), explains that the festivals have functioned as an important "chance for gays and lesbians to do something together" (quoted in *Aniisu* 2001: 53).

Taking visibility to the streets, Tokyo parades, replete with rainbow flags, outrageous drag queens, bare-chested women, gaggles of topless gym-built muscular male bodies in skin-tight shorts, and leather galore, could be pride parades anywhere. One major difference is the scale—just a few thousand participants at most, sometimes a hundred or fewer—compared to pride events in other major cities, such as New York, Sydney, and Berlin, where participant numbers sometimes reach tens, if not hundreds of thousands. The Japanese vocabulary used to talk about these marches and events is as borrowed from the Western LGBT world as the events themselves: *parēdo* (parade), *puraido ibento* (pride event), *reinbō māchi* (rainbow march), *puraido māchi* (pride march), *daiku māchi* (dyke march), *sekusharu mainoriti māchi* (sexual minority march), and Nagoya's own "Lesbian and Gay Revolution."[17] In effect, claiming American LGBT history as its own, a book commemorating the Tokyo Lesbian and Gay Parade 2000 begins its reflection on the history of the Tokyo parade by looking back to the uprising at the Stonewall Inn in New York City, remarking that it was this event that gave "explosive energy to the gay/lesbian liberation movement" (Sunagawa 2001: 186). However, these pride events have had a checkered history in Japan and have emphasized divisions within the queer community as much as they have enabled different groups to come together and forge a common cause, as Sunagawa Hideki's essay, "Reflections on the Tokyo Lesbian and Gay Parade 2000," chapter 18 in this volume, detailing his involvement in the 2000 parade, illustrates.[18]

TRANSGENDER LIVES

As we have seen, at different points in the prewar era, both FtM (female to male) and MtF (male to female) cross-dressing and transgender attracted public attention. In the postwar era, however, depictions of MtF cross-dressers and transgendered individuals have had a far higher profile in popular culture. The bold "coming out" of Torai Masae as an FtM transsexual in the mid-1990s, however, raised to a limited degree both the prominence of FtMs and public awareness of the hardships faced by those whose gender identity and sexed bodies do not coincide. In the 2001–2002 season of the Tokyo Broadcasting System (TBS) series *3-nen B-gumi Kinpachi-sensei* (Mr. Kinpachi of class 3-B), the identity struggles of a transgender FtM middle school student was one of the major storylines, which the network used to teach their viewers about transgender—even suggesting on their website that readers read books on transgender, including several by Torai.[19] In one particularly didactic episode the health teacher taught class 3-B—and thus the viewers—about the causes of transgender and why Nao wanted to be treated as a boy. Most students were in tears by the end of the scene. The news that Nao would not be able to have children after having sex-reassignment surgery, which he planned to have upon reaching the age of majority, provoked a powerful reaction of sympathy, demonstrating how the desire to dispel misunderstandings about transgender in this case was not accompanied by a similar desire to unsettle the centrality of the heterosexual family model, which would not be open to Nao.

Indeed, recent changes to legislation in Japan allowing the performance of gender-reassignment surgery for those diagnosed by the medical community as suffering from *sei dōitsusei shōgai* (gender identity disorder) and the ability of those having completed the surgery, under certain strict circumstances, to change their registered sex on official documents, have been criticized by many in Japan's transgender community for being overly normative. Firstly, many feel that the choice of the term *shōgai*, which in Japanese connotes a sense of "disability" and harm, is overly pathologizing and that the problem lies not so much with the individual "patient" but rather with a rigid two-dimensional gender system that does not acknowledge that gender expression can be multiple and varied and is not reducible to simple categories of "male" or "female." Also, many complain that the legislation, which allows only unmarried individuals without children to change their registered birth sex, is too narrow and is discriminatory against many in the transgender community such as Fujio Takafumi, whose story is reproduced as "How I Became an FtM Transgender Gay" in chapter 19 of this volume. As Fujio's life story emphasizes, the interrelation of gender and sexual identity is extremely complex and does not always follow the somewhat heteronormative narrative accepted by the medical profession and some within the transgender community. As he relates, he has experienced sexual relationships with both men and women (at one time having been married to a man and given birth to two children). However, after having undergone hormone therapy and further masculinized his appearance through a mastectomy, he is currently in a sexual relationship with another man. These complex identity issues are barely acknowledged by the medical profession and are seldom given voice to in popular culture.

The other contemporary transgender story offered in this collection is that of male-to-female academic Mitsuhashi Junko in "My Life as a 'Woman,'" chapter 20. Mitsuhashi's story is very interesting since it parallels changes in how transgender issues are understood in Japanese society that have been taking place over the last two decades. Mitsuhashi describes how her transgender interests were first given expression in the mid-1980s when she began to cross-dress privately before moving on to more public expression in the context of the Elizabeth Club, a private organization for "amateur" male-to-female cross-dressers. Her success in the club's competitions and events led her to professionalize her cross-dressing activities by working in cross-dressing bars that catered to a clientele of men interested in cross-dressers, going on to run large-scale events for Tokyo's cross-dressing community. So far Mitsuhashi's story follows a very common Japanese paradigm that situates sexual and gender variance in the entertainment world. However, her interest in the history of Japan's transgender communities led to her researching and writing a number of articles based on material that she had uncovered in the postwar *hentai* magazines. She later registered as a Ph.D. student at Chūō University and was one of the founding members of the transgender archiving project. Mitsuhashi now lectures at several Tokyo universities and has been a keynote speaker at international sexuality studies forums. On the whole her story has been respectfully reported on by the mainstream press, indicating that transgender issues can now be vocalized outside of the earlier entertainment paradigm.

The final selection offered in this collection, "My Life as a Hustler," chapter 21, comes from Akira, who was for a time a male sex worker. He offers some very touching reminiscences of his clients, and his testimony underlines the fact that sex work can be a personal choice and that what is traded in these exchanges is often much more than physical comfort.

WHERE NEXT FOR JAPANESE QUEER STUDIES?

As outlined at the beginning of this introduction, both "queer" and *hentai* have been taken up and made use of by Japanese researchers and activists in an attempt to articulate their local histories as well as to acknowledge the extent to which Japan, like any other nation, is also tied into global processes of change and transformation in the sex and gender sphere as much as in any other. This pioneering research is slowly making inroads into Japanese academic institutions and it is to be anticipated that a new generation of scholars, such as that now emerging from Chūō University's Postwar Transgender Study Association, will add greatly to our understanding of Japanese queer cultures as they developed over the last century.

However, more effort is needed to make this emerging scholarship available to the English-speaking world as well as to locate "queer studies" more centrally as a concern for Japanese studies as it is constituted in Western academic institutions. A possible role model might be the large number of excellent studies that have been made of women's lives in Japan since the 1970s; it is only to be hoped that over the next two decades a similar tradition of scholarship will develop that takes as its focus Japan's long-lived and varied queer communities so as to further advance not just our understanding of Japanese society but of global queer issues.

NOTES

1. "Hidden from history" was in fact chosen as the title of one significant collection of historical gleanings aimed at "reclaiming the gay and lesbian past" (Duberman, Vicinus, and Chauncey 1989).

2. English-language sources on male-male sexual practices in the premodern era include Pflugfelder (1999), Leupp (1995), and Watanabe and Iwata (1989).

3. Krafft-Ebing's *Psychopathia Sexualis* was first translated into Japanese in 1894.

4. The pronunciation *resubian*, most likely borrowed from French literature, was predominant through the 1960s before being replaced by *rezubian*, reflecting the influence of imported American pornography and lesbian feminist discourse.

5. Prewar eugenics are discussed extensively in Frühstück (2003).

6. A discussion of the development of discourse concerning homosexuality in Japanese popular culture from the 1930s can be found in McLelland (2005).

7. So-called *ianjo* or "comfort stations" employed women, most of whom had been forcibly recruited from Japan's colonies, who sexually serviced Japan's military. Shibata (1999) suggests that a better term for these institutions would be "mass rape camps."

8. Both pronunciations of the characters remain acceptable, however. While we are unable to ascertain the pronunciation the authors of the postwar articles included here had in mind, in this volume we have opted to go with *danshoku*, reflecting the post-Edo prevalence of *danshoku* over *nanshoku*.

9. *Kasutori* is literally a poor-quality wine distilled from sake lees. Drinkers were supposed to collapse after only three glasses—just as these magazines tended to fold after their third issue (Matsuzawa 1997: 59).

10. On developments in postwar sexual culture, see McLelland (2005).

11. During the Meiji period, *fūzoku* or "customs" was used in magazine titles to refer to contemporary customs or popular trends but began to be used before the war as a circumlocution for sexual customs, as a means of avoiding the censor's gaze (Matsuzawa: 1997: 61–62).

12. Another English account of this bar history can be found in Welker (2004). Other Japanese accounts include *Aniisu* (2001: 42–45), Shiba (1993), (1997), Nawa (1987), and *Gekkō* (1985).

13. For a description of the early *homo* magazines, see Aoki (2006).

14. A lengthier English-language history of the past three decades of the Japanese lesbian community can be found in Welker (2004). An outline of specifically gay activism is offered in McLelland (2005).

15. The retreats are discussed by Hara in chapter 12 in this volume.

16. See *Aniisu* (2001: 55). In "Japan's Lesbian Movement" (chapter 12 in this volume), Hara uses the term *nekkara* (from the root) to describe women who feel intrinsically lesbian.

17. Since its 2001 establishment as "Nagoya Gay Revolution," the name has remained written exclusively in Roman letters. In 2002, the event was transformed into Nagoya Lesbian and Gay Revolution, but the addition of lesbians seems an afterthought.

18. For an account of the 2005 parade, see Suganuma (2006).

19. See http://www.tbs.co.jp/kinpachi/series6/world_21.html (last accessed November 13, 2005).

1

A VISIT WITH YUASA YOSHIKO, A DANDY SCHOLAR OF RUSSIAN LITERATURE

Sawabe Hitomi[1]

She loved another woman without qualms. Here's a woman born in the Meiji Era[2] with a free and independent spirit.

On 20 June 1924, Chūjō Yuriko[3] wrote the following in a letter to Yuasa Yoshiko. It was around two months after they had met for the first time:

> When my heart is not occupied with work, I'm thinking of you. When I open my eyes in the morning, there's always a struggle over which will arise first, thoughts of you or thoughts of work. As I'm surrounded by work, most of the time, as planned, nine times out of ten, it's thoughts of work. When I write, I'm wholly engrossed. When I'm free, at those times, in my heart it's you who utterly prevail—in what I'm thinking, what I'm feeling, whatever I'm doing.

Chūjō Yuriko debuted as a writer at the age of seventeen with *A Crowd of Poor Folk* (*Mazushiki hitobito no mure*), and over the course of her

---

Translated and reproduced with permission from "*Dandi na Roshia bungakusha Yuasa Yoshiko hōmonki*," which was published under the penname Hirosawa Yumi in *Onna wo ai suru onnatachi no monogatari* (Stories of women who love women), *Bessatsu takarajima* no. 64, Tokyo: JICC shuppankyoku, 1987: 67–73. Translated by James Welker.

life penned many well-known books, including *Nobuko* and *The Banshū Plain* (*Banshū heiya*).[4] After meeting Miyamoto Kenji and getting involved in the proletarian literary movement,[5] she was a victim of severe persecution and died at the young age of fifty-one. And Yuasa Yoshiko was a famous scholar of Russian literature, known for her translations, such as Chekhov's *The Cherry Orchard* (*Sakura no sono*) and Gorky's *Childhood* (*Yōnen jidai*).[6] In her younger days, she was the model for the character of Motoko, who "swaggered around with a pipe in her mouth," in Yuriko's *Nobuko* and *Two Gardens* (*Futatsu no niwa*).[7]

When they met each other at Nogami Yaeko's[8] home on 11 April of the same year, in Yuriko's eyes, Yuasa seemed a completely mysterious figure, who was "hardly feminine or worldly, and I felt totally revealed." Yuriko wrote in her diary about Yuasa's unexpected visit to her home in Aoyama (Tokyo) ten days later: "[W]hen I was with her I stopped trying to show off, and I enjoyed being able to be myself." The two were quickly drawn to one another, writing letters to each other nearly every day. On May 28, when Yuasa visited Yuriko, who was then absorbed in writing at her country home in Fukushima Prefecture,[9] they had a marvelous time, just the two of them.

That summer, having put an end to her four-year marriage to Araki Shigeru, Yuriko set about writing *Nobuko*. "In the end, I should dedicate this work to you. It's something your heart let me create," she wrote to Yuasa. Ultimately, this work was born out of the pleasure she got from the love and understanding she shared with Yuasa. The two of them moved in together in January of the following year. Including their three years of study in the Soviet Union, which they began in December 1927, the pair lived together for a total of seven years, which ended in February 1932 when Yuriko married Miyamoto Kenji.

THE "DANDY" WITH AN ACERBIC TONGUE

Born in 1896, Yuasa Yoshiko is ninety this year. I was introduced to her through an acquaintance in October of last year. For a time after the war, Yuasa worked as a sharp-witted editor of *Fujin minshu shinbun* (Women's Democratic Newspaper).[10] When friends from that period of her life went to visit her, I was blessed enough to be able to go with them.

After nearly an hour on the bus from Hamamatsu[11] Station, we arrived at a rest home called Yūyū no sato (Tranquil Village). The eight-story white structure looked more like a high-class apartment building than a rest home. In the garden outside among the cosmos swaying in the breeze were some splendid cockscombs in full bloom.

When the elevator opened on the eighth floor, standing there was an old lady figure in a kimono, a striking "dandy" with a black beret on her head and a walking stick in her hand. It was Yuasa Yoshiko. At five feet (150 cm tall), she was a diminutive woman with beautiful white hair, but with the youthful way she held herself up straight as she walked, you'd never think she was ninety.

We got out of the elevator and went over to a "salon" across from us. Each floor had a place like this for receiving visitors. We all sat down, and after I introduced myself, Yuasa and her friends from her *Fujin minshu shinbun* days erupted into gossip about mutual friends.

"You—you look like a boy, don't you? I bet you have lots of women who like you."

That was the first thing Yuasa said to me. "*Hai* (yes)," I answered cheerfully. Now's my chance, I thought: "But it's the same for you too, isn't it, *sensei*?"[12]

"Nah. I was the one who always fell in love first," she replied, and everyone laughed.

"Those there—what kind of flowers are they? Gerberas? Those sure are pretty crummy flowers." The pink gerberas that one of her friends brought were looking a little droopy. Just as I had heard, her acerbic tongue revealed her offbeat sense of humor. In fact, though, she's a very open-hearted old lady.

EVEN IF YOU FALL IN LOVE WITH A WOMAN, IT WON'T WORK OUT

After dinner, when I take Yuasa back up to her apartment, I'm alone with her for the first time. A voice in my head presses me, "If you're ever going to ask her, now's your chance." "*Sensei*, tomorrow morning could

I talk to you about your youth?" I had heard the past, especially Yuriko, was something she didn't like to talk about, so my voice was somewhat tense.

Just as I expected, as soon as I said it, her own voice turned cross.

"Everything about my youth is all written down in books. I'm sure if you read what's already written, you'll find out what you want to know. I don't have much longer. If you're going to write about me, just do me a favor and wait till I die. Instead of bombarding me with questions, why don't you just get a feel for what you want to know during the course of our conversation?"

It figures—this isn't going to work. If I let this chance slip away, I'll probably never be able to ask her anything. Somehow I have to find a way to reach her.

On the sofa where Yuasa is sitting is a pile of the magazine *Fujin kōron* (Women's Debate). That afternoon I had made sure that the issue with an article I had written was among them. I quickly pluck it out and open it up to show her.

"Hmmm. . . . 'Attending a World Lesbian Meeting.'[13] Goodness. They have that kind of thing now?"

She looks over at me with her eyes wide open—she's intrigued.

"Seven hundred lesbians from around the world got together there."

When I say the word "lesbian" (*rezubian*), for a moment she looks as if she has awakened from a long dream. After that, slowly she starts to talk, one word at a time.

"I was always a naughty child—I guess it was because I only liked girls. So, if you were to say that I'm a lesbian too, well, I suppose I *am* a lesbian."[14]

This is a ninety-year-old woman, someone who's lived nearly a century. Her face, her hands, they're covered with wrinkles. The word "lesbian" flows out so naturally from a mouth that's as sunken and withered as a hollow on a tree. More than that, the word sounded so real.

"But at this age I don't like it . . . nah, I don't like it. The 'natural' (*shizen*) way is better. Surely, men and women together is natural. Of course, when I was young, myself, I liked women."

Sigh. Does she really think women loving women "goes against nature"? I'm a little disappointed. But I just met her, so it could be that she's being cautious with me saying it like that. And while I'm thinking this, still speechless, Yuasa continues.

"Even if you fall in love with a woman, it won't work out. Eventually, in the end, women end up with men, don't they?" she presses me. No. I'm not going to give in here.

"But, *sensei*, you loved women your whole life, didn't you? If you would talk to me about that, it would give countless women courage."

I'm desperate.

"Well, when it comes down to it, there's a woman living inside men and there's a man living inside women, so no matter who tries to like whom, it doesn't really matter, I suppose."

When she says that, I know I'm in luck, and things are starting to get juicy. The tension between the two of us has vanished and a smile is back on her face.

After all the talking she has been doing today and not having had her regular nap, she seems rather tired. Her friends come up to see how we are doing: "It's gotten so late, you had us worried that something had happened." I hold back the urge to ask just a few more questions and ask instead if we can continue tomorrow, and she goes back into her apartment.

THE FIRST PERSON I LIKED WAS A GEISHA

The next morning, the gray sky has but a tiny patch of blue cutting a hole through the clouds, but by breakfast time, the blue has spread across the entire surface of the sky and warm sunbeams are shining through the windows. We have french toast, salad, and tea. At this place, all meals are prepared well and they taste good. But, Yuasa says bluntly, "The food here is pretty bad at this rest home." On her face is the expression of a spoiled child.

After we finish eating, since it's important that the two women I came with not disturb the interview, they find somewhere else to sit and wait. I ride with my friend, just the two of us, up in the elevator to the eighth floor. At the entrance of her apartment Yuasa asks, "Whose shoes are these?" "Oh, those are mine," I reply. And to this she retorts, "Those are quite, hmm, large. Well, I suppose men aren't into you." And she proceeds to let out a loud chuckle.

From Yuasa's room you can look out over a vast stretch of the surrounding countryside. Yūyū no sato was built in 1976. Upon hearing
about the facility from a friend, Yuasa visited it, really liked this particular place here on the eighth floor, and decided on the spot to move
in. The apartment is fairly large, with four rooms including the kitchen.
Piled up on the desk and on the sofa are scores of new books that have
been sent from all over. It seems she also likes pictures, and on the wall
are paintings of Noh[15] performances, as well as portraits. On a bookshelf
near the entrance to her bedroom are *The Collected Works of Miyamoto
Yuriko* (*Miyamoto Yuriko zenshū*), nestled alongside several copies of
Letters from Yuriko (*Yuriko no tegami*), the latter of which Yuasa edited.

"The first time I 'liked' (*suki*) a woman was, I guess, around the age
of twelve or thirteen. She was a geisha called Tsuruoka-san—she was a
very beautiful woman. Well, when I say I liked her, it's just that I saw her
from afar and that's what I thought. The family I was adopted into ran
a restaurant, and when I was asked to go fetch Tsuruoka-san, my heart
always beat very fast as I went to get her—that's all.

"When a girl is born in Kyoto, her newborn clothes are made with
red on the outside and white on the inside. They say when I was born,
they were really hoping for a boy, so they made my newborn clothes with
yellow on the outside and white on the inside. And, as I was growing
up my mother always said to me, 'Oh, if you had only been a boy. . . .'
I was unruly like a boy, you could say. Being the kind who was always
getting pranks pulled on me by boys, sometimes I chased after them. Afterwards, my mother scolded me, 'That's not the kind of thing girls do.'

"At New Year's, I got *o-toshidama*[16] from my parents, but at the time
I didn't like to go thank my father. He was bedridden with a chronic
disease, and I was made to go up to his bedside and say 'thank you for
the present.' I hated that my parents made me say that. Now, I suppose
they'd say I was rebellious. And when I recall my grandfather, he was
always putting on airs—he was one to look down on people. This man
looked down on women too—Kyoto really wasn't a very good place for
girls to grow up."

Yuasa was born into a fishmonger family. Counting on her clever,
spirited temperament, when she was thirteen she was adopted into
the family of her aunt, the Inoue family, who ran a traditional restau-

rant. However, she didn't get along well with the boy they adopted at the same time with the hope that he would become her husband, and when her real mother was stricken with cancer, she returned to her birth home. In her late teens, she moved to Tokyo, and in her twenties, she worked as an editor while studying Russian. While her father was alive, he sent her an allowance, so she was relatively blessed economically. The home in Komazawa (Tokyo) where she lived with Yuriko had the luxury of a housemaid. Even given the cheap cost of labor at the time, when it comes down to it, she must have enjoyed a well-off bachelorhood.

I ask her about children, given that she was single her whole life.

"Did I ever want children? Nah. I never thought about it. I liked children—but not enough that I wanted my own. If there had been a man I liked, I supposed I might have wanted them, but I never found a man I liked. Japanese men are so feudalistic—they have no appeal. Plus, children are a whole lot of trouble—you see, I'm too selfish. My father never said a word about marriage, but he didn't seem to want me to be the kind of woman who would just get married. He never said anything directly, but as my mother had died long ago, there was enough money for me to continue with my studies, so after I graduated from the boring girls' school in Kyoto, I decided to go to Tokyo. I briefly went to Japan Women's University and Tsuda Juku University, but they weren't my cup of tea. So while working as a reporter for the magazine *Nippon ichi* (Japan—Number One), I studied Russian with my teacher."

As she talks, her eyes narrow and a nostalgic look comes across her face.

FOLLOW YOUR HEART

No surprise—she doesn't really want to talk about Yuriko. When I try to draw something out of her, she comes back with, "I can't recall." It's true that this all took place more than sixty years ago. And even if she has forgotten, that would be understandable. But somehow it seems that perhaps she doesn't want to recall.

Before meeting Yuriko, Yuasa had lived with a woman three years her senior in the Sarugaku-chō neighborhood in Kanda (Tokyo). She took in the woman, a geisha, in order to help her become independent. Yuasa encouraged her to become a singer of traditional Japanese songs, and when the woman had at last made a name for herself and was able to stand on her own two feet, she started having men over repeatedly. Yuasa was nursing the wounds she incurred from that when she met Yuriko.

> After Yuriko and Yoshiko met, they visited Kaiseizan[17] together, and on the first night the pair talked until late in the evening. Yoshiko spoke frankly about the circumstances surrounding the pain she had experienced in the past, and declared that, ultimately, a life together was not possible for two women in love with each other. At that point, the two were close friends. For whatever reason, while Yoshiko was drawn to the world of geisha, she was also very interested in Yuriko, for her intelligence and studiousness, and the two talked for hours on end, without becoming the slightest bit bored. Yoshiko had deep admiration for Yuriko, but somewhere their feelings weren't a perfect match, and Yoshiko didn't have the same feelings about Yuriko that she had felt toward other women in the past.

That passage comes from the afterword to *Letters from Yuriko* and was penned by Yuasa herself. I read this aloud and ask another question.

"So, if that's the case, *sensei*, rather than a 'lover' (*koibito*), it would be more on the mark to say that, to you, Yuriko was a lover who was like a friend, wouldn't it?"

"Well, something like that."

Yuasa nodded gently.

In 1925, when the two of them first lived together in a rented house in Takadaoimatsu-chō,[18] Yuriko wrote the following letter.

> Moya, in our life together, you should appreciate and value more the course of our relationship. In this life, my hope has been to succeed at but one beautiful love. I want you to feel this within yourself and never ever forget how sincerely I wish this. Little by little, I'm coming to appreciate more deeply the significance of what we have together, and I believe it can get better. I hold within me another hope, that our love can contribute a wonderful example, one that's not a lie, to society's understanding of love. Fostering love is truly a kind of work.

In Russian, *moya* means "mine" and it was a nickname Yuriko gave Yuasa. However much up to that point Yuriko had dreamed of the "perfection of love" between two people, a few years later she went off with

Miyamoto Kenji. The only way now to see the love they had is through several pictures of the two of them together and the 118 letters Yuriko left behind. But that's plenty—that's the feeling I got. Even if for only one part of her life, it's quite clear that the two of them loved each other, and sitting here in front of me is a woman who has lived her life proudly, our *senpai* (foresister).

"Yuriko was quite a talker—she was always gabbing. Plus, she was the kind who needed to be coddled. When Yuriko was working on a manuscript, I was always there working right beside her. Anyway, it's a real shame what happened to her. Misfortunate, perhaps. Kenji was a feudalistic man, and Yuriko wasn't the kind to grapple with him. Yuriko's foolishness, that was her true nature. She died without the two of us ever meeting again, and if you want to talk of regret, I do regret it, but I'll be seeing her again soon enough."

A gentle smile comes across her face.

"In life, you only truly love (*suki*) one or two people at most. I guess I was born too soon. If I had been born now, I might have had a different life. Anyway, what I thought I wanted to do in life, I did. People should follow their hearts."

When we go down to the office to buy some cigarettes, a seagull flies by, showing us its white belly.

"The seagull is a strange bird. It always flies alone. I've never seen a pair of seagulls flying together."

She mumbles this as if talking to herself. As she walks along humming a *dodoitsu* song, I follow behind the slight figure of a free spirit born in the Meiji Era, and I feel even now what an independent mind she has.[19]

Yuasa Yoshiko died in 1990 at the age of 93.

NOTES

1. This article first appeared under Sawabe's penname Hirosawa Yumi. Under her real name, Sawabe later published a book about Yuasa Yoshiko and her relationship with Miyamoto Yuriko; see Sawabe ([1990] 1996).

2. The Meiji Era was 1868–1912.

3. Writer Chūjō Yuriko (1899–1951) would later marry writer and activist Miyamoto Kenji (1908–), becoming Miyamoto Yuriko, the name by which she is better known. For a lesbian reading of Miyamoto's writing, see Iwabuchi (1995).

4. *Mazushiki hitobito no mure* was first published in 1917; *Nobuko* was first published in installments, beginning in 1924, and in book form in 1928; and *Banshū heiya* was published in 1947; see Miyamoto (1969: 537–39, 543).

5. The Japanese proletarian literary movement was at its strongest in the 1920s, with wartime oppression largely quashing it in the 1930s.

6. Yuasa's translation of *Childhood* was first published in 1929; her translation of *The Cherry Orchard* was published in 1950; see Sawabe (1996: 355).

7. *Futatsu no niwa* was first published in 1923 by Chūōkōronsha; see Miyamoto (1969: 543).

8. Nogami Yaeko (1885–1985) was a novelist.

9. Fukushima Prefecture is located northeast of Tokyo.

10. According to the newspaper's own website, it was founded in 1946, and in 1991 changed its name to *Femin*; see *Fujin minshu kurabu* (2005).

11. Hamamatsu is a medium-sized city less than two hours southwest of Tokyo by bullet train.

12. *Sensei* is a term of respect used to address such people as teachers, doctors, and experts.

13. Hirosawa (1986).

14. *Dakara watashi mo rezubian to ieba, rezubian nandarō kedo.*

15. Noh is a type of traditional Japanese theatrical performance.

16. *O-toshidama* is a gift of money given to children at the New Year.

17. A Shinto shrine located in Fukushima Prefecture.

18. The neighborhood, which no longer formally exists, is located in present-day Meijirodai, Bunkō Ward, Tokyo.

19. Sawabe notes at the end of this article that she wrote it with reference to *Yuriko no tegami* (Yuasa 1978) and *Miyamoto Yuriko zenshū* vol. 23 (Miyamoto 1979).

2

MY CAREER IN *DANSHOKU*

Notes on Sodomy

Kondō Takashi

As soon as the corporal's entreaties of love had ended, suddenly my body was forced down, and his well-honed muscles and the solid brawn of his body pressed down on me. I could only acquiesce to his rough embrace!

I was initiated into sodomy (*sodomii*) for the first time in my life when I was nine. My family ran a Japanese clothing shop in the city of K, among the clerks of which was one twenty-five or twenty-six year old, named Kinnosuke. He doted on me as though he might eat me right up. In the middle of one summer night, I had been put to sleep in a room apart from my parents. Kinnosuke came creeping into that bed, where I was alone. Since he always treated me with such affection, I wasn't really scared, nor did I refuse him. And then, Kinnosuke pressed tight to me from behind. The smell of Kinnosuke's semen, then—I was strangely excited. It remained in my nose for a while afterwards, and put me into a curious mood.

I first consciously felt "homosexual love" (*dōseiai*) when I was twelve or thirteen. I fell in love with a beautiful boy in my class, and even

Translated and reproduced from *"Danshoku henreki: aru sodomia no shuki," Fūzoku kurabu* (Sex-customs club), May 1954: 143–49. Translated by Micah Auerback.

after I had entered junior high school, the upper-division students always used to treat me as their *chigosan* (pageboy),[1] though we had no carnal relations. When I was seventeen, in my fourth year of middle school, there was a youth in the class above me, the son in a lumber merchant's shop in the town, named Hori. He took a liking to me, and one night I was invited to his house. He had a magnificent room of his very own for study, and there we two drank whiskey, and I wound up staying the night at his house in the end. It was then that he taught me mutual masturbation. Under the sway of a pleasant excitement the likes of which I had never felt before, I felt utterly intoxicated. After that, I never had such relations with Hori again, but I could never forget the excitement of that time, and I came down with the disease of fellowship with the same sex (*dōsei*).

After I graduated from junior high school, I went up to the capital and entered a technical school. I was a boy from the provinces, and the pleasure quarters of town were an endless fascination to me. Nearly every day, I walked, entertaining myself in Ginza, Asakusa, and Shinjuku. Having said that, all I really did was see movies, and I never went so far as to look for women.

When I was twenty, I was in a certain movie theater in Asakusa. In the darkness as the movie was being shown, the man in the next seat over slipped his hand onto my knee. For an instant, I was slightly surprised, but that man was a respectable-looking, middle-aged gentleman with a mustache, and I didn't think that his way of placing his hand was that of a pickpocket. Half scared of what he would do with his hand, half with a searching sense of curiosity, I did not refuse that hand. The gentleman's hand gradually worked its way up my lap. With his other hand, the gentleman took my hand and drew it toward him. It was the same action as before, with Hori, but with a tenacity befitting a middle-aged man.

Strangely, once I got started, I encountered this kind of activity in the movie theaters about ten times over the next two years. My partners were mainly men from their thirties to mid-forties, but among them there were about three young men in their twenties. Needless to say, our actions never left that spot, and as soon as I left the movie theater, I was always so frightened that I would sneak into the crowds as though I were running away.

When I graduated from the technical school, I got a job in a certain government office. As a working man, I had to consider appearances on the job and before my colleagues, and inevitably I was ashamed of having inclinations different from others, and I worked against myself to stifle such desires. As a way of sublimating them, I tried to camouflage myself with hard participation in sports. At some point I forgot all about such things, and soon after that I got my red draft papers, and I was immediately sent to Hankou in China. For the above reason, until that point, I had had many homosexual (*homo*) partners, but the length of my relationship with each was extremely brief, and dispassionate, so to speak. But while I was stationed in Hankou, I had some experiences in *danshoku* (male-male sexual relations)[2] that deserve special mention.

My first homosexual (*homo*) partner there was a corporal named Suda. Even in our detail, this corporal was a man with a violent reputation, but from the moment I arrived there, he treated me with kindness, and he demanded nothing of me when I was a raw recruit. I accepted his indulgence and, thinking how lucky I was, sometimes I skimped on jobs that I didn't like. One night, the noncommissioned officers and the soldiers gathered in the barracks and had a drinking party, eating the pigs requisitioned from the town that day. When the party was over, after most of the men had gone to entertain themselves in the "comfort station" (*ianjo*),[3] Corporal Suda took my hand while I was still drunk and led me to the next room, while nobody was there. Corporal Suda then made an appeal of his affection for me, doting on me.

As soon as the appeals had ended, suddenly my body was forced down, and the corporal's well-honed muscles and the solid brawn of his body pressed down on me. That night, I could only acquiesce to the corporal's rough embrace.

In the tight confines of the barracks, the rumors of the relationship between Corporal Suda and me immediately spread throughout the entire detail. When that happened, the corporal responded brazenly, and every night when he went to bed, he would draw me to his side and not let me go. Seeing which, the other men felt an abnormal curiosity about that activity, and *danshoku* became all the rage in our detail. At one point, our barracks looked just like a *danshoku* club.

The continuous, and intense, relationship with Corporal Suda was my first, and I was head over heels. Mysteriously, Corporal Suda, who had been so violent, became gentle even toward the others after he had begun to have a relationship with me. When people have their sexual desire satisfied, maybe they all change in such a way. I too gradually became drawn to Corporal Suda in an emotional sense, but before long he was suddenly ordered to transfer back to the Japanese mainland by our commanding officer. For the corporal, this was a bolt from the blue, but under the enormous pressure of militarism, the wishes and feelings of the individual were wholly disregarded. We promised that we would meet again, and parted reluctantly.

I cannot deny that I was assaulted by some feelings of loneliness after Corporal Suda left. Before long, two or three of the veterans talked me up, but none of them was the type I was looking for, and I wouldn't accede to their requests. However, after a while, my second partner came into the picture. One morning after I had been promoted to cadet rank, some new soldiers entered our detail, and one of them was assigned to me as my orderly. He was a sharp young man, twenty-three or twenty-four years old, of fair color and slight build, who exuded the sense that he was a "well-bred mouse."

He said that his name was Ise, that he was from the prefecture of Iwate, and that he had just gotten married. I took a liking to him at first sight, and after we had talked two or three times I had completely fallen for him. When I gave him something to do, I discovered that he was a really good guy; he had a frank disposition, was possessed of some breeding on account of his good upbringing, and was wonderfully smart. He accepted my feelings and was totally receptive. He would follow me anywhere. I wound up unable to pass my nights or days without Ise. In the end, although I felt sorry for the beloved wife that Ise had left in his hometown, one night I wound up initiating him in sodomy.

My third partner was a private named Kunio. . . . When we had been there for close to two months, we began to feel settled and started drilling. There was nothing special about these drills, which consisted of nothing more than walking through the parks and unfamiliar city streets in formation. I set out every day with a light heart. That was because Private Kunio was in charge of these drills. Even in our detail, he was a notably beautiful man—no, he was so beautiful a young man, with a childlike face, cheeks as red as apples, voluptuous and smooth, that I ought to call him a "beautiful boy" (*bishōnen*).

So of course he was pursued by the veterans, and even some of the officers seemed to have an itch for this beautiful private, but perhaps he was an "impregnable fortress," for until this point he seemed not to have become anybody's *chigosan*. At this opportunity, I resolved to make him mine. As I took him around with me every day, at some point Kunio started to attend on me even after I had returned to the barracks. Trying to smooth over my good feelings, I joked, "Now that I have two orderlies, I'm practically a regular commanding officer." And I was confident that Kunio liked me, too.

One night, I got dead drunk at my favorite drinking hole, the Li chen ren (Water moon), and I returned to the barracks drunk out of my mind, whereupon I fumbled my way into bed with Kunio. Kunio's eyes snapped open at once, and he looked at me with an expression of surprise. Unable to resist his cute expression, I grabbed him tightly. I don't remember what I did after that.

When we set out the next morning for drills, Kunio came to my side, and said, "Sir, you were in quite a temper last night," and gave me a faint, knowing smile. "Yes, I seem to have been rather groggy, and I don't remember anything that happened after I got back to the barracks. Did I make a show of myself? I don't care, just tell me." Kunio replied, shame filling his face. "Well, it was . . . terrible . . . to have you come at me naked, kissing me, licking my face, sucking on my lips, and then I can't say what happened next."

"Really, did I do such things to you? Well, Kunio, you must hate me now."

"No, not at all," Kunio contradicted me with haste.

And indeed he didn't, since after that point—even more than before—Kunio hung on to me and never left my side. When Ise, my orderly, would try to attend to me, Kunio's face would clearly register an expression I could recognize as jealousy.

From around then, the air raids gradually grew more severe. One time, the air-raid siren rang in the middle of the night, and when I rushed outside, Kunio took up my knapsack and came running after me in the middle of the confused crowds. And another time, I passed the night alone with Kunio on the embankment, and as we were indulging in our pleasure for two, we looked down on the city streets of Hankou, flashing with red smoke. Another time, we got covered with mud, crouched in the fields like a pair of sewer rats, indulging in our secret pleasure.

In this way, while I was sunk in my hedonism with Kunio, I was also continuing my relationship with Ise, but in both cases, I was always the one who played the active role, so I occasionally wished that I could be passively despoiled by some strapping older man. However, there was no prospect of finding a partner of the kind I liked around.

I still cannot forget when the city of Hankou was badly damaged by a massive air raid that year (18 December 1944). After the air raid, the streets of Hankou and the Japanese concession to the north were demolished without a trace, and the houses around the station transformed into flat scorched earth. Luckily, our barracks were spared the bombs, and our detail had virtually no casualties. In situations like that, people are selfish and care nothing for others, as long as they themselves have a place to live and enough to eat. We were all relieved, and our characteristic freedom from care began to rear its head. I still walked around the streets of Hankou, much reduced, every day. Sometimes I would take Kunio, and sometimes Ise. . . .

After all is said and done, Kunio and Ise were my salvation, my joy, and even my reason for living. All the other guys recognized my relationship with these two young men and went so far as to nickname Kunio my "page" (koshō). So I too was open about it, and we would sport with no care for who was looking. As we spent our days and nights in this fashion, the five months we were stationed there passed like some foolish dream. In the beginning of April of the next year, 1945, our detail said goodbye to the city of Hankou. Ise and Kunio were transferred elsewhere.

After I left Hankou, what awaited me was a succession of sufferings that I could not begin to recount. To do so would take me afield from the subject of these notes, so I will leave them out here. The war ended on 15 August of that year. After a hard period of living in a concentration camp, I was demobilized in July of the next year, 1946. I returned to the town of my youth, and for a while I rested with my mother there, but I was used to my dissolute lifestyle, and the constrained atmosphere of life in my country home was oppressive. After a month or so had passed, I packed a few things and came back out to Tokyo.

Knowing only the prewar Tokyo of my student days, I found postwar Tokyo so thoroughly changed that it was astonishing. The scenes in the street, human feelings and habits, everything, what stinginess! Everyone you could see was prying about nervously, looking as if eating was the only thing on their mind, or if not that, then with blank expressions of collapse on their faces. But since I had gone to all the trouble to come out to the city, I made up my mind to work hard in this Tokyo and to find a way to live. I found a six-mat room in Kanda and settled there. I didn't have any savings to speak of, and would have to work to live, so starting the next day I looked for job leads. I didn't want to work in a government office as I had before, but after four or five days I had a job in a certain commercial company in the Ginza—really just a black-market pharmaceutical company. About a month after that, through the relentless prodding of my mother in my hometown, I married Masako, a girl of twenty-two to whom I was betrothed. A large part of me is fairly normal, and our conjugal relationship went all right.

One day at the end of October, on the way back from work, my head was full of a feeling of constraint, and to take my mind off it, I got off at Kanda Station and dove into one of the stalls lined up in the area of the station. I downed three cups of sake lees and got straight drunk. As soon as I was drunk, my desire for *danshoku*, which had been dormant since Hankou, welled up all at once. Of course, I had not forgotten about those things since then, but I had no partner nearby, and particularly after I started my married life with Masako, I had had the common-sense fear that those things might bring disharmony to my home, and I had gone so far as to abstain from alcohol altogether. That was because I myself knew best that when I drank alcohol, my desire for *danshoku* was most fiercely incited.

Now, in order to take my mind off my feeling of constraint, insensible to my surroundings, and although I was out of my mind with drink, when the liquor had set in, my desires for that tantalizing love flared up, and I was no longer able to contain myself. Any passerby would be fine. I was so drunk that I wanted to embrace every man I was drawn to, though of course there was no way I could do such a rash thing.

Out of nowhere, I suddenly remembered something: an article on the society page of the newspaper that I had read some ten days before, saying that a certain man had been arrested for the crime of fraud and that when he had been interrogated by the police, he had said he was a "hustler" (danshō) in Ueno. At that time, there weren't many people who knew that there were hustlers in Ueno, and I too had thought it strange when I read that article. I hurried and ran to Kanda Station and bought a ticket to Ueno. I don't feel any attraction for people in the trade, like hustlers. There's no question that an honest man would be better. But then, there was nothing for me to do but seek an outlet in a hustler.

I arrived in Ueno. There was no way to know where they were, but I went ahead and climbed the steps near the bronze statue of Saigō Takamori. There was no moon out, but with the lights at the base of the mountain, the area was dimly lit, and I could see Saigō-san's carefree form, standing upright. It was an interesting turn of events to be looking for a hustler next to Saigō-san, who was reputed to have had a homosexual (dōseiai) relationship with the beautiful monk Gesshō: Thinking this, I was somewhat able to mollify my feelings. The weather was a bit chilly, and there weren't signs of people around me. I stood there for about twenty minutes but saw nobody who looked like a hustler, so at this point I decided to go further up into the mountain, and when I came to one side of the Tōshōgu shrine, someone spoke to me out of the gloom in a low bass voice, calling to me: "Mister, won't you play with me?"

A pure-white face came near. It was a rather nice slim face, with a perm and a one-piece dress. While we exchanged two or three words, I observed that my partner was indeed a male hustler, with his feigned voice and overly feminine coquettish figure. He didn't seem so bad, so I decided to spend the night in diversions with her (?) and was led to a cheap machiai (shelter) at the end of the lake. The result, of course, was that although I wasn't able to obtain anything like the intoxicating ecstasy that came from my fraternizing with Corporal Suda, or Kunio or Ise in Hankou, I was still somehow able to subdue my momentary lust. And one other thing I obtained from my diversions with a hustler that night was a certain hint: that even if I weren't doing it for pay, I could still stand on the street like a hustler, and find my partners that way. The next morning, I parted with the hustler, and on my way home, I made a momentous decision, fixing my mind on cruising the streets.

Thus, one day not long afterward, I made excuses to my wife, saying that work had gotten busy and that from that night on I would be working the night shift. From that night on, I cruised the streets. In my choice of location, I took care not to be seen by my colleagues at work, and considering the geography and the lay of the land, I picked Ikebukuro. For the first ten days or so, I came up dry, but after a while I got the hang of things, and from that point on I started to find partners in ones and twos. I was even able to have some homosexual (*dōseiai*) lovers.

I'll tell you about a couple of those men: A, the head of a section in a company, appeared to take an excessive liking to me from the very start. After two or three days, he came to where I was standing and said to me, "Why don't you come visit me at home now?" I didn't dislike him, so I went along with the invitation and was taken to his house. He was a pleasant man and introduced me to his wife and family as his masseur. From that night on, every night he would call me to his house and would openly indulge in dallying with me.

Then there was the student named B, who fell quite seriously in love with me. He was a student in the sciences at L University, but unbefitting his major, he was an awfully sensitive and pure young man. He had a deep-set, clear-cut face, and although the impression was different, B's face reminded me of Kunio—the Kunio of my days in Hankou. When we had a reunion, B pressed me, saying, "I can't get you out of my head, let's keep house together." When I replied, "I have a wife and couldn't do any such thing," he obstinately pushed the point and said, "Your standing here like a hustler is proof that you really don't love your wife, and to live on with a wife you don't love is immoral, so divorce her and live with me." He was so vehement that he said, "If you don't do as I say, I might kill you." He just went right ahead and did whatever he thought, so pure was he.

But while I might do some awfully wild things on account of my inborn habit of homosexuality (*dōseiai heki*), at heart I am a very commonsensical, family man. Therefore, although I was happy that B loved me, I just couldn't be with him to the extent of breaking up my family. So, I reasoned with B, telling him that it would be rash to break up my family all at a stroke, and that rather than doing that, it would be better to have a longer and less passionate relationship, and held his impetuous heart in check. Inwardly, B might not have been able to consent to what I said, but he seemed to have realized that it's no good for him to try to have his own way, and since then he hasn't pushed me to live with him. I am still seeing this B.

Well, I think I, a foolish man, will end my notes about my homosexual (*dōsei*) career here. Having finished recording it, I can't avoid the feeling that in my writing, I have overly enumerated the pleasures of attaining love. For one, my easygoing nature may have made me do that. . . . But, readers, you know that in this world, there can be no such thing as a succession of pleasures. Surely you will admit that behind all these delights, desolation and concerns hang in the air, like clouds.

NOTES

1. Originally, "the acolyte or *chigo* . . . [was] an adolescent male . . . often sent to serve in a temple or monastery in order to receive an education . . . [and whose figure] played a central role in medieval writings on male-male eroticism" (Pflugfelder 1999: 74). The implication that the *chigo* was both beautiful and the object of erotic desire, often homoerotic, remains in this twentieth-century usage.

2. Literally meaning "male colors," this traditional word for male-male sexual relations was pronounced *nanshoku* in the Tokugawa Era (1603–1867), but later came to be pronounced *danshoku* in popular discourse. See Pflugfelder (1999: 24–26, 184n114).

3. The euphemistically named "comfort stations" were actually mass prostitution camps where indentured women workers were forced to perform sexual services for the Japanese troops.

3

NOSTALGIA FOR MY TIME IN THE ARMY

Concerning Male Nudity and Sadistic Photographs

Morihara Taichi

The other day I saw the New Year's edition of your *Kitan kurabu* on sale in the store, and I was overjoyed and unable to contain my happiness on discovering friends who had the same tastes in collecting photographs as I do. I am taking the liberty of sending you six of the more innocuous of the photos that I've collected. They are extremely mediocre and unsophisticated works, but I would appreciate reviews from all of you who have been collecting these longer than I have. There are a lot of S/M pictures of women carried in your magazine, so I am sending you some pictures of men. They're really quite poorly made. They aren't posed pictures, but rather pictures I took while I was in the army. It's been nearly ten years since then. They developed oddly because at that time I couldn't get any photographic film and used x-ray film instead.

To explain simply: The model in these six photographs is a man who was my subordinate in the army, one So-and-so. We were split up at the end of the war and I haven't heard from him since. He was most attached to me, and now, seven or eight years later, he's still on my mind. I first met him in the summer of 1944, when I was sent from the academy

Translated and reproduced from "*Waga guntai jidai no kaiko: dansei nūdo to seme shashin ni tsuite,*" *Kitan kurabu* (Strange tales club), March 1953: 94–97. Translated by Micah Auerback.

as a cadet officer attached to a certain brigade. From among the new
recruits, I selected one who was still a student in the Faculty of Arts
at Tokyo Imperial University as my personal attendant. I couldn't say
exactly what it was about him that caught my eye, but his face had features as regular as anyone else, and then again I must have taken to him
because of his background—or maybe I had some fleeting jealousy for
that background, from which I had somewhere already derived some sadistic feelings for him. Later I learned that he had had excellent grades
in high school. His character was mild-mannered, and he gave me the
sense that he was a closely tended young child who had stayed that way
to adulthood. He was in all likelihood not the sort who would be promoted in the military. That was the time when the students were being
mobilized or some such, but he had not put in a request for the officers'
academy, nonchalantly entering the army as a regular private—not the
sort who knew the ways of the world.

He was shy and disliked appearing before others; he almost never
quarreled with anyone or did anything else of the sort. Whenever he
had to line up to receive something, which happened a lot at that time,
he was always spotted lining up at the very last place. I took a liking to
that temperament of his and indulged him liberally. Because of that, it
was a natural development that he and I would enter into homosexuality
(*dōseiai*). I had inherited a German Rollei camera from my parents, so I
took pictures of him in various poses. Then I would get really into it and
take pictures that today we would call male nudes.

Picture No. 1 is among those I took in the winter of 1944, when our
brigade was scheduled to join the Kanto Army, in high spirits. At that
point the air raids were gradually growing more severe in the home ter-
ritories, and it was said that Manchuria was a safer place to be. When
I think about it now, we drew the short end of the stick. At that time,
when we had such a large volume of preparations for the move, he made
a real mess of things. By which I mean this: They happened to tell us
that they were distributing cold-weather coats for the officers, so I sent
him to pick one up, but as always he stood at the very end of the line.
The coats ran out, there weren't enough for everyone, and he came
back empty-handed, reporting that he had been told that they would be
distributed after we had arrived in Manchuria. At once I yelled at him
and my irritation flared up, and this resulted in a pitiable picture like

No. 1. Now I think that I really did something cruel. If it had been his own coat, then things would probably have ended there and he wouldn't have complained about not having one. But the army of Japan in those days was a place with no human rights or anything, and terrible things would still happen for emotional reasons. And what's more, there was something sadistic somewhere in my heart.

At that time we were in a place where the sun shone warmly, but a howling north wind was blowing, and the gooseflesh on his shoulders and thighs was clearly visible. He was facing down, so I shouted at him forcefully: "Lift up your head! Now do you see how cold it is?" He raised his head, but his eyes remained averted. When I neared him, his eyes flickered up at my face, but then he averted them again immediately. He looked pitiful to me, so when I had thus exposed him for about half an hour, I untied him from the pine tree, intending to excuse him, but his unselfconscious expression of relief grated on my nerves—alas!—and I left his hands tied behind his back and forced him to lie down facing up. Then I grabbed his ankles and lifted his body up firmly, bending him over like a shrimp so that his two feet were planted on the ground on either side of his head. I stepped on them and pointed his ass up to the sky, and took live ammunition out of the pistol in my pocket. Loading it where he could see, I could feel his burning tension through my feet.

"You can't come until I say you can. Got it?" I thundered at him in a blast, and I dragged him to his feet and retied him and took a snapshot, which produced picture No. 2. As you can see, he wasn't on the heavy side, and actually had a rather feminine body with a light frame. After whacking him on the ass five or six times, I discharged the bullets and took the next picture of his privates with a close-up lens.

I still remember the flustered expression that he made when I first showed these nude pictures to him. But as I took more and more pictures, he got used to them, and later on, I would catch him peering at nude pictures of himself when nobody was around. Maybe he was gradually teetering toward masochism or narcissism.

Picture No. 3 is of the same person, but at that point I could no longer get magnesium, and the photo was taken indoors, so it's extremely dark. This is a work taken when I had gotten together with three of my colleagues to drink. At that time, we made our attendants entertain us, but mine alone wouldn't do anything other than the usual textbook things, so this is what happened as his punishment. At first we were just going to whack his ass in the manner of picture No. 3, but the alcohol got into us and we couldn't stop, and in the end we wound up turning him over and sporting with him as you see in picture No. 4. Aside from this one, all the other photos from this session were obscene. But then again, maybe this one might fit in that category too.

I made him help out when I developed and printed these photographs, and I made him pass them out to all the people who were gathered at that time. I suppose that that was in extremely poor taste. He passed them out bashfully, face averted. But from his attitude, I suspected that in his heart of hearts he might actually have liked it, and that he obtained joy from his exposure fetish. Later, when I embraced him with my hand to his heart, I would jokingly ask him how he felt when he was forced to pass out those nude photographs of himself. He kept his silence, but I could tell that his heart suddenly started to thump. Later still I would persist in asking him, and in the end he would confess that although he was ashamed, he also felt some kind of pleasure for reasons that he couldn't understand.

Picture No. 5 is not of S/M, but rather a picture of ourselves before our pleasure, taken by mutual consent. Perhaps some of you might retort: You might call this "mutual consent," but there's no mutual consent when you've got your clothes on, and he's naked and not wearing a stitch. So let's retitle it "A Picture of a Victim about to Be Sacrificed." Because of the effects of light and shade, it's hard to see his right hand, but as there's no way that I could retake this picture today, it is a precious keepsake for me. He is in a posture that seems most provocative to *danshokusha*[1] (those who engage in male-male sex) like us, though I suppose it might be unexciting for someone without such tastes. But I am drawn less to the squat bodies of women than to the straight lines of men—or, put negatively, you might say, to their flatness. Although I'm not unable to sympathize with the feelings of people who love the plump breasts and buttocks of women, I cannot but feel interest in the flat bodies of men—and this might just be me, but special interest in the nudes of men with light frames.

Picture No. 6 is of punishment. It's a bit difficult for me to tell you why I punished him, but I asked him to do something unreasonable and he hesitated, so I wound up torturing him again as a result. This one is also poorly lit as a result of the effects of light and dark and might look a bit strange, but for me it is a precious picture. I have enlarged it to portrait size and titled it "Super Secret." As you may see, he had round, plump features, and a commonplace expression, but sometimes he would look awfully cute, and would make a face that could be called less cute than noble. When I would go after him, at first he would be jittery and at a loss, but as he got used to it, he would work to affect a calm face, and make efforts not to change his expression. But—shall I say—I have bad taste, and whenever I saw him that way I would want to see his face change and treat him even more harshly. Sometimes, when it was too much for him, I would rejoice to see him creasing his brow, but it was extremely difficult to take a picture of this, since the changes to his expression were momentary. He would always return to his original, calm expression, and I would usually fail.

Picture No. 6 is of a time that I tricked him, tying his hands behind his back and forcing him to lie down on his back. I passed the rope through a hook on the ceiling and snapped the shutter at the exact instant that I pulled hard, raising him up, causing him to make this facial expression in spite of himself. Though he immediately returned to his calm face, it was already too late and I had captured his surprise on film. Later, when I was playing around with him and showed him this picture, it was also pleasant to see his facial expression.

He was, in short, an obedient boy. The second son of a landowner, he never considered the implications behind anyone's words. Something of his ability could already be seen, and I had a feeling that he was born into a race higher than mine, thinking at times that although he was my younger subordinate, he carried a sense of aloofness that made it hard to get close to him. At those times, I would be carried off by a reckless desire to torment him, and I would tie him up and strip him naked, gaze on that noble visage and the naked form joined to it, and gloat in my satisfaction. He was probably a normal man when we met, but the touch of my demonic hands, caressing every part of his body, must have gradually transformed his mind. I peered into, touched, and photographed every corner of his body.

It's been seven years since then. I cannot forget that man, who was pure of heart and to me always seemed like a child. I'm sure that if he knew my address, he would come racing back to me at once. And if he were looking for work, then I could have him work together with me. This time, I would like to associate with him as we gained a more democratic understanding of one another. But then, when I once asked him whether he himself consented or not, he said something to this effect: "When I am treated with no regard to my own will, there is the unease and anticipation of never knowing just what is going to be done to me, and I feel a thrill." Or maybe he would say that things were better when we were in the army.

My explanation, which was supposed to end simply, has instead become a long succession of nostalgic memories of the past. Apart from these I have about seventy or eighty pictures of him, and apart from those, I have collected a few pictures of Japanese and Manchurians in S/M or being punished, many of which I think might or might not count as obscene, so I'm not sure whether I should ask you to view them. But if it were permissible, I would like you to look at them and tell me your opinions. However, since the greater number of them are of my own creation, they are strongly linked to my tastes, and easily tired of, with no novelty. So I'm greatly counting on the photos and S/M pictures in your magazine.

For many years after leaving school, I was in the army or working, and the endless dreary lifestyle has dulled my pen and sent my thoughts into disarray and redundancy. I leave you with best wishes for your prosperity.

Respectfully yours,
Morihara

To: Head of the Reader's Column Division

Thank you for the valuable document and photographs. We wish that we had been able to publish all six photographs in the magazine, but conditions did not permit us to do so, so we have carried only picture No. 2. We would like to send you a more detailed reply in private, so please tell us an address at which you could be reached (a post restante *location is also acceptable).*

Someta Gen

NOTE

1. *Danshoku* (alternately read as *nanshoku*) literally means "male colors" and is a reference to male-male eroticism dating from the Tokugawa period (Pflugfelder 1999: 24–26); *-sha* is a nominalizing suffix. For a discussion of early postwar variants of this term see McLelland (2005: 81).

4

MINYAK KELAPA—A FRAGRANT BREEZE OF HOMOSEXUALITY

Namiki Sansaku

A beautiful local boy came to me with a thick amber-colored liquid in a china bowl. The feel of the liquid—*minyak kelapa*[1]—mesmerizes me as I remember it now.

It was 1944 or Showa 19, when I was nineteen years old—that means, so long as it is the Showa era, I am as old as the era—when I moved to Sumatra. The ship I was on board was the last one that made it to Singapore safe and sound. I moved there to be an apprentice of T Development Company after leaving MK gardening school in spring that year. This company already had farms in Southeast Asia before World War II. I worked on a farm on the outskirts of Palembang for half a year, struggling with the unfamiliar climate.

After a series of air raids in mainland Japan from May of the following year, 1945, the war situation got even worse for Japan. Most Japanese expatriates, except for the elderly, were mustered for war duty. I also joined the army with the adults—I was not yet an adult at that time.[2] Some of these men were in their forties. I was in a machine gun troop in B province facing the Indian Ocean. The barracks were in a rubber tree forest. I was provided with a military uniform—which was just a shirt and shorts, and we were

Translated and reproduced from "*Miniya karapa: sodomii no kazekaoru,*" *Fūzoku kagaku* (Sex-customs science), May 1954: 152–59. Translated by Takashi Fujita.

divided into teams. Once I got there, I felt as if I were swept far away. I felt unusually lonely and wondered when I could go back to my homeland.

The team leader was an old sergeant who fought in the Malay Campaign. He was eager to do his job. I do not remember the name of his assistant, but he was a scary, gangster-type corporal. The first month passed in a flash while I learned under constant pressure the operation and disassembling of machine guns. I experienced B24 air raids in the meantime. I could calmly witness enemy airplanes flying just three hundred meters above the air raid shelter. My body did not feel like my own anymore, maybe due to vigorous and constant military exercise.

Soon they decided to deploy the unit for combat, which was called "military exercise." Because recruits like me were not useful enough for that yet, we were told to stay behind and mind the barracks, and to be trained, which was important nevertheless. I soon became a foot soldier, and Indonesian soldiers were brought in to replace soldiers who left the barracks for combat.

Around this time, one day after I finished exercise, I felt a sudden chill and started shaking with my teeth chattering. I fell flat on my back when I was taking my gaiters off. As I had not been in Sumatra for very long after arriving from Japan, I had not yet become acclimatized. Working on a farm for half a year with vigorous exercise for a month in the tropical climate was hard enough even for a young man like me.

One did not have to be a doctor to tell right away that I had the symptoms of malaria. My fellow soldiers put five or six blankets over me, and one embraced my body to warm me. It should feel stiflingly hot if you are healthy, but I still felt desperately cold. After that phase, I felt very hot and felt my face flushing, and I also had a severe headache. I was feverish.

After a military doctor gave me a shot in my bottom, I was transferred to a hospital ward. It turned out to be a tropical fever that is one of the worst kinds of malaria. That is how I started to recuperate. I was half asleep and half awake for the first few days. I had no appetite at all the next week. One morning I felt better, but realized I still had a temperature of 101°F (38.5°C). I felt quite normal then with this fever, as earlier I had constantly experienced temperatures that were nearly 104°F (40°C).

There was only one Japanese army doctor, one army medic, and three Indonesian soldiers who were assisting the medic. The Indonesian soldiers took complete care of me. I was a private. The Indonesian soldier who spent the most time taking care of me was from Bojonegoro, Java. He was sixteen years old. His name was Tora. As *tora* means tiger in Japanese, he was called Harimau, which means tiger in Malay. However, he was too gentle and cute for such a nickname.

People know things better in Japan nowadays, but people used to imagine Indonesians as natives with dark complexions. But Tora's complexion was not very different from a tanned Japanese. He had nice features with impressively beautiful wet eyes and double-fold eyelids. Indonesians, who have been working in the fields for generations, have nicely balanced bodies. Tora was no exception. He was just five feet three inches (160 cm) tall, but his slim, long legs would make Tokyo women in the latest Western clothes jealous.

Tora was very attentive. It is probably because his brother used to work as a servant for the Dutch as he grew up, and Tora helped his brother in that environment. He was particularly kind to me for some reason. He said I was "not like other Japanese" because I never yell and am polite. I did not mean to behave that way. It was just that I was not strong enough because of the disease. Also, I felt guilty toward him because he attended to all my personal needs, which I had never experienced before. He must have sensed how I felt about it.

My Malay was limited, and so was Tora's Japanese. Yet we were able to communicate with each other smoothly. One day I woke up and felt thirsty during the day. It was still early for a meal or for medication. As I lay half asleep, Tora appeared with a glass of water out of the blue. It was rather eerie.

Although my fever had gone down in a week, I still needed to recuperate, as I was very thin after having no proper food for a week. Yet I don't think I looked terribly ill or weak as I used to be a good swimmer at school and had a good build. Food was not exactly abundant there, but I was lucky enough to be provided with eggs and milk, which were hard to come by in Japan. I regained my appetite in another week and got some of my weight back. The problem I had at this stage was that I had aches in my joints. I was able to make it to the toilet, but I felt slight pain around my lower back and groin when I got up and lay down.

When I told the doctor about it, he said, "Don't worry. It often happens after the fever goes down. Tora can give you a massage. He is a genius masseur." The doctor finished the consultation abruptly and left my bed.

Tora showed up smiling shortly thereafter with a china bowl that had a thick amber-colored liquid in it.

"What is it?" I asked.

"*Minyak kelapa* (palm oil)," he said.

After I asked him twice what he would do with it, he said he would use it for massage. The timing with which he appeared was too soon for the doctor to have sent him to me. It was sheer coincidence again.

Tora told me to take off my clothes and lie down with my face down. He put the oil on and made my back, waist, and thighs smooth. His massage was very skillful.

When I told Tora that the doctor said he was a great masseur, he looked happy and said, "*Saya tuan* (that's right)." He kept massaging and said he would do it with special care that day.

He let me lie down with my face up, and sat on my chest looking towards my feet. He started massaging from my chest. Soon I realized that he was certainly massaging with extra care. I felt it was a little bit strange. I was about to say "stop," but I could not reject him that way, considering how much he had been taking care of me. All I could do was to watch his round bottom moving up and down in front of me.

I should not have felt embarrassed because Tora attended to all my personal needs, using a beer bottle to carry away my urine. Also, his soft touch made me feel as if I were walking through a dream.

Looking back, I was under a charm from this point. I could have escaped it if I stopped him from massaging me. Thereafter, this massage business half turned into play (*asobi*).[3] Although my pain had already gone after a few massage sessions, I could never turn him away when he showed up with thick palm oil in a china bowl. I even started looking forward to it. When I felt the thick oil around my hips and his soft touch, I felt ecstatic and forgot everything else. Once Tora muttered casually, "You are alright. You are full of energy now." I blushed straight away, figuring out what he meant. I decided that we should definitely stop this play.

But in reality, it was hard to resist. Some invisible enticing hand reached to me and shut my mouth that wanted to say "stop." Thus we continued.

Meanwhile the war situation became even more intense. Part of the troop was transferred to barracks near the coast that were a former primary school. They were there to monitor the Indian Ocean and the sky. Rumor had it that British troops would land on the island. One night, we heard a distant murmur and then footsteps rushing toward the yard in the barracks, which echoed horribly in the rubber forest.

Wondering what was happening, I got up, left the hospital ward, and looked for Tora.

It was a dark night without the moon. As I approached the flickering light of a cigarette in a field, I found Tora was lying down and chatting with his fellow soldiers.

"What was that noise?" I asked them.

"We don't know," all three of them replied. There was a tranquility that made me feel embarrassed about my nervous expressions. Even after I concluded it must have been a night exercise, and went back to the hospital ward, my heart was beating in a cowardly way. It was indeed just a night exercise as I gathered later. But there was an unusual atmosphere that traveled 220 yards (200 meters) to the hospital ward.

The war situation bore a sense of urgency that made us feel unsettled. This sense of urgency reached its peak when we heard reports of the Soviet Union joining the war. Even the military doctor who was usually calm got unusually excited and told me, "How can you stay in bed with malaria forever?" It made me get up and almost cry.

We heard of the air raid of a special bomb on Hiroshima, from "the Front Herald," which is the information recovered from incomplete telegrams. I thought I might not see my homeland any more. Whether Japan won or lost the war did not matter to me any more. Soon I began to accept my fate, that of someone dying in this tropical land with nobody realizing it.

I was not as desperate as you might think, and I was almost calm at this stage because of the presence of Tora. Tora was the only family and lover for me. I trusted my whole life to Tora and was living in a sweet dream. I should have questioned myself. In this situation, putting a loathsome label on yourself as being unpatriotic and questioning your behavior would be very natural for a young man, let alone for a soldier at this time in Japan. But I did not care about such business any more. The magic of the thick amber-colored liquid *minyak kelapa* had captured my body and soul.

Then it was the fateful day of 15 August. All soldiers were in the exercise field near town due to an inspection, and the barracks were very quiet on that day. The play with Tora was not just being massaged with *minyak kelapa* any more. There were all sorts of play. As the enclosed bed had enough space for two, Tora came to the bed and got all over me like a snake whenever he had time.

I had experienced a woman just once. I lost my virginity the night before I left Japan to a woman in a port town. As you might figure out, I was not particularly keen on this business. Bad friends of mine—in fact all of them were already married—got drunk, and decided that I should experience a woman and dragged me into a whorehouse. The whore under the bedside lamp with a red shade looked so old and ugly that she would make the legendary old demon woman in Adachigahara[4] look young and beautiful. She had thick makeup to cover wrinkles and poisonously painted red lips. While she might have been excited by the young, nineteen-year-old, naive body, I lost interest in her as she showed her coquetry. It was unfortunate for me that the first experience with a woman turned out like that. My expectations and imagination were shattered. I concluded there was nothing special about the secret of love as I imagined it to be. It was a big turnoff.

On the other hand, the interaction with Tora was something totally different. There is no way that the ugly old woman, even with every trick of hers, could possibly achieve the pleasure of the play I experienced with Tora that started with him massaging me with that slick oil. Unlike the flat rice-cake-like body of that woman, Tora had a lean, flexible body like a female leopard with the curves and softness only boys have. When I smelled the subtle palm oil scent from Tora's body, I felt like I was in a dream and forgot about everything else.

On that day, two other Indonesian soldiers joined a military exercise as assistants along with the Japanese military doctor and an army medic. Only Tora and I were left alone in the hospital ward in the rubber forest. Both of us were lying down dreamily, chatting about trivial things. Neither my Malay nor Tora's Japanese was good enough, but we were probably communicating beyond language. When we looked at each other's eyes, we understood each other. We leaned against each other's shoulder, listening to the sound of the breeze going through the forest and the sounds of birds unfamiliar to me.

When we heard the roaring sound of an airplane out of the blue, we got up and gingerly looked out of a window. The airplane was flying high above from the ocean toward us, then passed the forest in no time. We ducked onto the floor, covering our ears as we were trained to do. However, we heard no sounds of bombs. Not even air strafing was about to happen. After a while there was a murmur from the direction of the barracks where Indonesian soldiers were. Tora tchicked and walked away. It was selfish of me to feel that I could not rely on someone like Tora at that moment.

Then Tora ran back to me with a piece of paper in his hand. He said the airplane dropped it. It was news saying that the emperor accepted the Potsdam Declaration.

"What does it say?" Tora asked me, looking at me with a worried expression. "The war is over," I replied with utter surprise.

After some fuss, we were ordered to demobilize. We were not ready to leave just yet. It was not easy to swallow what we had just heard. We could not believe it so readily. We just looked at each other. Five days later, on 20 August, I was released from the hospital ward. Those who were recruited locally were discharged all of a sudden.

I felt relieved simply because I was free from the military bind, even though I felt uncertainty about the future now. On the other hand, the fact I had to leave Tora was heart-wrenching.

But the restless atmosphere around me did not allow me to indulge in the sentiment.

The troop order was to go back to your workplace, follow orders, and not to act carelessly. That kind of vague order made us even more restless.

I had no idea what Tora was doing around this time. I had not been able to see him since the day we heard the news. I did not need any special care any more, as I was not expected to come down with a fever again. Even so, I could not figure out why Tora, who used to come to see me whenever he had time, had disappeared.

I guess those Indonesian soldiers had their own situations to deal with. Maybe Tora figured out something that let him avoid me. Maybe our friendship was too insignificant, like dust in a big cold wave of reality like this.

I gave up. In fact, I began to think it might be better not to see Tora any more.

But Tora appeared in front of me out of the blue when I was about to leave the hospital ward. He took away whatever I had in my hands. He followed me, almost looking angry. We walked without a word toward my squad on a little path in the rubber forest. We knew that if something was uttered we would embrace each other and cry.

Tora forced himself to smile and, at the entrance of the barracks, told me, "Don't forget." His voice was so weak that it was hardly recognizable. But what he said was very clear to me. "No, I won't. Never." I replied with a strong tone.

Tora stood still and made a Japanese army-style salute that he had just learned.

My smile at him froze and was wiped away when I looked at him trying not to show tears in his eyes. I replied to his salute and expressed all my feeling by saying, "Thank you, Tora." It was the last moment we were together. Our separation was unrealistically simple after we had given our bodies and souls to each other.

The next day we were carried on the backs of trucks toward Palembang and other towns around it.

This is my little memory in the barracks in a rubber forest near the Indian Ocean on Sumatra, far to the south of Japan, around the time Japan experienced the fateful day of 15 August 1945. The memory is so fragile that I now feel as if I were dreaming. It is not only because of the malaria. The rubber forest, the hospital ward made of reeds, the sound of the breeze blowing through the forest, and the sounds of unfamiliar birds—all of these seem like an illusion far away from me. Even Tora's figure that I should not forget looks vague in my mind now. But there is just one thing I remember vividly. It is that thick amber-colored oil, *minyak kelapa*, with its distinctive scent and feel.

NOTES

1. The Indonesian term for coconut oil.
2. In Japan the legal age of majority is twenty years.
3. The term *asobi* (play) has a sexual connotation in Japanese.
4. Adachigahara is a legendary demon that lived on human flesh; she is featured in a famous Noh play.

5

CONFESSIONS OF A PROBLEM

A Roundtable Discussion with Male Prostitutes

Setoguchi Torao (discussion leader); Masako, Ranko, and Otoki[1]
(male prostitutes); and a reporter for Ōkē magazine

Men who deny they are men. Why do people in general not look warmly upon those who cry in the shadows with the loathsome name of male prostitute (*danshō*)? . . . Listen to their true cries!

SETOGUCHI: Based on the fact that I know Otoki and Ranko, I came to be the discussion leader after having been called here in haste, so please speak frankly.

RANKO: It's my personal wish that, while there have been many discussions like this, today we will speak about our true feelings and our true lives.

BACKGROUND

SETOGUCHI: As for the order of the discussion, let us first hear about your childhood.

RANKO: When I graduated from elementary school, I only played girls' games. When I was sixteen I fell in love with a man for the first

Translated and reproduced from "*Danshō zadankai: mondai no kokuhaku*," *Ōkē* (OK) 2, no. 5 (August 1949): 6–12.[2] Translated by Wim Lunsing.

time. It was right about the time when the song *Oka wo koete* (Crossing the Hill) was a big hit and I lived in Minami Sakuma Ward. One
night, when I was browsing in the shops, a gentleman followed me. I
fled in fright. Another time the same thing happened but this time I
thought that the man wasn't so frightening and I went along with him.
In the end I gave him my naked body that night. As a result I felt that
the things I had been troubled by had been resolved and I became so
absorbed with it that I couldn't bring my hands to work. From such
experiences I became obsessed with this world. And seventeen years
later. . . .

SETOGUCHI: That's a long time. How long has it been for you, Masako?

MASAKO: Since 1933, but there was a break of six years.

SETOGUCHI: How old were you when you started in this trade?

MASAKO: Twenty-two. As far as playing around is concerned it was
much earlier. That was in the first year of junior high. I matured early.
When I was little, I was often called a girl. Around the time when I was
in the sixth year of elementary school, there was someone I loved.

SETOGUCHI: Was this person male?

MASAKO: Of course. It was a classmate. Although I loved him, he took
no notice of me. So I pushed him. Then he came after me. I fled. In
the end, he came after me and caught me and hugged me. I was satisfied with this in a happy but shameful manner. From my earliest times
I had some feeling of being perverted (*hentai kibun*).

REPORTER: Weren't you interested in female classmates?

MASAKO: No, I wasn't.

SETOGUCHI: As for living together. . . .

MASAKO: My partner was one year older than I. After I learned this
way of playing around, I left my parental home. I wasn't in good
health. I started reading through pamphlets and so on looking for a
cure for my pleurisy and tuberculosis, but there was none. I got the
feeling that if I was to die anyway, it would be a waste to die without
doing what I loved and I became acquainted with the fact that there
was a society like this in Asakusa. While I was earning some money and
living without thinking about it, I found someone I loved. He became
my "patron" (*patoron*). I had made it.

SETOGUCHI: Your financial master.

MASAKO: Yes. This person is now over sixty years of age. I continued with this man for about half a year. Then I found another man to love. In Asakusa there is a roundup once every month. Because the man I loved was a member of the *yakuza* (Japanese mafia), he got caught and I had to send some things to the prison to some extent. I needed money. I extorted it from the other old man. I thought that he might get enough of me this way, and, with the intent to separate, I asked him to buy this and buy that but, in spite of this, he warmed up towards me and didn't want to separate. In the end I ran away. After this I suddenly met a young man and without holding anything back I was drawn to him and after a while he was called in front of his older brother. When he was asked by his brother: "What is this, you getting together with a perverted man who acts like a woman?"[3] I overheard this and was offended, and so I said, "Isn't it you who brought me to this place," and he became angry and stuck a knife in my left arm. When I was struck, I didn't feel pain but when I touched it I felt a warm substance like water—I bled terribly. I loosened my stiff sash and I stopped the bleeding by binding it around my arm, but because the brother of this man was a respectable person, he showed his true feelings and lowered his head in a bow. Being the hothead that I am, I sharply retorted: "As I have no use for you, stay away from me," and left the house. Afterward I thought that being in Tokyo was boring and went to Osaka. However, recently we met again by chance.

SETOGUCHI: How was it when you met? Had he become like any other person?

MASAKO: It was like the old embers of our love were rekindled between us. However, his family situation didn't allow for it. And in the end it was just a feeling.

SETOGUCHI: About when did you return to Tokyo?

MASAKO: In 1942.

SETOGUCHI: I had known Otoki for about ten years but at some point we met coincidentally at the exit of the Keisei Railway. I didn't recognize her at first. Otoki puts so much into her good looks. I didn't ask about it at the time, but when did you become a woman?

OTOKI: I was born a woman mentally.[4] I began working in the trade after the end of the war. That was because I had nothing else to do.

SETOGUCHI: And until the end of the war?

OTOKI: I was a backstage dresser. After the end of the war, our house was burned down and my family had been evacuated to the country-side. I was alone. The house of my uncle was in Takinogawa and I had been placed under his charge. But my perversity (*hentaisei*) became a problem and I stayed for a while at a hotel in Kurumazaka in Ueno (Tokyo). At that time I got to know Ranko. Ranko had drifted to the vicinity of Ueno before male prostitution began to flourish there. After a short while Ranko went to Osaka. At that time I didn't even think about entering the trade. Maybe she will be angry when I say this, but I looked down on her.

RANKO: (*Nodding in agreement*) That's true.

OTOKI: Working in kabuki didn't even earn enough to buy food. My borrowing also increased. I was told that giving away my body might just give me a lucky break, so why didn't I try it? but over and over again I refused. I didn't have the confidence to get into the trade like a woman. The techniques were explained to me by Ranko at the time when I was living at the hotel, so I roughly understood. I had no money to make a kimono then, so I borrowed kimonos from Akashi (near Kobe) from a fruit seller. As there were no beautifully attired people at the time, my appearance came out first class. So if I went out, I would get a client immediately. I was too afraid to climb the hill in Ueno. When I was down, clients came to me. I needed money, so I had no choice. But I was worried about what to do if I would be found out and ended up refusing all the clients that came. The next day the same thing happened again and I was called "doll Otoki" as in: "What's with her? She's always standing there like a doll."

REPORTER: Photos of you appeared in a magazine, didn't they?

OTOKI: Yes. Thereafter I took a man and he didn't find out at all. Then my self-confidence grew and I started taking one client after another.

REPORTER: Isn't this around the time when there was a lot of attention given to Otoki in the newspapers?

OTOKI: About that time, one day we got word that that night there would be a police roundup and, dressed nicely, I was having tea in a coffee shop with the girls. When we wanted to leave, a police detective came and stopped the girls, saying: "You there, wait just a minute." As their faces were known, there was nothing to do about it but I was a new face so he didn't know me. But when he asked me, "And who are you?" to which I replied, "a friend," he said, "Then you come along too." And I was nabbed and made to go with them. When I went, there were many reporters and in the newspapers of the next day it appeared on a large scale and at once my name became spread around widely. Without me knowing about it, they had made tape recordings. It was embarrassing.

SETOGUCHI: Isn't it about this time that you started appearing in Shinbashi (Tokyo)?

OTOKI: From before Christmas until February this year I was working at a cabaret but I had no income. Then I made my comeback in Shinbashi.

I WANT TO BE SOMEONE'S WIFE

REPORTER: Do you really like it, or rather do you do it because you need to earn your livelihood?

OTOKI: No, I do it to earn a living. I like a homey lifestyle. I want to take hold of a man, become his wife and prepare his food.

MASAKO: That's an ideal. Will it ever . . .

RANKO: We have many sorrows.

MASAKO: Last year I was so fortunate to get a man who supported me, but, as he went bankrupt, I had to start working again.

SETOGUCHI: Masako and Otoki are different from Ranko. Doesn't Ranko love to do it more than that it's to earn a living?

RANKO: Yes. If I feel sexually lonely, I get to feel that any man will do.

MASAKO: Ranko, please tell us about your romance.

RANKO: It concerns the office chief of a small company who began turning up at my place. He tells the women in the neighborhood that they're too good to be on the street. He also says that they should stop their way of life. One day, thieves entered my place and everything was stolen. At that time this man had clothes made for me and was very nice. We got together and I cooked and washed with all my might with the feeling of a real couple. I made great efforts, thinking for instance about what side dish to make. I didn't even buy one shirt. In this period it happened that things didn't go well and he didn't return home for five days. At this time I developed a motherly love like feeling. When he returned the fifth day having drunk alcohol, it ended up with talking of separation, by my saying, "I think you have some secret, if you meet a woman you like, that's alright." Although we tried to separate, we couldn't. At the time I really thought seriously that I would have been better off being born a woman. As he was supposed to come on New Year's Day, I waited for him without touching the food with my chopsticks but he never came. Thereupon his company went bankrupt and he became a vagrant and turned up again. I found him pitiful and bought alcohol and entertained him. I also give him pocket money. But I refused to return to our former life.

If he had come even once since our separation it would have been alright, but as I didn't even hear from him once, I refused.

SETOGUCHI: The book *Danshō no mori* (Grove of Male Prostitutes)[5] tells about women who can't become mothers and men who can't become fathers. When you heard that, how did it make you feel?

RANKO: It's really the same feeling. Why wasn't I born a woman—I've thought this over and over.

PHILOPON ADDICTION

SETOGUCHI: Otoki told us about his worries about being found out to be a young man and that in the beginning he was afraid. Have you ever been found out?

OTOKI: Never ever.

RANKO: Apart from the men who know that I'm a man when they mess around with me, up to this point, I've never aroused suspicion.

SETOGUCHI: Wow. How come?

RANKO: I've been in this business for seventeen years.

SETOGUCHI: If they touch your breasts, it would be rough.

RANKO: It's part of our technique not to let them touch our chest. Even when our clients sleep, we simply don't allow ourselves to fall asleep. That would mean trouble if a client were to wake up in the night. So we mostly take or inject philopon.[6]

SETOGUCHI: This is a big trouble. And if you get a marriage proposal. . . .

OTOKI: It happened to me.

RANKO: There is a case in which a person who was asked to get married as a woman and did so because she didn't know what else to do. After three or four days the stress was too much and she confessed and fled. . . . It became a bit of a problem and she was even accused of marriage fraud. She didn't tell the truth until she actually got married. She was that resistant to telling him that she was a man.

REPORTER: Do you have no interest in women whatsoever?

MASAKO: Only to the extent that I think that woman can be beautiful.

RANKO: In my case my interest extends to noting the woman's clothes, hairstyle, and style.

REPORTER: You have no sexual interest at all in women?

OTOKI: No, not at all. If a woman looks at me, I shudder.

RANKO: I feel no more than friendship.

REPORTER: Are you all virgins in relation to women?

OTOKI: Yes.

REPORTER: Your feeling of loving men is the same feeling as we have of loving women. What sort of man do you find interesting?

RANKO: Until I experience them I don't know whether I can love them or not.

REPORTER: And as for stars?

OTOKI: I like the brusqueness of Sano Shūji.[7]

REPORTER: And Ranko?

RANKO: Hmm, I like, for instance, Ryū Chishū.[8] The way in which he gets a bit angry without saying a word.

MASAKO: There are also men you think you like at first sight but when you talk with them, you dislike them.

REPORTER: Now on the opposite track, seen from your side, men are fickle, but [what] do you most dislike—that is, the worst thing about men?

MASAKO: Even if they're unfaithful I'm not jealous. It's good to have someone with whom you have similar interests. If not, life isn't enjoyable.

SETOGUCHI: In that case, what sort of men do you dislike?

MASAKO: Men who don't know etiquette.

RANKO: If I see a man wearing an aloha shirt I feel like whacking him.

OTOKI: A clean man is good.

REPORTER: When you say that, it struck me when visiting your place, Ranko, that your room was very neat and tidy.

SEXUAL DESIRE AS A MALE

REPORTER: I've been wanting to ask you, how is your sexual desire as a man?

MASAKO: That varies. It varies with the person and with the way of playing with clients.

REPORTER: How about Ranko?

RANKO: If I love someone I get excited. However, I definitely can't get naturally satisfied when having relations with a client.

OTOKI: I'm simple—when I feel like getting satisfaction with a client I love, we get satisfied together.

RANKO: With me it's no good. If it doesn't go a step further it's no good.

MASAKO: When working in the trade, feelings don't get across. When I can't control myself or get dragged along, and even though I think that I should not let my feelings go, I let them go and get satisfaction.

REPORTER: Can't you be satisfied with women?

OTOKI: That would be disgusting.

SETOGUCHI: Otoki said recently that she wanted to get out of the trade, run a bar or something, and settle down. I think everyone thinks that. You think about what you'll do when you grow older.

OTOKI: I want to make a living running an *oden*[9] shop. How about Ranko?

RANKO: That's not possible without a patron, though, is it?

SETOGUCHI: So what do you plan to do when you get older?

RANKO: I will continue in this life as long as I can. I can't throw away the pride that brought me here. If I were to become a vagrant . . . I couldn't sink so low.

MASAKO: We're condemned to potassium cyanide.

OTOKI: That's for sure.

MASAKO: At first I didn't think about suicide. At the end everyone is alone. If there is someone I love, I want to die surrounded by the feelings of that person. I want to die of heart failure or something like that.

REPORTER: Why did you think of committing suicide?

MASAKO: I planned to go to the temple of my family when I grow old. There I would be happy to sweep the fallen leaves and make a bonfire. This was all I planned. But it appears that this temple has become ruined and empty. As there is no one I can depend on, in the end I decided upon potassium cyanide.

SETOGUCHI: Is there no way out, no way to live?

RANKO: As we in the end can't become men, I think it's no good unless the world understands us.

SETOGUCHI: Otomi became an actor. That's really a way to start again.

RANKO: I don't think Otomi can start over.

OTOKI: Hasn't Otomi ended up doing dead-end jobs?

RANKO: Our ideal is to lead the life of a couple.

REPORTER: Is it your goal to lead the life of a housewife or to really find the sexual desire as a woman, which is it?

RANKO: The first goal is sexual.

OTOKI: There's also the night trade but for my own pleasure both are included.

SETOGUCHI: It's Otoki's dearest wish to get out of working for her livelihood, and into cooking and washing for a man she loves, and being taken care of by her husband.

OTOKI: Having become a woman, it's impossible to return to being a man.

REPORTER: We're reaching our conclusion here, but how do you want to be seen by the world?

OTOKI: I don't want to be looked down upon. I want to be thought of as a pitiable person.

REPORTER: How about Ranko?

RANKO: I think we need compassion. In this sense, the people of Tokyo don't have much understanding. In the incident of the assault on the commissioner of the metropolitan police, I felt that the treatment in the newspapers was bad too.[10] If this would have happened in the Kansai region, I think it would have been regarded in a light-hearted manner, like: "Ha ha—Look at them go at it."

REPORTER: Is Kansai really better?

RANKO: There's more understanding.

REPORTER: How about the past and present?

RANKO: In the past, I didn't work as a prostitute like I do now. The way things are done has changed.

REPORTER: How?

RANKO: Hmm . . . it was like the no-good girls on the streets. They put makeup on and walk in the Ginza area. They look at the display windows and hunt for clients.

REPORTER: That's not hunting for a client for one night but for a patron.

RANKO: Yes. If possible someone who has money. . . .

REPORTER: Let's leave it here. Thank you.

NOTES

1. These are all female-sounding names.

2. The editors would like to thank Micah Auerback for bringing this article to their attention. A copy of the magazine can be found in Waseda University Library.

3. *Hentaina onna mitaina otoko.*

4. *Seishintekina onna wa umaretsuki yo.*

5. Sumi (1949). This book describes cross-dressing prostitutes in Tokyo's Ueno Park.

6. Philopon is a methamphetamine.

7. Sano appeared in nearly 150 films from the 1930s to the 1970s.

8. Ryū appeared in countless films from the 1930s to the early 1990s.

9. *Oden* is a stew of fish, tofu, and vegetables served in a fish broth. It used to be sold from carts during wintertime but is now available from most convenience stores.

10. This probably refers to the police raid on male prostitutes gathered in Tokyo's Ueno Park on the night of 22 November 1947. The police raid was motivated not so much by the fact that these were male prostitutes as by the fact they were seeking customers outside the designated red-light zones. Rather than accept being moved on by the police, the male prostitutes staged a riot during which several policemen were injured. The incident was widely reported in the press.

6

GRAND *SODOMIA* CONFERENCE

A Discussion of the Joys and Agonies of Homosexuality

Ujiya Tomiyoshi (the voice of Fūzoku zōshi), Kabiya Kazuhiko (a writer for the Fūzoku zōshi), Fujii Seiji (a barboy, age twenty-two), Sugita Hitoshi (a grocery clerk, age thirty-two), Yamamoto Tatsuo (a salaryman, age twenty-three), Yoshimura Yutaka (a bar owner, age forty-two)

This conversation took place in the afternoon of 10 October 1953 at a bar named Yakyoku in Shinjuku. It was part of a series in the magazine *Fūzoku zōshi*.

We are having a conversation with Mr. Yoshimura, master of the bar Yakyoku (Nocturne), which has the longest history in the city of Tokyo. This magazine endeavors to have a roundtable discussion on behalf of all the *homo* (homosexual) brothers throughout Japan. This magazine has made the first attempt to conduct such an event, which we hope will be appreciated by all our readers.

THE HISTORY OF THE SODOMY PARTICIPANTS

Ujiya: Thank you very much for gathering during your busy schedules. *Fūzoku zōshi* has received the most overwhelming response from readers about our essays on *homo*. Also, we have received so many requests from readers in rural areas asking us to help facilitate the ex-

Translated and reproduced from "*Danshoku no yorokobi to nayami wo kataru: Sodomia dai zadankai*," *Fūzoku zōshi* (Sex-customs storybook), December 1953: 165-78. Translated by Joseph Hawkins.

change of correspondence and to set up a dating association for them. Today, we have the owner of the *homo* café and bar Yakyoku, which has the longest history in Tokyo, along with the barboy Fujii, and our readers Sugita and Yamamoto. I'm going to ask Kabiya to be the moderator today, and others to please speak up and don't be shy. So then, Mr. Kabiya, would you please begin?

KABIYA: It seems that [this magazine] *Fūzoku zōshi* has an editorial policy which is supportive and understanding of homosexuality. As for myself, a person interested in sexual phenomena as a *homo*, and as for those who are in some conflict [about their homosexuality], I think this is a very good thing.

People say that homosexual (*dōseiai*) behavior increases after wartime whenever and wherever throughout history. The same situation can be found in Japan where the number of *homo* after this war has increased significantly, to the extent that people are even considering it to be a trend in some rural areas. Therefore, those who have such tastes are gathered together today here in Tokyo. We'll discuss their experiences and also their considerable presence in Tokyo without embellishment. Through this article, we would like to share this enlightened moment with readers all over Japan. As this is the reason for today's discussion, please disregard all the constraints of logic and theories and such. I am just going to be a listener and leave you, the main participants, to speak. First of all, please talk about your own history of sodomy (*sodomia*) and your homosexual tendencies (*homo no keikō*). How about you Mr. Sugita, are you an *ūru*[1] or a *pede*[2]? How do you define yourself?

SUGITA: I think both. At any rate, in my case my actual experiences of this matter are few. I only started out mixing with those people since this past September, although I had some tendency [toward homosexuality] before then.

KABIYA: So what about you, Mr. Yamamoto?

YAMAMOTO: Me? Well, probably I'm an *urning*. And in terms of age preference I have no interest in younger guys, only men, in other words, over thirty.

SUGITA: I'm also the same way. I'm thirty-two years old but I prefer to have a person who is the same age or older than me.

YOSHIMURA: We have many customers coming to our place who are interested in young guys. And people who like middle-aged and older guys go to Asakusa. There are bars like this one in Asakusa but there are no coffee shops. A person who likes young people generally goes to Shinjuku and drops by this area.

KABIYA: Master,[3] is your main tendency to be a pederast?

YOSHIMURA: (*Blushing*) If I were to choose, I prefer manly types in general.

KABIYA: How about your customers?

YOSHIMURA: They also prefer manly men with a direct manner. Those who like men are feminine so their psychological makeup is very similar to that of females. Therefore, they like manly types in the same way as women do. Accordingly, they prefer rough trade to those that look like dolls.

KABIYA: When you had your first homosexual experience (*homo no keiken*), what was it like. . . ?

YOSHIMURA: It's an innate trait isn't it? In books from the old days there were many obvious articles about homosexuality and there were some in the magazines. I used to read them and I'd get excited. I felt I was a *homo* about the age of around thirteen or fourteen and I had my first experience at that time.

SUGITA: It's the same for me. I've developed since then. However, like I said I started to go out as of September of this year.

YOSHIMURA: That's a very slow case for someone who lives in Tokyo.

SUGITA: No, actually I grew up in the countryside and came to live in Tokyo after the war.

YOSHIMURA: This sort of thing has spread in a big way after the war.

UJIYA: Do you have a family, Mr. Sugita?

SUGITA: Yes, I do. I married into the family of my bride.[4] I made an ill-informed decision to marry after the war. I have two children. However, my wife doesn't have any interest in having sex. While I was suffering from mental agony because there was no way to obtain sexual satisfaction, I found places in Shinjuku and Asakusa where "those people" gathered. I started to go to Shinjuku and experienced that world for the first time. However, that first time I was scared and I came right back home without doing anything.

UJIYA: What was the first experience for you then?

SUGITA: At a movie theater. I got to know a guy there and he told me there were some *homo* places in Hibiya and Ginza.

KABIYA: When was the experience in the movie theater?

SUGITA: It was in the first week of September.

KABIYA: Was your partner older?

SUGITA: There were many young people there but I wasn't interested in younger people much. Older people also came there but I felt some insecurity, so I came back home.

UJIYA: When did you start, Mr. Yamamoto?

YAMAMOTO: Yes, it was about junior high school—second year. I was about sixteen years old. The teacher from my school did stuff like that to me. I wasn't at all conscious at that time about homosexuality (*dōseiai*) and also I didn't understand, so I just thought, "He's treating me with affection." However, during the war, because I was in a group-living situation while I was working in a factory as a student, that sort of thing also happened there. It wasn't like it is nowadays with everybody being aware that this sort of thing goes on. I didn't know too much about it.

KABIYA: Master, don't you have any love experiences with women at all?

YOSHIMURA: No. (*laughs*)

SUGITA: I had been seriously involved with a female while I was in the military. While I was in the army, I sometimes got as many as four letters in one day from that lady. Some military members and officers who were in charge frequently became angered by the situation.

UJIYA: Did you have any love relationships with women, Mr. Yamamoto?

YAMAMOTO: I started to be aware of this after the war—in 1949. So, I was the same as ordinary people before that, and I had relations with women, but they didn't work out. If you're going out with a female then it is already assumed that you are on course for marriage, isn't it? However, living this way the situation is more complicated and somehow more interesting too. Having said that I didn't think "how disgusting" when looking at women either. Of course they are beautiful and I feel something of an attraction for them. However, I think homosexuality (*dōseiai*) is much better.

HOMOSEXUALS AND MARRIAGE

KABIYA: Do you want to be a single man for the rest of your life?

YOSHIMURA: It's too late for me to think about marriage now that things have come to this stage.

KABIYA: How about you and marriage, Mr. Yamamoto?

YAMAMOTO: I'm going to marry someone, just like ordinary people do.

KABIYA: Is that what you want to do?

YAMAMOTO: Half of it is my own will. The other half is in consideration of my parents' wishes. If anything, my character might be optimistic, I don't get distressed too much. I've thought about it for a long time now, but I am going to get married and have a family soon.

KABIYA: Do you think you will have a good relationship with your female partner?

YAMAMOTO: If I were in that situation, I think it would work out.

SUGITA: In my case, it's been an extremely happy home. The youngest child is five years old right now. Since we had a child I've never had sex with my wife, but also we've been sleeping in different rooms after that.

KABIYA: And marital love?

SUGITA: If you trust in each other things are harmonious, I think.

KABIYA: Does your wife know of your homosexual tendencies?

SUGITA: No, she doesn't.

YAMAMOTO: In the cases of the people whom I've gone out with so far, their wives know all about most of these things. These men tell their wives about themselves and I've heard that they understand.

YOSHIMURA: As I heard, Mr. Sugita married into the family of his bride, correct? It is common among the customers who come to my shop to have a similar situation. Although they have been married to their wives for five to eight years, there are many cases among those men who leave her all alone. The situation for the wives is really pitiful.

SUGITA: In my case, if anything, my wife hated the marriage relationship.

UJIYA: Doesn't she say anything about not sleeping in the same bed?

SUGITA: She doesn't say anything at all. In either event my wife is meek. There are six in our family. In my situation everything in the household, from clothing to almost everything, I buy everything to give them. My wife barely goes outside almost the whole year long.

KABIYA: Are you hiding your homosexual tendencies in the company that you work for, Mr. Yamamoto?

YAMAMOTO: Yes. I don't think it's necessary to show that there.

KABIYA: How about to your parents?

YAMAMOTO: I don't think they know. They think I'm just hanging around with my friend.

KABIYA: Master, you said you like manly types. Were you talking about appearance?

YOSHIMURA: Appearance and character also I would say. And it makes me happy to conquer them.

KABIYA: Master, do you go out with your customers?

YOSHIMURA: I'm trying to avoid doing that with my customers as far as possible. There are some people who try to get me but I believe that's not a good thing for the business and I'm patient without taking action. I often get letters from customers after they return to the local rural areas, and they ask me to use them as a barboys when they're visiting here. Yet the people who talk like this have a tendency to float around so I've never used them.

SODOMY AND ROMANCE

KABIYA: Where do you usually meet your lover—is there any specific place for that?

YOSHIMURA: Not specifically, it varies.

KABIYA: Excuse me for asking so bluntly but how do you have sex? How about anal sex and masturbating each other?

YOSHIMURA: . . .

KABIYA: How about you, Mr. Sugita?

SUGITA: Like I said, I am still kind of new to this world, so I can hardly show my feelings to anyone aggressively yet.

YOSHIMURA: I prefer one at a time—it has to happen when we are in love. But of course I know some people who go to hotels with four or five people to have fun.

SUGITA: There are such people—in my case when someone asked me to have a three-way I refused.

UJIYA: But how about you, Mr. Yamamoto. Can you be satisfied to go somewhere with someone without having sex?

YAMAMOTO: Well, it depends. Sometimes we end up having sex, sometimes not. But most of the time it doesn't happen.

UJIYA: How about the place?

YAMAMOTO: We usually go to hotels.

KABIYA: When you go to those kinds of places they think you're odd, don't they?

YAMAMOTO: Everybody these days knows about it.

YOSHIMURA: Recently, all of the maids at the hotel know about this sort of thing.

SUGITA: I just started to do this recently so I'm sort of embarrassed when I go to some hotels. Even if they ask me, I won't go to someplace where I've been before.

UJIYA: Of course you have foreplay before actually having sex, don't you?

YAMAMOTO: There would be no fun without doing that. . . .

YOSHIMURA: Recently lots of young people are going out with Americans. They have very rich sex lives so much so that we traditional Japanese would be surprised.

YAMAMOTO: Among male prostitutes, some like foreigners and others don't. But even among them, there also seems to be the pattern that the younger ones have more sex techniques than the old ones.

KABIYA: Are you passive, Mr. Yamamoto?

YAMAMOTO: In my case, I prefer older people, so that means passive, doesn't it?

KABIYA: Do you have anal sex?

YAMAMOTO: How embarrassing. (*laughs*)

KABIYA: I get notes from people and often they write about the details of their sex habits. I find the vast majority participate in mutual masturbation and fellatio.

YOSHIMURA: Yes, after the war the foreigners came and these days sex is getting more hard core. It's strange but foreigners lick all over your body, even between the toes. The foreigner who comes to my bar took a young boy and went out with him. Later the young boy came back and told me, "Mr. Yoshimura, I was shocked. The foreign guy asked me to pee into the glass many times. I didn't want to do it but I did. Then he drank it." Another person who was out with a foreigner told me that the foreigner asked him to shit and so he went to the toilet. The foreigner followed him. The guy got angry when the Japanese boy tried to wipe his ass. So, the Japanese guy came out without wiping his ass and the foreigner licked and kept saying, "Good, good."

KABIYA: That's called a urine-drinking habit. I heard there are many cases.

YOSHIMURA: There are many men who like to drink semen.

UJIYA: I assume performing mutual masturbation at the theater is easy, isn't it?

SUGITA: That's why people are doing it in the theaters, isn't it? I've often seen it.

UJIYA: Still, the sexual participants who do this kind of stuff in the movie theaters must get a surprising thrill doing this and it might be preferable, mightn't it?

KABIYA: For the partner then there is something inspirational about sexual preference, isn't there?

YAMAMOTO: Yes, that true. Somehow, the precise inspiration comes to me.

YOSHIMURA: So, it isn't only the appearance is it?

YAMAMOTO: Yes, that's right. The face is really not a problem for me. But an expressionless face is out.

SUGITA: And then, if they aren't clean, I don't like it.

YOSHIMURA: On the other hand, there are those who like uncleanliness. For me, I like neat people of course when we go to the hotel together. When the other person takes off their clothes, if he is wearing pure white underwear I will suddenly get an indescribable excitement. On the other hand, if the person isn't clean I will be disappointed.

UJIYA: Master, because of your vast amount of experience it must require a great deal of foreplay for you before ejaculation mustn't it? Because of your sophistication, you must thoroughly enjoy the experience.

YOSHIMURA: It depends on my mood at the time. When it's quick, it's really quick. When I think about it there are also times when I've enjoyed myself for up to an hour.

KABIYA: In the case of *homo*, are there also forty-eight body positions?[5]

YOSHIMURA: Everybody looks at those illustrations and does it, but in the end, isn't it the same case as female and male?

KABIYA: Historically, male prostitutes are said to be serving customers performing doggie style (*bakku*),[6] nowadays do regular amateur people do it from behind?

YAMAMOTO: Many people hate having anal sex and because of that there are many people who do everything else to the exclusion of that.

YOSHIMURA: These days, the most common occurrence is blow jobs isn't it? Before I had this bar, all of the people in the entertainment industry were into anal sex so I believed that there were no other styles than the ones in those relationships. Then, I started to go out with many different kinds of people after the war and most of them didn't do doggie style so I began to realize that the most popular form of sex was fellatio. I can't say that with absolute certainty because sometimes it depends on the person's individual style—with one it must be anal intercourse, for another they must have fellatio. Anyway, after the war kissing and giving blow jobs became popular.

KABIYA: Sugita-san, when you're having sex with your wife are you consciously thinking of her as a female?

Sugita: Well, I fantasize.

Kabiya: Do you fantasize your partner as male?

Sugita: Yes.

Ujiya: Master, have you had any experience of marriage or experiences with females at all?

Yoshimura: No.

Sugita: Didn't you think at all about how the people around you thought about you?

Yoshimura: When I was in the entertainment industry, the people around me never recommended that I do that. However, since I started in the bar, there have been some conversations about marriage, and some arranged marriage meetings, and I passed each time. There was a time when I was approached insistently. However, I was only doing it because of the expectations of society from the beginning and I rejected the offers every time. I felt sorry for the other party.

Ujiya: Were you in the entertainment industry long?

Yoshimura: I was in it for ten years.

Kabiya: Were you playing the *onnagata* (female roles)?

Yoshimura: Yes, I was.

Kabiya: It seems there are many of this type, aren't there, in the entertainment industry?

Yoshimura: Yes, there are a lot. Most of the *onnagata* are this type.

Kabiya: I've heard that one of the groups called S in the Kansai region has many of that type.

Yoshimura: All of those people are my friends, when they come to Tokyo they come here to see us.

BEHIND THE SCENES IN THE BOY WORK

Ujiya: When did you start working at Yakyoku, Mr. Fujii?

Sugimura: It's already been five or six years. During that time I've been a "bride" (*oyome*) once.[7] (*laughs*)

KABIYA: Fujii-san, do you get a loving feeling from boys (barworkers)?

FUJII: I don't feel it.

KABIYA: Is it because your *homo* tendencies are the same? Like *ūru* friends?

FUJII: It's not specifically that.

KABIYA: What would you do if the customer had similar tendencies to yours? Would you take some offense?

FUJII: Not especially. Customers either like it or they don't.

KABIYA: Do you get male and female couples as customers?

YOSHIMURA: It's no mystery that normal people don't come to my place. Occasionally male and female couples do come by and we usually think they don't know what's going on, but it often turns out they've heard a rumor and have come by to check us out. (*laughs*)

YAMAMOTO: Normal people go to the Brunswick[8] or the Ibsen.

SUGITA: The people who know about those places are a small portion of the total population, aren't they?

YOSHIMURA: There are people who don't want to come to these places although they know about them. Even *homo*, isn't that right? Therefore there are a lot of people who go to movie theaters and parks and so on.

KABIYA: Can you describe one experience when you went to live with someone. Was it your customer's place?

FUJII: Yes.

YOSHIMURA: (*Although the question is asked directly to the barboy Fujii, Yoshimura, who is the owner of the club, takes over the task of responding.*) It happened like this. Three or four customers came into the bar and asked me to lend this particular boy to them. However, I told them we have a policy that we will never let them have him while the business is open. Then, he said, Master, it's OK, we are only going to have a cup of tea. If there had only been one customer, I wouldn't have let him go but there were three or four. Then, I wondered and worried about what had happened to him because he never came back for three days. And then, on the fourth day he came back as if nothing had happened, so I asked him, "What happened?" "Actually," he replied, "The man will make my life happy forever and he's going to give me a position in his own company where I will work hard." Then, I said, "Go then, if that's what's going to happen." And then I gave my permission to let this boy go to that customer. At first, the company was running smoothly. The patron (*patoron*) had rented a room for him. He was commuting to the company from there, but it was a small company and it wasn't going well. The company closed, so the owner took him to his own house. His wife didn't know what was going on. Anyway, it seems she didn't want to let him stay there because he was just a boy that her husband had employed in his company. So she treated him coldly and harshly. Afterwards, the boy came to talk to me and I told him he could stay at my bar, so he's here now.

KABIYA: Was the customer older?

YOSHIMURA: About forty years old. . . .

UJIYA: It must be fun when you are working at the bar.

YOSHIMURA: It is fun, isn't it? Anyway, if you don't drink as much as a cup of coffee, you can't stay in the bar. And the boys are getting a salary. However, I wouldn't let these boys do anything lewd.

UJIYA: In places like yours, it seems like if you hire beautiful boys there must be many customers who come by who are focusing on just one particular boy, aren't there?

YOSHIMURA: Yes, that's right.

KABIYA: (*Speaking to Fujii*) You must experience lots of temptation from the customers, mustn't you?

FUJII: Yes, there is a lot.

YOSHIMURA: But if you are working in the business for a long time you get to know the psychology of the customers and you begin to know their true feelings and if they are telling the truth or not.

KABIYA: So what would you do if a love were real?

YOSHIMURA: If that's the case even the owner of the business can't stop it. I don't want to interfere in someone else's romance.

UJIYA: There are many requests in the form of letters asking us to arrange a barboy who looks like the one in the enclosed pictures. (*To*

Fujii) It might be difficult to talk because the Master is present but can you speak your mind about the fun things and the hard things?

FUJII: Really, there aren't any particularly hard things.

YOSHIMURA: I think it must be hardest to reject the offers from customers who are aggressively pursuing what they want.

FUJII: It's a business thing. So I don't want to offend my customers. And at the same time I don't like to trick customers to make them pay a lot of money either. . . .

UJIYA: Anyway, there are many readers who are begging for arranged meetings.

YOSHIMURA: That's right, isn't it? In the countryside many people are troubled by not finding someone.

UJIYA: You're happy when a customer you like comes in, aren't you?

YOSHIMURA: Of course, even I get lighthearted. (*laughs*)

KABIYA: When did you start to be aware of your homosexuality, Fujii?

FUJII: At eighteen.

KABIYA: Was it an older man as I assumed?

FUJII: He was in his twenties.

UJIYA: What kind of temptation do you receive from your customers? In the regular bar the customer shows money to make the invitation, but. . . .

FUJII: That's not how it happens.

YOSHIMURA: Actually, it depends on the person. They might invite them to the movie theater and then slowly. . . . Then again, there are those who are aggressive and say, "Won't you spend the night," as well. But, if from the first time the person is too aggressive and the offer becomes too businesslike, we decline. Well, these things start out as beautiful love romances, then when they get to know each other they have sex, don't they?

UJIYA: If three or five customers get attached to you it's troublesome, isn't it?

YOSHIMURA: There usually aren't three or five people. (*laughs*)

TOKYO PLACES TO HANG OUT FOR SODOMY

KABIYA: By the way, how many coffee shops or bars like yours exist in Tokyo?

YOSHIMURA: Well, quite a few new ones opened last year. There are four in Shinjuku, and in the Ginza district—from Ginza to Shinbashi—there is a place that opened a week ago. If you add that, there are about four or five. After the Pacific War, I started to do this in 1946 and at that time there were no other places like this that existed in Tokyo yet. As a result, the number of customers was particularly big. After that, here and there, places like this one began to appear dispersed throughout the city. But, people coming from the countryside heard about my place and they came here. Because our place is old, customers who haven't come for a while still sometimes show up.

YAMAMOTO: Mishima Yukio used Ginza's "B" bar [i.e., Brunswick] in his novel. It was publicity but it also caused problems, they say. Over there, those people would go to the second floor, and the regular people who didn't know anything about it would stay on the first.

UJIYA: In these places the treatment of the customers sometimes took great care, didn't it?

YOSHIMURA: Yes, that's right. Ten people have ten different colors and also they are from various class levels.

KABIYA: What were you thinking when you went to these kinds of places—like Mr. Yamamoto, for example? Were you simply taking a break? Or was there another purpose?

YAMAMOTO: No, I just stumbled in.

KABIYA: Wasn't that because you could meet some pederasts among the customers?

YAMAMOTO: Yes, that's probably true.

KABIYA: Master, in this kind [of] business there are lots of handsome boys and it's good for those customers who like the "beautiful boy" (*bishōnen*) type, but what about those who like masculine kinds of men?

YOSHIMURA: There are boys who have well-built bodies in this kind of place.

YAMAMOTO: This place is more comfortable if you compare it to the others. That's why the customers don't feel the pressure to be so strident when they come here. Master, Koharu, the other branch of Yakyoku, is vastly different in terms of the atmosphere, isn't it?

YOSHIMURA: Yes, it is. That place's customers are comparatively older.

KABIYA: Could you give one example of your tough experiences in the treatment of the customers. You must have tons of them, haven't you?

YOSHIMURA: Yes, I have. Like I said just now, if there are ten people, there are ten different ways of doing things and we have to judge. For example, there might be a customer who looks like a gentleman because he is dressed well but who turns out to be a savage beast. (*laughs*)

SUGITA: Do other people in this kind of business come to your place?

YOSHIMURA: Sometimes I see them. Although they only come occasionally they usually bring a partner they found somewhere else and they bring him here to drink peacefully in my bar.

BOYS WHO ARE LIKED BY WOMEN TOO

KABIYA: You aren't attracted to women at all, are you, Mr. Fujii?

FUJII: I think they are beautiful, but sex is a different story.

YOSHIMURA: That is why occasionally, on his day off, the waitresses in the neighborhood invite him out or treat him to a movie.

KABIYA: Oh, so the women like you then, do they?

YOSHIMURA: Yes, that's right. They say that all of my boys are particularly beautiful. And the neighbors say that so many of my customers are good-looking too. The people who come to my place are not that special, but they like the fastidiousness of their appearance.

YAMAMOTO: Compared to the regular world, many of them are very sophisticated.

UJIYA: In the case of enticement from females, do you change suddenly?

FUJII: The boy will try to crack jokes, but the customer often doesn't get it and becomes overbearing.

UJIYA: Despite being hassled by women, you don't feel any sexual desire?

FUJII: I feel that male and female relationships are much scarier than male-male ones.

KABIYA: One of the causes of homosexuality (*dōseiai*) must be the feeling of dread toward women mustn't it? To be close to women is difficult and man-to-man relationships are much easier.

YOSHIMURA: There are occasional cases of young people who are going to have sex for the first time and become impotent because of fear. In that same context, they may feel that women are unclean, or that they are fearful of them, don't you think?

SUGITA: Do people come here asking to be introduced to prospective partners?

FUJII: Yes, they do and in these cases I'll be the matchmaker.

SUGITA: That must be pretty difficult, if that's the case.

FUJII: Afterwards there were some people who left word saying that the matches were unsatisfactory. (*laughs*)

UJIYA: If customer A says that was good and B says no, then that can be difficult, can't it?

YOSHIMURA: If we do that, then there are a number of problems that can arise.

SUGITA: Is there anyone who starts to go out with someone they don't like from the beginning?

YOSHIMURA: If they dislike them, they wouldn't go out in the first place, don't you think?

KABIYA: Is there anyone who has become "a bride"?

YOSHIMURA: Yes. (*laughs*) A boy who was here until recently was loved by his customer so much and the customer was from the countryside and as he came to Tokyo he made the boy take a vacation to drag him around with him. When I said, "That is really making trouble to do that," then the patron gave this boy a monthly stipend so that he quit the place and he's being taken care of. It is odd to say but the boy belongs exclusively to this guy anyway.

SUGITA: But those situations don't last a long time, do they?

FUJII: This guy was not a Tokyoite, he's from the countryside and he usually has a distance between him and his boy instead of living close together, that way the relationship lasts longer.

UJIYA: When you were a bride were you happy, Mr. Fujii?

FUJII: I wasn't all that happy. For some reason, it didn't go as well as I'd hoped. The person I like doesn't want me, but the person who likes me I have no interest in.

SODOMY'S PERVERSITY AND VARIETY

UJIYA: By the way, Master, are their any bullies and bullied among same-sex practitioners?

YOSHIMURA: Yes, there are. There are people who like to tie up another person's body to make them happy and also there are those who become ecstatic from being bound.

KABIYA: Among the people who like being bound the *urning* type is most common, isn't it?

YOSHIMURA: Yes, that's correct. There is one foreign guy who wants—while he's giving fellatio or making someone else do it to him—to be whipped with a leather strap. He says that when the welts get red it feels really good.

UJIYA: Fujii-san have you ever had to go with a perverted customer?

FUJII: No. But I've had customers who pestered me.

UJIYA: But if you like him, then it isn't unpleasant is it, even if he is persistent?

FUJII: But I don't like persistence too much.

UJIYA: Even if Americans are homosexual (*dōseiai*), they are not satisfied with normal things, are they?

YOSHIMURA: It seems that way.

UJIYA: Yamamoto-san, how about foreigners, you don't like them very much, do you?

YAMAMOTO: I don't dislike them, but I don't understand the language perfectly and they don't take baths as much as Japanese so they are filthy. (*laughs*)

FUJII: It is a different physical constitution to that of Japanese, isn't it? But there are those who like that.

SUGITA: If you are doing it with foreigners, aren't you uneasy the first time?

YAMAMOTO: Even among foreigners there are good and bad people. Therefore, there is little meaning in distinguishing them from Japanese to me.

YOSHIMURA: Foreigners appear very kind. Japanese are quick to turn away after the sex is over and sleep, but foreigners have a good technique in the aftermath. That's why, with one person I know in the Japanese case—he only likes young guys but with the foreigners anyone is OK and there is no discrimination based on age.

UJIYA: Sugita-san you aren't very experienced, so you probably don't have any experience of perversities either, do you?

SUGITA: I have no experience. One man offered for me to go to a public bath somewhere and to stay and wanted to caress me while I was sleeping.

HOMOSEXUAL (*DANSHOKU*) TECHNIQUES

UJIYA: Are there a lot of techniques you naturally come to know?

YOSHIMURA: Especially young people. Older men use them as toys and ten different people have ten different styles, so after you've been with ten different people you remember those ten different ways of doing things.

KABIYA: Each person's style is different, but what kind of technique is the most popular?

YOSHIMURA: There isn't too much difference in the case of heterosexuals.

KABIYA: Anyway, one is masculine and the other is feminine. By the way, Master, the person who has a tendency to be *urning* has in a sense a stronger masochistic character and a strong exhibitive tendency, so they must be pleased with the doggie style.

YOSHIMURA: Yes, that's right. It depends on the person's constitution. Some people even though they are young can't do it no matter what. And then, there are older people who can do it without pain calmly.

There is a story from a long time ago where a movie actor had difficulty getting the things he desired. He came to drink a cup of tea by chance and he was adored by a veteran of this way and was forcibly tempted to a hotel or somewhere, and after two or three days the veteran came back and he said he could really do everything. "Wasn't it the first time?" I asked. Although it was his first time, he told me, his muscles were flexible and therefore everything was fine. There was an incident like that. There are males whose constitution is like that of females itching to have anal sex, but on the other hand, there are people who have no sense, they do it just for the money.

UJIYA: When they do it doggie style, do they put something on?

KABIYA: Lubricating oil. From the old days, male prostitutes used oil for swords when they had anal intercourse.

YOSHIMURA: However, once you are a veteran you don't have to use it.

UJIYA: Still, for people who like to take it in the behind, that's the best isn't it?

YOSHIMURA: Really, for some men who are tired of women but don't necessarily have a tendency toward homosexuality, there are those who convert. Anyway, in the army, during the war, among the recruits, these things became widespread. Then after the Americans came, and more newspapers started to write about them, so many people know about these things these days.

UJIYA: If you read Mishima-san's book, pomade or some sort of similar thing like that was carried around as it was written in the book. In those days, they had a particular or special oil for anal sex didn't they?

YOSHIMURA: Is that right, I wonder how that was? As I listen to the conversation, I remember that some people used cold cream and penicillin ointment. And in the old days there was no cold cream, so people used Vaseline instead. Since we produced cold cream, it smells very nice too. And also some people who are more concerned about sanitation, even if they get hurt, they can manage pretty well if they use penicillin ointment.

UJIYA: If you like men, or the phallus,[9] it is best if the appearance is perfect, isn't it?

YOSHIMURA: Seven or eight out of ten men are made happy by the larger size.

UJIYA: Do you get a lot of excitement from the phallus, Yamamoto-san?

YAMAMOTO: Of course.

UJIYA: Mr. Fujii, among the customers who come to the bar, there must undoubtedly be those who are mischievous.

FUJII: There are those who on every occasion come to touch my penis.

KABIYA: Do you let them touch it?

FUJII: I'm not letting them touch it. On the other hand, if I am attracted to the other person, then it's a different story. Actually, that seldom ever happens. However, if I begin to like them then our shared understanding becomes conspicuous.

UJIYA: Sugita-san, how do you feel about getting it from behind?

SUGITA: I don't like it. I was asked to do it once, but I said no.

YAMAMOTO: I hate it too.

UJIYA: For the beginner, in the case of a rear entry, the possibility of injury is of concern, isn't it?

KABIYA: I've heard that the rectum can be injured.

YOSHIMURA: There's that, but if you get a bacterial infection of the colon it's just like gonorrhea where pus might come out and it hurts. I heard of a case where someone thought it must be gonorrhea, so they went to a doctor to get an injection of penicillin but it didn't work. Then, they told the doctor the real story and he told them it must be a bacterial infection of the colon and he gave them medicine and it seemed to go away. That's the reason why I'm not too enthused about taking it from the back.

KABIYA: By the way, don't people who are homosexual (*homo keikō no hito*) want to be cured?

YOSHIMURA: There are some who do.

KABIYA: How about you, Master?

YOSHIMURA: I am becoming aware that I won't be cured until I die. I was born like this, so it is an instinct for me to love someone who is androgynous. There are those who believe they can fix it by getting married, but year by year they return to their former ways. However, I admonish them not to cross the line even once, don't abandon your families! Then, I also lament the cases where the really young commit crimes for profit. To do it for love and romance is wonderful, but to do it for material things is. . . .

KABIYA: Yamamoto-san, what do you think about treatment?

YAMAMOTO: I want to fix it. Although I may not be able to cure it completely, I hope I can decrease it by experiencing sadness and disillusionment to some degree.

YOSHIMURA: So that's the way you've come to think. In point of fact, despite your feeling of disillusionment and guilt now, at some time after a couple of years you may want to have that feeling again.

KABIYA: Sugita-san, do you have the will to change?

SUGITA: I'm probably about the same as Yamamoto. In my case, I think about my family especially and I don't want to break myself away from it.

UJIYA: Fujii-san, do you have the desire to cure yourself? But you must be enjoying yourself, aren't you?

FUJII: Yes, I am happy.

UJIYA: In the case of heterosexuals, it seems that their sex takes a longer time, because the sensitivity of the female is very sluggish. How about in the case of homosexuals?

FUJII: If it is someone you like, longer is better.

KABIYA: Do homosexual people have training to increase their sexual capacities? Like drugs?

YOSHIMURA: Yes, they do. (*laughs*)

UjIYA: I've heard when this type of people meet and make arrangements they are different from heterosexual people in that they are impatient.

YOSHIMURA: Yes, that's right. If the person tries to pick up A and that doesn't work then he'll try B, and if not B, then he'll go to C. However, each of these people must feel as though they are being toyed with. In the end, the person won't get anyone.

SUGITA: In movie theaters there's a lot of that. When a person finishes with one partner he will move on to another almost immediately, it's like that. But that's really disgusting, isn't it?

UjIYA: So what's your way of deciding which man in the theater is what you are looking for?

SUGITA: In the case of normal people, they usually don't like to have their bodies touched, but the type at the theater, they like to touch. Furthermore, the places are predetermined so if you go there they are almost surely in the place where they were assigned to sit. So, then, if you don't like doing that, you have to step to the side or some other area of the theater.

UjIYA: Finally, can you tell me something about the varieties of techniques used by homosexuals?

YOSHIMURA: Yes, there are many.

FUJII: *Urning* on top, or *pede* on top. . . .

YOSHIMURA: That's why there isn't even a small difference from males and females.

FUJII: There are some people who like rub your chest too.

YOSHIMURA: I heard that for some people that really brings ecstasy.

SUGITA: Probably depends on a person's constitution.

FUJII: Still, even if it is a man if you rub the nipples they become erect.

UjIYA: Yamamoto-san, what turns you on?

YAMAMOTO: Probably, if they are a good kisser, it's good. Of course, if you like the other person, after a while whatever he does, you will get turned on.

UJIYA: But, even if you don't like them what can make you give in? Do you have a weak spot?

YAMAMOTO: Nothing. If I don't like the person, no matter what they do nothing will happen.

KABIYA: In the end, for the *homo* and for the *urning* the perfect person doesn't exist. In conclusion, the homosexual's affection is mainly based in the mind. That's the main point.

UJIYA: In conclusion, this is probably it about here. Thank you for speaking about many real subjects that usually we won't get a chance to hear about—this will serve as a good precursor for later discussions.

NOTES

1. An abbreviation of Karl Heinrich Ulrich's (1825–1895) term *urning*, designating a female soul in a male body. The term was popularized in Japan during the Taisho Era (1912–1926) when a range of sexology magazines popularized terms then current in Europe. In this case, *uru* is probably best translated as "bottom."

2. An abbreviated form of the word "pederast," which in its Japanese usage at this time referred to men interested in transgender as well as younger men. In this case, *pede* is best translated as "top."

3. Here, "master" refers to Yoshimura's position as the bar master rather than indicating a subservient position on the part of the questioner.

4. That is, he was an adopted groom, taking on his wife's family surname—a common custom in families without male heirs.

5. This refers to a traditional and popular set of illustrations in which male and female couples are positioned in forty-eight poses during sexual intercourse.

6. The original uses the English-language word "back" in Japanese transliteration. "Back" refers to anal sex, most often meaning what in English argot is called "doggie-style" sex, or when the insertee is mounted while on all fours.

7. In this case the *oyome*, or bride, refers to a boy who is taken home on a "permanent" basis by his desiring patron.

8. The Brunswick was a gay bar located in the Ginza area, made famous by Mishima Yukio in his novel *Kinjiki* (Forbidden Colors), where he refers to it as "Rudon's." The bar had two stories, a first floor where regular heterosexuals

gathered and a second-floor bar for homosexual clientele. See chapter 7, this volume, for a detailed description of gay bars during this period.

9. Although the magazine's representative is referring to penises, he uses a polite linguistic device that means "symbolism." I have chosen to translate it in an approximation as "the phallus."

7

LIFESTYLES IN THE GAY BARS

Kabiya Kazuhiko

PART I: THE NEIGHBORHOOD OF SHINJUKU

Feelings of love are not just between men and women. Furthermore (male-male sexuality) is taking on a semi-professional character in today's world.

The existence of tea houses and bars catering to male homosexuals (*danshokuka*)[1]—places today colloquially referred to as gay bars or gay shops[2] in Tokyo and other big cities—is known by many people through newspaper and magazine articles (half of which are either phony rumor or just briefly glanced at). Rumor aside, the places I actually know are in the city of Tokyo, and one can count twenty or so of just those that I have verified; what is more, they seem to be on the increase.

It is said that in every age and in every country, the number of homosexuals (*dōseiaisha*) increases after war, and Japan in the wake of World War II is probably no exception. Given that the homosexuality[3] curve seems to be climbing remarkably, as might be expected, it is probably

Translated and reproduced from *Amatoria* (Studies in Sexual Customs), June 1955: 68–75, July 1955: 38–47, and August 1955: 146–55. Translated by Todd A. Henry.

fair to say that gay bars (*gei bā*) are and will increasingly become places of pleasure for these numerous sodomites (*sodomia*).

What is interesting is that this kind of gay bar, at least in this country, is a product of the end of World War II, and that it did not exist during the prewar era. I had been thinking for some time that I wanted to leave an accurate record of the particular manners and customs (*fūzoku*) of the postwar gay bar for future *fūzoku* historians. Having received a request from the editorial office of this magazine (*Amatoria*) to write something with this title, I would like to take this opportunity to at least make a report of the current places only in the Tokyo area in the most detailed and accurate manner possible.

The Place, Structure, and Character of Gay Bars

It is natural that, as a form of business, the gay bar occupies a place in the city's many bustling districts. Broadly classifying this phenomenon by area, let us first take a look at the neighborhood of Shinjuku.

There is a tea house/bar called Yakyoku (Nocturne) in a secluded place off a narrow alley behind Nikō, which is in front of Shinjuku Station. Relatively old and already in existence during the war, this place featured girly boys (*onna bōi*) at the time, but began anew as a gay bar immediately after the war and remains as such to this day. It is fair to call this place the pioneer of gay bars, and one can discern an established presence befitting it. However, the inside is quite cramped. Upon entering, there is a counter on the left and the only customer seating areas are on the right side and in the back.

The owner is a stout, large-framed man of fifty-five or fifty-six; as a former performer of female stage roles (*onnagata*) and with a proclivity for homosexuality as a passive type (*ūruningu*), his words and actions have an incredibly gentle air to them. One feels a mature sex appeal emanating from his entire body. It is as though his body has acquired such a sex appeal. According to what young customers say, one can sense something of a mixture between the paternal and maternal when one comes in contact with the owner. That is the feeling one gets, and, in fact, he is quite good at taking care of others. He really puts his heart and soul into it when it comes to his trade. He is indeed skilled at business.

It seems that I have a bit too freely written about the owner's personality, but that, in short, is because his character shapes the character of the place.

There are currently four barboys (*bōi*), all of whom are around twenty. (I will explain their nature in the next section.)

Ibsen, located right behind Daiei Studios, is the second oldest bar next to Yakyoku. If one proceeds nimbly up the stairs from the alley facing the street, one of the barboys opens the door. The inside is small and rectangular in shape; all corners of the room slightly protrude; at one corner is a seating area, while at the others are arranged three sets of tables and chairs.

The appearance of the thirty-five or thirty-six-year-old owner is slightly dark and that of a dominating type (*pede*); he always wears a rough, checkered, button-down shirt. His way of speaking itself is masculine, but the tone of his voice is quiet. Before opening this place, he was a regular at Yakyoku.

I have barely seen this phenomenon at other gay bars, but this place sometimes takes in ordinary couples (*futsū no abekku*)—this is to say, a couple consisting of a male and a female customer. I believe that this may be because this place is on the street behind the cinema district, a location easy to spot, and perhaps because intellectual couples are fond of the name Ibsen; regardless, the sight of male and female couples indulging in love talk at this kind of establishment somehow makes one feel a sense of pity and thus something strange about the whole thing.

Located in front of the Shinjuku Ward office in the middle of what is commonly called Shintenchi (the underground prostitution district of Hanazono-chō) is a new face, Adonis, having opened last September. Its owner used to be a regular at Yakyoku, and, catching the wave of the gay bar boom (*gei bā būmu*) he opened this place; however, it is interesting that the place he chose is at the very heart of where hookers congregate.

Mr. K, the manager of this place, is a young man currently enrolled in a philosophy department at some university and is an aspiring writer who came to contribute his own diary to the magazine of the homosexual social gathering I organize; as the milieu of this place is discussed, let me quote a passage from it.

Establishments with a vulgar color, the entertainment district. Three gas lamps and four decorative street lamps in the middle of a blind alley illuminated at dusk. Boldly wearing lurid makeup and clothes that please them, women catering to foreigners and Japanese line up chairs outside of every door. In gay voices, they call out "Mr. Spectacles" and "Mr. Company President" in Panglish[4], which is the same in every erotic district. Young foreign dilettantes reach their climax and are quick to say OK [let's do it] when women put their arms around their waist and lean on them coquettishly. A "short-time" [fooling around with these women] is as simple as a quick bowl of ramen. *Interaction between men and women is conduct that is quite natural* [emphasis in the original].

Behind the view that interaction between men and women is "quite natural conduct" lies the doubt that relations between men are not. As he has experienced sexual love with other men and constantly witnesses many other relationships like it, one ought to pay attention to this author's impressions.

Because this place was planned and constructed with three floors, it is tall enough to look up at. Inside, there is a counter downstairs which takes up a large area, and so the customer seating is extremely cramped. The upstairs area is oblong and somewhat spacious, with a few chairs and tables along the wall; the passageway is wide enough for two or three couples to dance.

The owner, aged forty, is very honest-looking and wears plain clothes. He appears to be busy with his main business (a café) and, therefore, does not show up much at the bar. His taste is for catamites (*chigosan*)[5] and he is said to be a dominating type (*pede*). The manager, Mr. K, is also a fan of young boys. This is perhaps the reason for naming this place Adonis (the name of the beautiful boy who appears in the Greek myth).

If one considers Yakyoku and Ibsen as specializing in tea house/bar operations, Adonis has the quality of a club and a deep flavor as a social meeting ground. However, all three establishments reflect the local feel of Shinjuku, which does not put on the airs of Ginza, nor is it open to the public like Asakusa.

The Character and an Analysis of the Barboys

It is difficult enough to write about the world of the barboys who work at gay bars without the reader first knowing what should be called the argot used among them. Doing otherwise would make this world utterly incomprehensible.

For example, words that we utter in the gay bar like *pede* (pederast) or *ūru* (*urning*) have no currency whatsoever. We call the equivalent of *pede*, *otachi*,[6] and that of ūru, *onē* (big sisters). Words like *homo* and *sodomia* are not used. Rather, we call them *ikken*. (It is unclear whether this term is written with the characters meaning "at first glance" or those for "one case".)[7] People with a taste for *chigosan* (catamites) are said to be into "pediatrics" and those who like older men and the elderly, to be into "otorhinology" (*jibika*). The etymology of the latter comes from the fact that the elderly are hard of hearing. Those who not only like men but also women are called *donten*,[8] and money is referred to as *ritsu*.[9] Those resulting in a pricey tab are thus referred to as *ritsuya*. In this way, these words seem to be nearly the same as those used among male prostitutes (*danshō*). About half of the barboys at gay bars utter this kind of jargon—some on an everyday basis (those who are long-standing in the barboy profession), others in a proud way (those who are new to the profession).

The self-confidence that "we are not amateurs of this persuasion; we are professionals"—the self-assurance of being seen as experts in various matters is, I think, nothing but a manifestation of that which they conceal inside themselves.

Upon hearing a discussion of the cause of homosexuality (*dōseiai*) I had with a member of my social gathering at the table of a gay bar, a barboy once complained about us to his buddies, saying that "those guys are talking about childish things"; this is a sufficient example to prove the "pride" they possess, as I have been discussing.

Now, if one were to record the characteristics of the barboys at Shinjuku's gay bars, first, in terms of age—the four at Yakyoku, five at Ibsen, and four at Adonis—of a total of thirteen, as many as twelve are in their teens. One is sixteen, he's the youngest. One is twenty-one, he's the oldest; most are eighteen or nineteen.

Because one is entering this kind of place, most individuals are homosexuals (*dōseiaisha*) or are those with a proclivity for homosexuality (*dōseiai no keikō*); however, something deserving special mention of late is that Yakyoku has hired non-*ikken-san* as barboys—that is to say, those without a homosexual persuasion (*homo no keikō*).

Why did Yakyoku do that? I have not questioned the owner about this matter, but I would conclude in this way.

Barboys with homosexual proclivities (*dōseiai keikō*) have a tendency to fall in love with their customers. If a customer shows up who is a barboy's preferred type, the barboy's eyes immediately light up and he is absorbed. Falling in love is a weakness. He can no longer be demanding. He stops forcing an enamored customer to spend as much money as he can. Even if they go to a hotel together, he cannot boldly pester him for money. In this way, in other words, it is unprofitable for the bar.

Another example is the not-so-infrequent expert of this persuasion who, as a form of stimulation, has the habit of enjoying himself by showing young men without homosexual proclivities the appeal and pleasure of cavorting in this world. Considering the trouble of this practice, it must indeed increase the enthralling sensation. The purpose of this business practice is to lure this type of customer.

A master of these things from experiencing a long career in the gay bar business, the owner of Yakyoku thus hired straight (*homo de nai*) barboys. Or, as a veteran of this persuasion, he might have even deeper reasons undetected by an amateur like myself, but I do believe that the speculations I have made above are not totally off the mark.

Let us go a bit further with this issue—namely, whether a barboy lacking a homosexual temperament (*homo ke no nai*) is, in fact, fit to work in this type of bar. As outsiders (*shirōto*), ordinary people might think that a boy like this would feel oppressed after a day of work or would be shocked and end up quitting. Of course, there are probably those who disappear after one disgusting experience. However, the truth is that not even one of the barboys now employed at Yakyoku has quit.

I have two or three personal views on the nature of this phenomenon, but I will omit logical explanations and attempt to let the words of a semi-pro (I will explain this term in detail in the next section) twenty-one-year-old student who frequents gay bars explain the reason on my behalf. I should first say that this young man does not have homosexual proclivities (*dōseiai keikō*), and so he says he does not understand the world of homosexuality.

"So, why are you doing these things?" In response to my inquiry, he answered in the following straightforward, really straightforward way: "For one, I am bored. Also, because it is, by and large, amusing. Another reason is because it makes money."

I think that straight barboys continue working at gay bars for one of these reasons.

When Ibsen recently put out a recruitment ad in the newspaper, about three barboy applicants showed up, more than half of whom were not of the homosexual persuasion (*kono keikō de nai*). This is also ultimately related to money, a practice induced by today's "economic downturn." Work at a gay bar or anywhere, as long as it makes money—teenagers' present outlook on life is indeed foreign to that which adults hold.

So, do the barboys at gay bars make that much money?

Depending on the bar's policy, they either live in or commute. For example, at Yakyoku they all live in, at Ibsen they all commute, and at Adonis there are both live-ins and commuters. The set salary is 2,000 to 3,000 yen for live-ins and 4,000 to 6,000 yen for commuters, which seems to be the going rate in Shinjuku.[10]

The entertainment fee is cheap. But, among them, many have regular jobs and work as barboys part-time. In this way, they work at a company or a store during the day and make a quick change into barboy by night. Or, they attend university by day; some study dressmaking with a private teacher.

As for additional income, they receive tips from customers at the bar, payment for spending the night at a hotel with a desiring customer, etc. Barboys cannot speak freely about the financial rewards of the latter, but based on what I hear from others, it is higher than that of (female) prostitutes. To be more precise, there is no such thing as a market price, which is determined by the individual customer.

Occasionally, some barboys have husbands—that is to say, a particular individual who is his regular. I will have the chance to comment in detail on this phenomenon.

In terms of their homosexual persuasions, *urnings* are by far the most numerous. Because *urnings* willfully take on feminine sentiments, their attitude and speech toward customers naturally becomes womanlike. Even when they are not coquettish like a woman, something in their facial features or bodily appearance manifests itself in a seductive way; at times, so-called sissy (*onē*) expressions like "exactly, honey" or "that's right, darling" fly right out of their mouths.

One time at Adonis, I heard the blustering words of an inebriated barboy, which, like the *urning* himself, were somehow soft.

Because work is work, their looks are generally neat. Many *urnings* can be described as lovely rather than handsome. I always think that if they were not homosexuals, they would be rather well sought after as girls. Due to their beautiful looks, they are generally narcissists. They are fully confident in their looks and appearance, and seem to adore themselves. What they have in common with masculine homosexuals is their penchant for hygiene, never missing a day in the bath; they always wear clothes pressed neatly by an iron.

Finally, in terms of the kind of service they provide to customers at the bar, besides delivering ordered drinks, they sit next to customers with an interest in them or beside those who are their type and make conversation with them; if it looks like there is a money-making customer, they must also provide various erotic services. Like hostesses at regular bars and cabarets, there is no way out when it comes to business, but there is also nothing funny or laughable to spread rumors about it in tabloid newspapers and such.

The Characteristics and an Analysis of the Customers

From the perspective of customers in Shinjuku's gay bars, the difference between Yakyoku and other places is that the former holds fast to its regulars as an established bar.

At one time, foreign customers appeared at Yakyoku, Ibsen, and other bars, firing out money with a bang; lately, however, those "aliens" (*gai*) (the way foreign customers are called in this society), have altogether disappeared, perhaps drifting to high-class gay bars in the Ginza area.

If pressed to say, Yakyoku has more middle-aged customers than young ones, while Ibsen is the reverse, filled with young, salaryman types. Adonis, on the other hand, is overwhelmingly occupied by students.

Yakyoku and Ibsen are good for a tête-à-tête, while Adonis is suited for dancing and revelry. Whenever one goes to the second floor of Adonis, young customers and barboys are cheerfully dancing the mambo in a small area, whereas at Yakyoku and Ibsen, one frequently comes across the sight of customers and barboys tucked away from the seating area, engaging in sweet whispers.

Because the majority of barboys are passive types (*ūru*), one would think that many of the customers are dominating types (*pede*), but this is not the case; rather, the number of customers with *urning* inclinations is greater. Some people probably find it doubtful whether an *urning* like this would be satisfied by a barboy companion with the same proclivity.

However, by and large, the customer does obtain his satisfaction. Because the homosexual is always hiding his own feminine inclinations, which are different from those of society and the people around him, the ill feeling of this secret tends to settle in his heart. He is thus satisfied by simply coming to a gay bar and, all at once, spewing out this gloominess in his heart. There is no need to hide one's sexual orientation (*seikō*), as everyone here is a "comrade" (*dōshi*). If one can chat with like-minded barboys and customers, dance, and expose one's true self, the ill feeling inside is suddenly relieved. And, at times, there are even cases wherein the customer's (*urning*) sentiments match that of one's preferred type of *pede*. In this way can one's desires be released.

The reasons for going to gay bars can roughly be divided into three categories:

1. One has his eye on a barboy
2. One somehow wants to dispel his melancholy
3. One is in search of a sexual object among the customers

However, to this has been added a new trick of late (such was also the case before). As I touched on a bit earlier, this involves those semi-pro types who themselves come with the aim of finding a customer for "business."

These types are a motley crew: those without an occupation, the unemployed, salarymen, or students who do it for part-time work, and even some *ikken-san* (but like the students mentioned above, many are not homosexual). It is, in short, a money-making enterprise, and when it comes to business, anything goes.

PART 2: THE NEIGHBORHOODS OF KANDA, GINZA, AND SHINBASHI

The Neighborhood of Kanda

An Owner with the Name "Mama-san."
One can first mention Silver Dragon (Shirubā doragon) among Kanda's gay bars. This bar opened in 1949 and for about two years did a quiet

business for a small clientele of foreign customers. But, from 1951, it finally became known among homosexual lovers (*shudō aikōsha*) and is said to have become busy. As for the location, it is on the right side of the Imagawabashi streetcar stop in Muromachi, about one city block down the alley from the bakery on the corner. They hang a small sign that reads "Ginryū" (silver dragon). [11]

Small eateries and one-shot bars uniformly line both sides of that neighborhood. When I said the name Silver Dragon about two years ago while having a shot at a nearby bar on my way home from my first visit there, the barmaid grinned and said with a wry smile, "Oh, that place of homosexuals (*okama-san*). . . ." This narrow attitude toward homosexuality (*danshoku*) is not restricted to the women at that bar; this limited level of understanding is commonplace among people in general. The difficulty for this gay bar to get along with the three establishments on either side is likely a source of anxiety.

So, when one opens the door to Silver Dragon and walks in, there is a big counter to the right of the staircase; small, however, are the seats. In the back, there are stairs that lead upstairs. It is here that customers remove their shoes, check their hats and overcoats, and then proceed to the second floor. There is an eight-*tatami*-mat (approximately 13 m²)[12] room here with benches, tables, and other furnishings suitably arranged. The lighting is slightly dim, and the face of the person sitting in the corner is only visible in an ash-white color.

The owner is called "Mama-san" here. Although tall, a bit plump, and with a slightly dark complexion, he has a round and gentle countenance. At first glance, he looks no older than thirty-something, but apparently born in 1911, he is really forty-three or forty-four. Because he is a complete *urning*, his body type is characterized by light facial hair and an adam's apple that cannot be seen. With a small lower jaw and a shapely body, he has, in large measure, taken on feminine characteristics.

However, his personality is extremely open; he is not secretive and is without airs. "It is because I am a woman. . . ," he boldly proclaims. He dislikes formal clothing and wears a gaudy Hawaiian shirt all year long. In terms of having his own thoughts on male homosexuality (*danshi dōseiai*), this Mama-san is probably the best-known gay bar owner in Tokyo. Without borrowing from others, he maintains his own opinion.

He thus seems to be on the mark in the training of his barboys (I will explain this point in detail later).

During his youth, this clean-cut man, valuing harmony with society and finding it difficult to dismiss his mother's propositions, is said to have married without choice; after a few months, he eventually divorced without ever laying a finger on her.

He currently lives with his mother. What "filial piety." One cause of his homosexuality may, however, derive from this very condition (mother complex).

Mama-san says that his desire is to make his place into a club rather than a bar, and, yes, one can feel a pleasurable air in the upstairs atmosphere where customers, barboys, and the owner amicably intermingle.

And next, one more place. . . .

Until now it was the Silver Dragon when one thought of gay bars, but just two or three months ago a place called Shangri-la recently opened its doors in the same area around Kanda Station. When you hit the alley directly in front of Silver [Dragon], turn right and walk twenty or thirty paces along the wide road and then turn the corner at the pharmacy? [sic], which will be on your left side; you will soon see a small, faint green sign with the name of the place in white letters. The place is on the second floor, a climb up the stairs directly off the street. Once inside, there is a small counter on the left and the seats are big; the place is arranged in bar style with benches, small tables, and so on.

I have not met the owner, but he is a thirty-five- or thirty-six-year-old foreigner. As this is the first foreign-managed gay bar in Tokyo, it seems there is a unique quality to this place. But, as I am unfamiliar with the details that ought to be mentioned, I shall stop simply at information about its location.

Interaction between Barboys and Customers

At present, there are five barboys at Silver Dragon who range in age from twenty to twenty-five. In terms of their homosexual inclinations (*homo no keikō*), one is a dominating type (*otachi* or *pede*) and the other four are *urnings* and *onē-san* (big sisters). Here, the *urning* barboys take on female names such H-ko and C-ko.[13]

Just as the owner is "Mama-san," the "women" (onē) of this establishment play the female role. Most of the barboys here engage in other occupations by day or are studying as apprentices. What is different about them in comparison to the barboys of other places is that they seek jobs with a relatively productive dimension to them. This seems to be the influence of Mama-san's training.

When new barboys come into service, they are always edified as follows: "Although you are pampered by the customers because you boys are young, it is a big mistake for you to think like that forever. They will no longer pay attention to you when you reach a mere twenty-five or twenty-six. Only when a gay barboy is young is he a flower. So, you must prepare for getting old by taking up some kind of work. The problem is that because you are barboys at a place like this, everyone thinks you want to do ballet or make your living doing Japanese-style dance. But, here is where you go all wrong. This is, in fact, a sign of your lazy habits. Rather than yearning for such things, you had better learn to take on a more steady and reliable job."

This kind of "training" seems to be having an influence on the way in which they conduct their lives.

Mama-san also says the following to his barboys: "Homosexuals (ikken-san) are always thinking about men, but enough with that kind of passion—you should try to devote yourselves to other things."

In other words, he recommends the sublimation of feelings for the same sex. Those words were by all means reasonable, but needless to say they were not really being carried out.

It is a fact that the desire to seek a same-sex partner among sodomites is by far stronger than that of ordinary people (futsūbito) seeking a partner of the opposite sex. If one begins to discuss from what this derives, this discussion will become both drawn out and miss the point of this article, and so I will restrain myself; suffice to say that this feeling also occurs among the gay barboys who are assumed to be able to easily seek the objects of their love.

The barboys of this establishment do accompany customers when invited to a hotel, but for homosexual (ikken-san) barboys, this is not necessarily done simply for the sake of making money. Incidentally, although I did not put to paper accurate statistics in the last installment (Part 1, above), the market price for the love a customer provides to a barboy is currently said to cost 1,000 yen. Next, in speaking about the customers of this place, the number of foreigners was overwhelmingly high at one time; however, it seems the ratio today is about two foreigners for every eight Japanese. Hence, barboys who are preferred by Japanese have replaced those types who fancy foreigners.

In terms of the age range of customers, people in their twenties and thirties seem to make up the largest proportion. As for region, there are a variety of customers, including people from Ginza and Asakusa.

The atmosphere of the place is free and flexible—it takes on a Japanese style if, on that day, the person who sets the mood has a Japanese taste, and if the person likes Americans, it has a Western flavor. Once, when cavorting on the second floor of this place, a slim young man who is said to be a master of Japanese dance suddenly stood up, told me to play the record "*Musume dōjoji*" (The maiden of Dōjo temple),[14] and danced a few steps to the rhythm. I recall watching over him after everyone there quieted down. Although it was Japanese dance in Western clothes, there was not the slightest oddity about it; it was, on the contrary, a dance full of "girlish" glamour. However in demand, this elegance cannot be seen at ordinary cabarets in the Ginza area, to which unrefined company officials are taken by the heads of construction companies. This is certainly not a biased view of mine. It is unmistakable. This is a fact.

As I have said numerous times, gay bars are places of real comfort and shared pleasure for their customers.

Neighborhood of Ginza

Brunswick and Others

"A mediocre teahouse named Rudon, located in an area of Yurakuchō, opened after the war and from some point it became a club for followers of that path (*sono michi no hito tachi*). But, some customers knowing nothing of this come in, drink a coffee, and without realizing a thing, walk out the door."

By chance, some people know that this place called Rudon, described above in Mishima Yukio's *Forbidden Colors* (1951),[15] is Brunswick, which is located in Ginza's Owarichō. You will see this place directly on your left if you go about half a block in the direction of the Sanbara Bridge from the Ginza yon-chōme intersection, turning right at the corner of the kimono shop in front of Ono's Pianos. Whether you are a woman or a man, if you stop in front of this place, a door boy from behind a transparent window will open the door with "Please, do come in." Willy-nilly, you must go inside.

By day or night, the interior has a dazzlingly bright feeling to it and a playful sensation like a movie set. Toward the back there is a counter and six or seven lovely tables with relatively spacious seating; a multi-colored and many-sided chandelier hangs freely from the ceiling. On one pillar hangs a wide-brimmed Cuban hat with a gaudy ribbon, and on the other a model airplane. Somehow it has the air of a teashop where one encounters young girls or middle-school students.

On one shelf a ball-shaped duckweed said to be taken from Lake Akan fills a glass container with a deep and dark green, and, in the big glass container where customers pass, tropical angelfish remain still with their two long feelers drooping down.

I have no knowledge of tropical fish, but as far as I have heard, these small angelfish have incredibly keen senses; indeed, they do not miss the minutest of sounds, and they recall the face of their owner with this keen sense. It is interesting that, with their acute nerves, they somehow are thought to resemble sodomites.

As Mishima Yukio also mentions, this place, due to its location, is frequented by male-female couples (*abekku*) and fellow females who stroll along the Ginza—the feeling is that passers-by know nothing about it [being a gay bar]. That young female customers are particularly numerous is, like the sweet red-bean paste place Orizuru (Folded-paper crane) in Shinbashi, probably just because the barboys are young and handsome. If this is indeed true—namely, that the female customers come in with their sights on the barboys—then, that the former, who know nothing about sodomites (*sodomia*), who hold neither fancy nor interest in their lives, are somehow typical.

To return to our subject, near the door there is a staircase that leads above ground. Upstairs on the second floor is the veritable headquarters of the gay bar Brunswick. When the patrons who follow that path (*sono michi no kyaku*) enter this place, they immediately go upstairs without looking around on the first floor.

The second floor of this place is more spacious than the other places already mentioned. At the top of the stairs there is a counter and chairs lined up all the way to the back door leading outside. There are seven or eight sitting areas. Because the passageway is wide, there is enough room to dance in groups of three of four.

The owner of this place is forty-five or forty-six. He has a modish mustache below his nose and long hair. And as can be gathered from the decorations of the place, he likes rather flashy clothing. It is said that he managed a café in Ginza long before the war. At home, he has a child and a wife who runs a store specializing in sweet red-bean paste. Even though he has a wife and children, he is, of course, a homosexual (*shūdo*) lover; in terms of his sexual proclivities, he is a dominating type (*pede*) who seems to have taste for beautiful boys (*bishōnen*). However, when he first opened this establishment, he had no plan for a gay bar; he simply settled on nice boys who were to his liking and put them to work. But, before he knew it, people of this persuasion began to congregate here. The oldest bar in Ginza, this place, as one might imagine, seems to have a good clientele.

Brunswick probably figures within the category of "high-class" bars, but as for places that one can walk into with relative comfort, there is one called Ranya.[16]

If one goes two or three minutes in the direction of Yuraku Bridge from Sukiya Bridge, the last stop on the city tram, turning right at the church, Ranya is just before the tempura shop.

This bar also consists of two floors. The downstairs area is very small, and so most customers are shown to the second floor. The second floor is also narrow and long, and the illumination is dim like other places. Chairs and tables are lined up all along the wall, and barboys come and go diagonally across the narrow passageway. Patrons dance with barboys here, as do customers with other customers. This probably increases the extreme sense of closeness.

At thirty-five or thirty-six, the owner is rough-skinned and has the feel of a dominating type (*pede*). There is another gay bar in the neighborhood with the (assumed) name "B." I will withhold the actual name and location of this place according to the owner's wishes, but I will go ahead and make note of its unique features from my own point of view. That is to say, "B" operates as a regular teashop by day, but when the night curtain comes down over the neighborhood, it turns into a gay bar. This is indeed an interesting way of doing business.

At around 7:00 p.m., the curtains are all tightly closed, the door securely shut, and "ordinary" (*futsū*) customers are no longer allowed in. Only those who happen to know—that is, customers familiar with "this way"—enter through the back door. It has both an upstairs and downstairs; the interior design and furniture is simple.

The owner's forehead is balding, but he is still young; with clear-cut looks like a Noh mask and neatly dressed, he is certainly an emblematic Ginza type and has the feeling of a typical sodomite. Night brings out the *homo*—with an understanding of the secrecy of such sodomites, this owner perhaps chooses this kind of business practice.

The Role of Barboys as Comedians

There is one amusing barboy in Brunswick. He has a small frame of just over five feet, a light complexion, and a countenance that is slightly more humorous than charming. His age is maybe twenty-five or twenty-six. Insofar as he has given himself the name "the comedian Bonta,"[17] his way speaking and attitude is entirely clown-like; he is always singing jazz in a loud voice when customers are not around. For a part-time job, he sometimes sings at an Asakusa cabaret.

What is more, he encourages intermingling between customers as well as between customers and barboys. Hence, as soon as he encounters someone, he asks, "What type of person do you like?" With a tone full of a particular humor, he solicits his interlocutors without arousing in them a feeling of shame. He asks in a homey way, as if he will quickly find one a partner.

I think this kind of comedic personality is rare among sodomites. Generally, the personality of sodomites is introverted and neurotic, and, externally, they keep a straight face. That is because most of them do not have an iota of burlesque.

Bonta's comic disposition feeds into his spirit of service. From this spirit of service must stem his penchant for and commitment to channeling the love of others. Or, his comic service is, perhaps, a commercial stunt, but I think there is nothing wrong with that.

At present, Bonta seems to have the position of head barboy at this place. There are thirteen barboys from ages fifteen to nineteen—that is, the point between adolescence and early manhood.

Hitherto, this place tended to hire thin and delicate beautiful boys (*bishōnen*) who were fancied, but recently this has changed and it is staffed by barboys with masculine countenances and figures. According to Bonta, "Beautiful faces like those of dolls are out of style nowadays. Customers are unhappy unless the boys are handsome and have a dark-skinned, clean-cut look. In other words, those with a Cuban style, if you know what I mean."

Once seen, young, dominant-type (*otachi*) boys are welcomed by their clients. However, this is not to say that the number of *urning* customers has increased. Whether sodomites are passive (*ūru*) or active (*pede*) these days, the aforementioned type of man is, for the most part, being sought after as the object of love. As a result, it has become all the more difficult for feminine (*onē*) men to find partners.

So, the barboys at this place all work in uniforms consisting of a white-style coat and black trousers. However, Niwa Fumio,[18] who freely makes use of a variety of eccentric materials, portrayed a Brunswick-like atmosphere in a short story called "Blue Streets" (*Aoi machi*) from a year or two ago. As he makes reference to the barboys, let me extract this passage:

> . . . in [the bar] therapy, the feeling that one is, in particular, being ogled at coils around one's skin, and it does not go away. Maybe that is because they are not casually looking at one. Which reminds me that all the men at this place deliberately make one feel as if they are aiming at some kind of effect. This may be too much thinking on my part. From their standpoint, they are probably behaving naturally. There was, in fact, something in common with the feeling that I got from Shin.

And so on and so forth. It seems apparent that even someone like Niwa Fumio is in a state of bewilderment at the uncomfortable mood of this place. Hence, for straight people who are not of this persuasion (*kono michi de nai mono*), there is something in the atmosphere produced by the gay bar that they perhaps cannot stand to bear.

The barboys of this place usually go to school in the afternoon. About half of the barboys commute while the remainder board at the owner's home.

Moving on, Ranya has four or five barboys, and "B" has close to ten. At both, the age is about twenty, but the performance fee is highest at "B," from about 5,000 to 10,000 yen.

Turning to the makeup of the customers at these three places: First, Brunswick, which has a ratio of about one foreigner to nine Japanese, used to abound with students and young office workers, but now middle-aged men seem to make up half of the clientele. In other words, it is likely that students who are dependent on their parents and young workers eventually run out of money cavorting at this type of "high-class" bar.

The head barboy, Bonta, explains it like this: "Yeah, this place maintains its pride as a Ginza establishment, but does not make impecunious customers spend unreasonable amounts of money. If a customer initially admits that he only has a certain amount of money, we try to show him a good time within his limits. . . ."

There is this tradition that if a customer loosens the strings of his pocketbook and cavorts at "high-class" gay bars, then a large sum of money will indeed stream forth.

The son of an old shop owner in Ueno who shows a passion for the barboys at this place and goes there repeatedly is known to have spent several hundred thousand or several million yen.

Next, as for Ranya, many of its customers are young men in their twenties and thirties. I once happened to see Mishima Yukio at this place. Although half are Japanese, foreigners are known to come occasionally. Most of the customers are Japanese, but individuals with strange-colored hair seem to stop by on occasion.

The Neighborhood of Shinbashi

Bobby's Club

As of now, there is only one gay bar in Shinbashi, called Bobby's Club, which is on the third floor where Orizuru is located. Just like the gay bar "Y" in the Torimori area, there are almost no homosexual (*ikken*) customers now and so it is no different than a straight bar.

If, after leaving the west gate of Shinbashi Station, one goes out onto the street along the Tamura-machi-Shinbashi segment of the streetcar, there is a sweet red-bean soup shop hanging a sign that reads "Orizuru" on the side toward Ginza. Alongside is a staircase facing the road; by swiftly going up from there to the third floor one will arrive at Bobby's Club.

There was a nude photography studio here until the summer of 1953, but after it went out of business, a gay bar called Lira Boy opened. However, this place closed at the beginning of this year; two or three months ago the manager changed, and thus was born Bobby's Club.

Inside there is a small but gorgeous hall. On the right side immediately after entering, there is a check for storing one's coat and personal items, alongside which is a large counter with a precious feel to it; benches and small tables are arranged next to the window.

Although the owner is a man named "Mr. Bobby," he is not a foreigner; he is bona fide Japanese. According to calendar years, this owner is said to be already over fifty-five, but when one sees him under the light of this place, he invariably looks just over thirty. The sound of his voice is a somber bass, but it is youthful. He has a tall, fit figure, and his clothes are chic, like those of a stripling.

When I met this owner, I recalled Oscar Wilde's novel *The Picture* of *Dorian Gray*.[19] It seems that this owner has somehow said goodbye to becoming an old man.

The number of boys exceeds ten, all with nice builds; they are handsome striplings of around twenty years of age. All of them elegantly sport a coat and necktie. It would seem that more of their appearances are masculine (*otachi*) rather than feminine (*one*). Most of the customers here were foreign since the time of Lira Boy; even now, the ratio is said to be six foreigners to four Japanese.

According to what the gay bar owner hears from his barboys, most of the foreign homosexuals (*ikken-san*) are *urnings* (*ūru*). It is said that one frequently runs into those who, with a big build and stern look, invariably have the look of a dominating type (*pede*) but actually play the female role. Therefore, dominant (*otachi*) barboys were chosen at this place, a situation slightly different from that of the aforementioned Brunswick, where many boys with a masculine (*otachi*) air about them were hired.

PART 3: THE NEIGHBORHOODS OF UENO AND ASAKUSA

The Neighborhood of Ueno

From former days, the lands of Ueno have had an extremely strong connection to *danshoku*. There was the homosexual (*danshoku*) incident between the great Edo-period (1603–1868) actor Sawamura Tanosuke[20] and Ueno Myōō Inshōkai that caught the public's attention at the time. Although it died out in other areas during the Tempō Reforms (1841–1843), this persuasion flourished in the male catamite tea houses (*kagemajaya*) in the precincts of Edo's Yushima Tenjin Shrine until the Meiji Restoration (1868); and, much later, it immediately reemerged after World War II, as male prostitutes gave rise to numerous talking points, and so on. . . .

Despite the strong connection that homosexuality (*danshoku*) has thus had with Ueno, there is only one gay bar where aficionados of this persuasion gather. Located in Yushima Tenjin Otokozakashita, Yushima is that one place. It used to operate at Ueno Yamashita but last year it moved to Yushima, as the sign reads.

It is usually said that the owner of this place, who is a huge fan of the new school, took the name from one of his favorite *kyōgen*[21] narratives, "*Onnakeizu*" (Genealogy of a woman), but another theory has it that it is probably due to the fact that in former days male catamite tea houses were lined up along Yushima.

In which case, it must have been the bar owner's cherished desire to run a business that matched his own homosexual proclivities (*dōseiai seikō*) with that alluring name, Yushima, while appreciating the entangling emotions of male catamite tea houses located around there. Well, the owner's name is Y K, and he worked as a male actor of female roles (*onnagata*) in the Soganoya Gorō troupe; he still dresses as a women at the bar. But, he did not wear the female hairstyle when the place was at Yamashita; rather, it is cut and parted in a masculine way. However, all the clothes he wears are for women.

His carriage, attitude, and language are also feminine. He is a woman through and through. He is very sensitive, and I feel that to be a woman's sensitivity. I think this belongs to something of androgyny (feminization) or eviration (demasculinization), rather than to being an *urning*.

Although his age is just over forty, he has few whiskers, no wrinkles, and his looks are of a gentle man's body. He is also an affable person, but I think that on the inside he harbors a sense of resistance that does not easily yield to people.

It's discernable that the structure, design, and management style of the place clearly pronounce his personality and that he does not see eye to eye with other such businesses.

If one descends the stone steps of Yushima Tenjin Shrine's Otoko-zaka, there, on the left side of a tranquil, narrow street in the rear of the neighborhood, quietly sits Yushima. It is a drinking establishment with a sober and relaxed feel, not closely related to what might be called a "gay bar." When one opens the black-painted entryway—it is not a door—one finds a counter and chairs in a small, three-*tatami* area (roughly 16 ft² or 5 m²), and so the seating for customers is terribly cramped.

There is another room behind the counter. There is a bench and a small table in this Western—which is to say, Japanese-style Western—room, which has the feel of four-and-a-half *tatami* mats (roughly 24 ft² or 7.25 m²). When the store was opened, this room and the former were one, but they were divided into two last summer. Maybe it was a "golden cut" undertaken as a management strategy.

On one wall in this room is a circular window, hollowed out in the shape of a crest called Uraume; on the other side of that window is Mama-san Y K's living room.

There is a second floor. Before there was only one room on the up-stairs level, but after remodeling there are now two guest rooms. They are four-and-one-half *tatami* mat rooms suitable for light drinking while facing one another across a table.

All this is arranged according to Y's tastes, and in the establishment's remodeling, one seems to be able to see some shifts that Y K's mind has experienced.

One cannot understand Y K without knowing the struggles and troubles involved in running an unusual bar with the determined will of a woman (?) in this rigid society.

As Y says, "My real ideal is to hire two or three young barboys in their teens, making them up in the image of the traditional catamite (*wakashu*) or something, and have them entertain customers. But, that, as you know, is a dream. There aren't such boys in this day and age.

Speaking of young ones nowadays, they are all Western wannabes with long sideburns, curled hair, and, if not, try out a crude haircut like an American soldier; they smell of Westerners and there is not even one who resembles the catamite (*wakashu*) type. Furthermore, in terms of service, homosexual (*ikken-san*) boys often play footsie under the table with customers and some even touch each other. I could not possibly do such things."

Turning his hand to the side, Y makes a face showing his impatience.

This is not to say that he denies any intimacy; he does not mind some people becoming sexually intense like animals if the two are covered by a curtain or a veil; yet his hope is that everyone is "plain and romantic" in his bar.

Because alone he cannot handle everything himself, Y has hired barboys two or three times, but none of them seems to have fared well.

Having apparently given up on male barboys, Y has now hired two authentic girls to serve the alcohol. Given this, Yushima will probably take a different trajectory than a so-called "gay bar."

It wouldn't matter much, as many customers come to his bar just because they favor Y K's personality, not because they are after the barboys or some aim like that. And, so, it is not a problem. However, it might become a place not associated as a pleasure ground for sodomites.

The Neighborhood of Asakusa

Asakusa also has a strong connection with homosexuality (*danshoku*). Although unrefined, there were catamite tea houses (*kagemajaya*) during the Edo period and a male prostitute den in the area of Yoshino-chō during the early Shōwa Era (1925–1989).

Centered around the sixth block near Asakusa Park are a number of theatrical houses and movie theaters; not a few of the actors and entertainers performing in these playhouses—generally referred to as playhouse performers—have homosexual proclivities (*homo keikō*). And, even if they do not clearly have this proclivity, many among people who work in the playhouses or in the performing arts consider sexual relations with women (*joshoku*) ordinary, and thus choose homosexuality (*danshoku*). One can view this among playhouse performers as an anticustomary spirit, if one were to go so far as to call it that. Borrowing their words and putting it simply: "Women (*suke*) are strange and cannot be dealt with. It is better to have sex with men, of course."

I have just remembered and so I will write it down here: Although people know well that the wandering Hiraga Gennai[22] was fond of catamite youths (*wakashu*), my view is that his penchant for them derived, in part, from his anticustomary spirit.

To return to our story, there are many aficionados of this persuasion in Asakusa, and, as written above as regards those individuals associated with playhouses, rather than hiding their homosexual penchant, they triumphantly flaunt it, which is probably why it is easy to operate gay bars in this area. As a result, there are more bars here—numbering eight at present—than in any other amusement quarter of the city.

As for the quality Asakusa's gay bars have in common, the local flavor is also reflected in their plebian character. They are accessible and genuine without any airs. One can feel free going there in Western clothes and Japanese wooden clogs.

Well, let's take a look into the establishments one by one.

Four or five houses before taking Nakamise from New Nakamise Boulevard, which passes directly from the side of Asakusa Matsuyayoko to the movie district around the sixth block, there is an alley on the right. The narrow lane can be almost described as a gay bar alley (*gei bā yoko-chō*), which has four or five such establishments in a row.

On the right side, the first is Tamatatsu, the oldest such establishment here in Asakusa. At the entrance, there is a large paper lantern on which is written the bar's name. Passing through the divided curtain, the inside is relatively spacious; on the left side is the counter, which one often sees at outdoor stalls selling *oden* (vegetables, fish cakes, dumplings, and other items served in a broth), and on the right, chairs and four or five tables—a common layout. It is not stylish, doesn't pretend to be chic, and is without a serious appearance.

This is OK for Asakusa. On second thought, it is just right.

The owner is a sturdily built man of about fifty who, as his hobby, makes dolls. According to the manager, who seems to have a solid homosexual relation with him, the owner was not originally a homosexual (*ikken-san*). I would like to probe his views on homosexuality, but maybe the owner's penchant for this persuasion results from a state of mind

like the playhouse performers mentioned above or, knowing the allure
of both male and female persuasions, perhaps he has arrived at a mental
state in which "women are boring and men are more interesting," as Itō
Harusame used to often say.

L, with the position of manager, is around thirty years of age; he has
a round face and, having shaved himself nice and blue, he is a rather
handsome man who, at first sight, has the aura of an *urning*. It is not that
he uses feminine jargon (women's language) but is very *suave* [emphasis
original].

He has the same hobby as the master—dollmaking—but another
of his pastimes is to entertain and work as a matchmaker between
customers. Based on a commercial mindset, this spirit of offering his
services is, above all, due to the fact that he has already firmly acquired
someone of his ideal type (he is an "otorhinologist," which is an argot
for one who fancies old men). If he were sexually unsatisfied, it would
be difficult for him to help others.

There are three barboys (I will discuss barboys in detail in the next
section).

The next bar is Futaba, which is diagonally across from Tamatatsu. Its
façade and layout is, more or less, like that of Tamatatsu; the only difference is that the former is a bit less spacious.

I am not sure if someone drew it, but on the lintel in the corner hangs
a design of a naked man. Interestingly, a small leaf (a real leaf) has been
placed over his private parts.

The owner says, "Come, Mr. Detective, for it is rotten to be scolded."
That is very Asakusa-like and quite charming.

The owner, T, is a tall young man only twenty-eight years old. He
fluently spins out feminine language, answering any question.

"This thing of M+W[23] is in fashion these days; if you were to gauge,
what is your approximate ratio?"

"Hmm. About 30 percent M and 70 percent W, I would say (*kashira*).[24]
But, you know, in the bar I talk in this way, but when I go to charge a
customer, I become a respectable man."

"So, you change your use of language inside and outside the bar?"

"No. It is not that I do it consciously, but when I leave the bar maybe
it's that I don't want to be ridiculed and I straighten up; inside the bar,
everyone is a homosexual (*ikken-san*), you know. I naturally feel relaxed,

and because I have many feminine characteristics by nature, I just feel at home."

"What's your ideal type?"

"All people of this persuasion have two things, their 'actual ideal' and their 'ideal.' Their actual ideal, which is to say their complete ideal, is an ideal person who they dream about, someone they would jump at if they could encounter him. One cannot possibly come across that kind of person. So, where possible, they compromise with their emotions, and look for someone as close as possible. That's what they call their 'ideal.' . . . The ideal I seek out is someone who is about forty and of a medium build. I despise chubby body builds to the point of shuddering. After that, I fancy thick eyebrows and beautiful eyes. By far, I like those who have a slightly dirty look."

By slightly dirty, he doesn't mean unhygienic; T underscores someone whose appearance includes disheveled hair, Western clothes, and Japanese sandals.

I learned a lot from what he had to say.

There are also three barboys who work at this establishment, none of whom are much older than twenty. They are lively boys with high spirits.

Right next to Futaba is a bar called Kiyoshi.

This bar used to be called Nitta Minoru's Place, as Nitta Minoru, the former actor in Shōchiku's films, used to manage it; now, a man named K K runs it.

On the right side is the counter; on the left, chairs and tables; and in front of a one-half *tatami* mat area (about 8 ft^2 or 2.5 m^2), a counter for making *okonomiyaki* pancakes.

The owner, K, an intellectual who used to work at a small newspaper company, is a fair-skinned, handsome man of thirty-four or thirty-five, or a "beauty" as they are called in this world (of course, in the case of sissy types). He is a person with a nihilistic feeling. He has a wife and children, but his wife knows about his sexual proclivities and the nature of the bar, perhaps an exception in this world where everyone keeps their homosexuality a secret from their families. By the way, he is also into "otorhinology."

Due to the fact that this place appears to have exceptionally good dancing, one can always find two or three couples boogying in the cramped seating area.

People dance in a very Asakusa style: with their bodies pinned to one another and their faces rubbing against each other, they really enjoy the intoxication of dancing.

There are three barboys—two are middle-aged, and one is in his twenties.

Hakataya, a hop, skip, and jump from the Nakamise area, is on the left side of the street if one takes an immediate left from the street that passes through the sixth-block movie district, which is directly opposite the International Theater (Kokusai Gekijo).

As might be expected, the bar is designed for the masses—a large, cavernous establishment indeed. The counter is ridiculously large, so that customers can huddle around it.

A man with a shiny, oily face, the owner is fifty-five or fifty-six, a native of Hakata, Kyushu. It is said that like the owner of Tamatatsu, P—not a lad, but a thirty-five year old—plays the wife's role for him, and they are in a good relationship.

There are also two barboys around thirty years old.

Also in this area, behind the Hongan Temple, is a bar called Loberiya.

Serving drinks and *okonomiyaki* pancakes, this place used to use only the second floor for customer seating but was recently remodeled to include an underground, salon-style room. In the front is a counter, and as for customer seating, there are five or six sets of chairs arranged throughout the room.

The owner, S, is thirty-two or thirty-three, an active man with a darkish complexion. His homosexual proclivity is that of a dominating type (*pede*), seemingly taking as his objects of desire those about ten years younger than he.

The character of this bar is one wherein a barboy is in constant attendance on his customer. In other words, it adopts a cabaret-style entertainment strategy: Barboys must cater to customers' likes.

Which reminds me, there are four or five barboys in addition to assistants.

In addition to what I have mentioned above, other bars include Nagasaki, which is right off of Kokusai Gekijo Boulevard, and Momoyama and Kisen, which are close to Tamatatsu. They are all, more or less, like the many bars already mentioned, and so I will omit them.

I forgot to mention that most gay bars in Asakusa have a second or third floor, which are sometimes used for customer seating or as a bedroom. They give off an Asakusa-like, a very Asukusa-like particularity. Which is to say, if people take an interest in one another, they prefer to quickly become acquainted in a forthright way without putting on airs or frills.

As mentioned above, although unusual, middle-aged barboys work in Asakusa's gay bars. This is something one cannot encounter in the bars of other areas. One of the middle-aged barboys at Kiyoshi is thirty-four or thirty-five, and the other is about forty; at Hakataya, they are thirty-five or thirty-six, but none of them can be called attractive, even in terms of their flattery.

It is interesting that all of these individuals make it brilliantly working as barboys.

Among Asakusa customers, there are many who are said to be "otorhinologists" or who "specialize in older men." In other words, those who seek the love of fifty-year-old men or people of older generations; among these customers are those who, as mentioned above, by and large fancy older barboys.

In terms of these older barboys' ideal type, A at Kiyoshi (forty years old) says he likes mafia types who are about the same age; B (thirty-four or thirty-five) says he likes young ones in their twenties; and P at Hakataya, insofar as he has a deep commitment with the owner, is of course devoutly into otorhinology.

Futaba and Loberiya are places that offer only young barboys.

If, by way of experiment, we were to attempt to inquire into the fancies of these young barboys. . . .

C at Futaba says he's twenty-three but, at first glance, is a nice barboy, pale-faced and slightly chubby, who appears no older than eighteen or nineteen; he says that aside from men over fifty, he feels absolutely no affection.

"I am especially enamored by white-haired men. My real ideal is someone with silver hair and who tends to put on a bit of weight," and so on, answers C. Could it be said that he has a silver-hair fetish?

Generally speaking, it is a fact that sodomites are extremely sensitive to the hair on their partner's head and body. The have a deep interest in the hair on one's head, eyebrow hair, facial hair, underarm hair, chest hair, shin hair, pubic hair, etc. Naturally, the more dense the hair, the more attraction they feel. Among homosexuals, it is not at all an uncommon occurrence for them to suddenly lose interest in someone simply because of a sparse endowment of pubic hair, in spite of the person's ideal looks and body type.

The barboys at Loberiya are between about twenty and twenty-three, none of whom are as extreme as to be "pure otorhinologists"; generally, it seems that they are into older middle-aged men to the age of about forty.

As the owner of this bar interprets it, "but most of them can barely stand it; if they were to speak their mind, I believe their real motive is for the money."

That is, in fact, probably true, but it is also a stern reality that among homosexuals there are those who love older men.

Asakusa's plebian character is also manifest in the appearance of the barboys and in the look of the bars.

The majority of the barboys have their hair stylishly trimmed.

In winter, they are often seen in a windbreaker or jacket, and in summer in a Hawaiian or polo shirt; they are almost never seen wearing a suit. With few shoes, they either wear slip-ons or Japanese sandals.

In terms of their conversation, they use many arcane, feminine words. That feminine language is not softly spoken; rather, it is used bluntly. What is interesting is that this feminine language sounds more virile than masculine language.

In this area, sissies indeed become masculine. That effeminate men become masculine is a convoluted way of saying it, but it can be broken down as follows.

Being called a sissy (one) or *urning* in this world indicates individuals with a feminine sentiment in their mind, but that doesn't severely damage their personality or their overall character.

That a sissy-like barboy uses feminine language means that he has naturally acquired that which derives from a commercial mindset and that a he wants to be treated as a woman by customers, although his true personality is, after all, that of a man.

I understand that this kind of masculinity naturally expresses itself in the open and ostentatious atmosphere of Asakusa and produces a virile resonance in their feminine language, manifested in the complex form of an "energetic feminine manner."

Although it is unclear whether the barboys are conscious of this or not, but that kind of sissy hot temperedness (*tekkasa*) is better appreciated by customers over and above their pure feminization (*joseika*).

Another particularity of the barboys in Asakusa is that they do not perform part-time jobs during the daytime.

Why don't they do part-time jobs or go to school? It might be laziness, lack of diligence, etc., but the most important reason is that the majority of Asakusa gay bars, which do not look favorably on barboys doing part-time jobs or going to school, are live-ins.

In terms of the financial guarantee, the salary fixed by the bars is about the same as in other areas, or even less.

So in order for them to earn more money, they have to provide ample services to their customers. If requested by a customer, they have to carry out amorous exchanges from time to time. Those kinds of exchanges inevitably become numerous. And, even after returning from a night out with a customer, they still have to take care of business at the bar. These kinds of chores are the reason why they are forced to abandon doing part-time jobs or attending school.

Let's take a look at the customers in Asakusa's gay bars.

Looking at their age, there are many young clients at Loberiya whereas at the four bars Tamatatsu, Futaba, Kiyoshi, and Hakataya, most seem to be older, middle-aged customers.

Let me explain the case of the latter.

The reason for numerous older customers at the latter four bars is, as mentioned earlier, because the owner and many of the barboys are "otorhinologists," as are many of the customers.

Many customers fancy young men of the same sex, based on a state of mind in which, in terms of their age, they search for what they have lost. However, because there are young barboys in these establishments who are "otorhinologists," a romance becomes possible if compromises are made to some degree.

Although young customers come to these four bars, most fancy men in their forties or fifties. Hence, young ones go to those bars looking for older barboys and middle-aged owners, and even middle-aged and older customers come. Based on the good offices of the owner, love connections are made between customers and barboys and between customers themselves.

And, in this world, there are absolutely those middle-aged men who seek out middle-aged men and older men who seek out older men. There are quite a number of such customers at the gay bars of Asakusa. Which is to say, species who call out to and gather with their own species; here, these types of customers can fairly easily find their fancy.

The "focus on older men" is thus truly in its heyday at Asakusa's gay bars. As one store owner went as far as to convey with a serious face, "A thirty-five- or thirty-six-year-old barboy or one about forty is, to a certain extent, not good enough. I desire an even older barboy."

Looking at customers in terms of their place of origin, there are few from this area, but as regards other areas, it seems that many people come from the downtown areas of Nihonbashi, Ginza, and Kanda. It should go without saying that the reason why there are few locals is because of sodomites' particular sense of secrecy whereby being seen by an acquaintance is undesirable.

In addition, customers from the countryside are fairly numerous. This is because Asakusa's plebian character makes it easy to approach for people from the countryside.

When homosexuals (dōseiaisha) from the countryside come to Tokyo, they want to go to the gay bars, but because both the barboys and customers in the places around Ginza put on airs, they cannot blend into that kind of atmosphere. And soon after, they will become afraid of how much they will be overcharged. At which point they pick up and naturally head for Asakusa, which is frank and has neither an air nor a secret. That is because they can easily find a partner there, even if it is for a brief romantic exchange. The reason for this is because the owners of Asakusa's bars are busy channeling customers' affections.

If we inquire into customers' professions—storeowners, business employees, factory workers, students, entertainers, playboys, etc.— many, as is the area itself, are of the plebian class. Sometimes policemen also come as customers.

"I was allured by the prosecutor's keen eye," as one bar owner put it; those with the looks of a police officer are lionized in this world.

Even in Jean Genet's The Thief's Journal, homosexuality between a police officer and a sodomite is taken up. In the story, a young urning man—the Genet-like "I" of his work—has romantic feelings for a police officer and follows him around day after day; two years later, he admits his love for the police officer, and, in the end, they come to love one another.

Due to his profession, the police officer might be hiding it, but I think that among them there are surprisingly many who likely have homosexual proclivities (*dōseiai keikō*)—just as homosexuality (*danshoku*) was prevalent among soldiers who carried out a communal life solely among men. . . .

One can often see a playboy look among the customers not only of Asakusa's gay bars but also in the bars around Shinjuku; I feel like I can understand their homosexuality (*dōseiai*).

If one simply thinks of the cases of gamblers and "knights of the town" who have traditionally led an all-male, communal life; of the strong bonds between boss and follower and between elders and their patrons; of the feelings of awe and attachment of the latter for the former and the deep feelings of affection of the former for the latter; and of the sense of contempt for women one can sometimes see in them—whether they are conscious of it or not—homosexuality (of course, a spiritual thing), in spite of its different manifestations, is thus thought to have arisen.

But, even if there are those who, let us say, are conscious of that, as in the case of policemen, it is probably that their "stubborn" nature suppressed those kinds of feelings without them appearing on the surface.

CONCLUSION

In conclusion, I would like to add my personal thoughts on what I have enumerated above in surveying the essence of gay bars. Thinking through everything:

1. The management is too commercial.
2. The business has no room for improving.
3. The managers' ideal toward homosexuality (*dōseiai*) is shallow.

Omitting the details, I can broadly summarize these three points.

To begin with, let's first discuss the first point.

Being what it is, it is natural that business is businesslike, but its over-commercialization is, instead, a cause for losing customers.

As I mentioned in the first installment (Part 1, above), because homosexuals want to dispel the frustration in their hearts, many go in search of the gay bar, which is, at best, an artificial place. Considering them the same as cabaret customers, they cannot be overcharged 30,000 to 50,000 yen for a bill of under 1,000 yen at a bar for the masses. As that would hardly last for workers, they naturally end up staying away.

These are words that most apply to so-called high-class bars. . . .

Point two refers to the fact that most of the establishments are either bars or pubs.

The manager of Silver Dragon mentioned his hope: He thought, for example, that it would be nice to have at least one club-like bar—a bar where anyone could feel free to go inside, meet like-minded customers gathering in one place, and chat and drink with one another.

One can say that the second floor of Silver is almost like this.

Point three is that the owners of gay bars have nothing but a shallow ideal about homosexuality. To this day, some of them even hold an inferiority complex.

I think that in terms of their raison d'être, gay bars should be given far higher praise than regular cabarets and bars.

Note: For those with questions or concerns about homosexuality (*homosekushuarite*), please inquire at the following address (with a self-addressed, stamped envelope): Ekoda 2-974, Nakano-ku, Tokyo.

NOTES

1. Literally meaning "male colors," this traditional word for male-male sexual relations was pronounced *nanshoku* in the Tokugawa Era (1603–1868), but later came to be pronounced *danshoku* in popular discourse. See Pflugfelder (1999: 184n114). By the 1950s, when this article was written, the term was falling out of favor. A *danshokuka* (or *nanshokuka*) is someone who engages in male-male sexual practices. As *danshoku* was the favored pronunciation by this time, that is the transliteration employed here.

2. In the original these terms are referred to in capitalized Roman script as GAY BAR and GAY SHOP.

3. The term here in katakana is *homosekushuarinii*, probably a typo as this spelling does not feature elsewhere.

4. The English spoken by pan-pan girls.

5. A *chigo* was traditionally a young pageboy who would wait upon senior Buddhist monks and samurai. The subcultural use of this term to designate the younger partner in male homosexual liaisons lasted well into the twentieth century, as its use in this instance shows.

6. This term is apparently related to the term *tachi* (top), widely used today in Japanese lesbian and gay communities.

7. As the author's confusion over how to write the term suggests, *ikken's* etymology is unclear. An article on "*Okama* expressions" published in the scandal magazine *Hyaku man nin no yoru* suggests the term is to be written with the characters for "one case/item" and that it was a slang term for the penis among homosexuals. See *Hyakuman nin no yoru* (1963).

8. That is "flip-flops" or "reversibles," men who would take on both active and passive roles.

9. Literally a rate or a percentage.

10. The figures here are presumably per month. For instance, in 1953 when televisions were first introduced to Japan, they cost 15,000 yen per set—a figure that placed them out of the reach of most consumers.

11. "Ginryū" is made up of the two Chinese characters for silver dragon. In contrast, the term "Silver Dragon" as written in the Japanese syllabary for foreign terms (katakana) would likely have had a more fashionable ring at the time.

12. Room size in Japan is often measured in terms of a standard-sized *tatami* (straw mat), which varies from eastern to western Japan but is roughly 6 ft. (180 cm) by 3 ft. (90 cm).

13. The character *ko* affixed to Japanese names typically indicates the female sex.

14. *Musume dojōji* is one of the great dance-dramas of the kabuki stage. The ancient legend of a young woman possessed by unrequited love provides the framework for a series of solo dances that take the girl from innocence, through frustration, to her transformation into a vengeful serpent-demon.

15. *Forbidden Colors* (*Kinjiki*) describes a marriage of a homosexual man to a young woman.

16. *Ran* means "orchid" but is also used as an abbreviation for Holland (*Oranda*) and so the name could be translated "Dutch House."

17. This may be in reference to the contemporary comedian Tokyo Bonta.

18. Niwa Fumio, 1904–2005, was a novelist who published over eighty books in his long life.

19. *The Picture of Dorian Gray*, the only novel by Oscar Wilde, was first published in 1890 and tells of how a portrait of the eponymous Dorian Gray is marred because of his many sins, becoming old and disfigured, while he himself remains young and perfect.

20. It is unclear to which incident Kabiya is referring here. He may have confused the name of the actor. Sawamura Sōjūrō (1685–1756) was a famous kabuki actor who founded a dynasty. His descendant, Sawamura Sōjūrō V (1802–1853), was an accomplished onnagata.

21. A brief play performed between Noh plays to provide comic relief.

22. Hiraga Gennai (1728–1780) was a polymath who experimented in both science and literature. His *Nenashigusa* (Rootless grass; 1763) is a satirical tale of Enma, Lord of the Dead, who falls in love with a kabuki actor and dispatches a demon off to the world of the living to kidnap him.

23 M(en) + W(omen) refers to mixing feminine and male language.

24. The Japanese term *kashira* conventionally marks feminine language.

8

ROUNDTABLE: FEMALE HOMOS HERE WE GO

Saijō Michio (chair), Ōgiya Afu (writer), Ueshima Tsugi (bar owner), Miwa Yōko (company employee), Kawakami Seiko (company employee)

Homosexuality is not just for men! Among women it is also a splendid rage!

WOMEN ARE SECRETIVE

SAIJŌ: Shall we get started? We had planned to see Professor Ōta Tenrei[1] and the writer Ōgiya Afu[2] this evening but unfortunately Dr. Ōta has an emergency case and cannot attend. As I expect Mr. Ōgiya to arrive any moment now, shall we begin? Welcome again to all of you who came during this busy season. I have long hoped to have this kind of opportunity to discuss female *homo* but it was quite difficult to assemble women. That we could gather three women tonight is all thanks to the painstaking efforts of Miss Ueshima, so firstly I wish to thank Miss Ueshima profoundly.

UESHIMA: Oh, it was nothing. As both Miss Miwa and Miss Kawakami are young women, unlike myself, it will be a problem if they appear in magazines and so forth. Therefore they only agreed after I said that they could appear under pseudonyms rather than their real names.

Translated and reproduced from *"Zadankai: josei no homo makari tōru," Fūzoku kagaku* (Sex-customs science), March 1955: 148–57. Translated by Wim Lunsing.

Until yesterday, Miss Kawakami said she was alright with this, but today she suddenly became reluctant and it was quite a big struggle to make her come along. (*laughter*)

KAWAKAMI: Well, after all, it is difficult.

SAIJŌ: Thank you so much for making the effort. And, as it is the busy period just before the New Year, thank you all the more. As we know, there are various texts on male *homo* from olden times,[3] and of course we are aware from recent newspapers and magazines that in the present day as well, it is quite a widespread fad. However, whether or not it is because women have an extraordinarily secretive character compared to men, we don't hear a word of their situation. It is definitely not the case that there aren't enough such women to merit talking about. In fact, on average, every third day I receive a letter from a different female reader asking me to increase the coverage [in this magazine] on female *homo* or to create a group for female *homo*. As I brought some of the letters, let's look at two or three. This one is from a woman who talks of "the female *homo* party" of Tokyo: "Mr. Saijō, I read *Fūzoku kagaku* [this magazine] every month. I wonder why, although there is the FKK social club for male homosexuals (*dōseiaisha*), you haven't established a social gathering for women? I would like you to set up such a group as soon as possible, however much it costs. If the membership roster approaches a hundred people, I am prepared to cover the total cost of the dues. . . ." (*laughter*)

UESHIMA: What an enthusiastic person.

SAIJŌ: I don't know who it is but I receive a similar letter from this person every month. As I don't know her address, I have no way of contacting her. . . .

UESHIMA: Let me have a look at the letter. Maybe it's someone I know.

SAIJŌ: The postmark is from Minato Ward [Tokyo].

UESHIMA: Well, the handwriting is different. However, the letters that come to my address are also from a very enthusiastic person who asks me to create a club and says that she will pay for it all.

SAIJŌ: What kind of person is she?

UESHIMA: I can't say exactly, but it is the wife of a wealthy man. I think she is about thirty-six or thirty-seven years old, though, at a glance, she seems no older than about thirty.

Saijō: Indeed, such enthusiastic wishes do not stop with just one or two people. All right, let me read another letter. This is from a female painter from Urawa City [near Tokyo]. In the first part she writes about herself but if I read from about the middle, it says, "Every time a man asks me to marry him, I feel so disgusted that my hair stands on end and I run away, but in order to make a living by the paintbrush, I have to negotiate with men and when I negotiate with men, they invariably ask for my love or for me to marry them. On such occasions I nearly have to throw up and end up never wanting to set foot into the male world again. Even for the sake of my livelihood there is a limit. Isn't there an older woman in this world who will love me with all her heart and let me paint without having to worry about my livelihood?"

Miwa: I understand that sort of feeling very well.

Ueshima: Certainly. I wonder whether there is an unexpectedly high number of such women.

Saijō: In short, that thing called man is, quite simply, disgusting?

Ueshima: Please forgive me, Mr. Saijō, but I think it's something like that. (*laughter*)

NEVER HAVING LOVED A MAN

Saijō: This evening please think of me as androgynous. Or else I'll become jaundiced and end up not being able to say anything. (*laughter*) In the case of men, it appears that a dislike of women can be inborn or acquired, and, unsurprisingly, it appears to be the same in the case of women. How is it in your case, Miss Ueshima?

Ueshima: In my case? I was married once.

Kawakami: To a man?

Ueshima: Of course.

Kawakami: Oh yuck! (*laughter*)

Ueshima: I really didn't know anything about women. I'm from a family of six, with three older and two younger brothers, and my mother died when I was young. So, I grew up among men all the day long. And when I was twenty-four, I was forced to marry, of course through a matchmaker. I didn't even have a look at him [before we married]. He was the only son of an honest oil shop owner and ordinarily I was happy but when night fell I was running away from him, and it was my mother-in-law, more so than he, who became angry, and it ended in divorce. I felt relieved, but even now I can't return home, and I ran off to Tokyo.

SAIJŌ: So then, your dislike of men was inborn.

UESHIMA: I was brought up among boys. So, even when I got married, men had no charm for me. It's not that I dislike men as such but if I think of sleeping with one, I start to tremble. (laughter)

SAIJŌ: How about you, Miss Kawakami?

KAWAKAMI: Hmm, what should I say?

UESHIMA: This child learned to be that way.

KAWAKAMI: What? That's not true.

UESHIMA: Well, if it hadn't been for Yukiko. . . .

SAIJŌ: Now, now. Please let her speak for herself.

KAWAKAMI: I think that it was a part of me from when I was small. One could say that in most cases a girl experiences something like feelings of love for a boy in elementary school but I never had such an experience.

MIWA: Now that you mention it, me neither.

SAIJŌ: So, you've never once loved a man?

MIWA: Of course not.

KAWAKAMI: Me neither! (laughter)

SAIJŌ: How about having been loved by a man?

UESHIMA: Even asking such a thing is in bad taste. Such situations cause us a lot of suffering. Even though there is nothing as refreshing as brushing men aside.

SAIJŌ: Of course—or rather, it seems plausible. What next, then? I think that seen from your perspective there are quite a lot of women in this situation.

UESHIMA: Quite a lot. In particular young women's musical theater troupes (shōjo kageki)[4] are well-known for them, but there are also many in the dormitories for students at girls' schools as well as those for factory workers. Apart from that, there are also unusually many among cabaret[5] waitresses and girls of the blue- and red-line districts.[6]

SAIJŌ: This occurred just two or three days ago. When returning home from an end-of-year party, I felt that I hadn't had quite enough to drink so I was hanging out in an area of Shinjuku [Tokyo] with a number of bars. I thought it was about nine o'clock but in reality it might have been closer to eleven o'clock. Given the current economic slump, it appeared to be quiet everywhere but when I looked casually into one establishment, I was given quite a start. Two girls were holding each other tightly and kissing passionately. (*laughter*) I had heard rumors of this but as it was my first time to see such a place, I opened my drunken eyes wide and gazed in rapture. However, the two were entirely indifferent to whether someone was looking or not. They were completely lost in their kissing for a while but eventually paused. Then they looked intently at each other's faces. And after about a minute they started kissing passionately once again.

UESHIMA: You were watching very closely, weren't you? (*laughter*)

SAIJŌ: Seeing this, I became convinced that there must be quite a number of female *homo*.

THE FOURTH SEX

UESHIMA: As Mr. Saijō saw it for the first time, he was taken aback, but it's very common, right?

MIWA: Yes, there is a lot of this.

SAIJŌ: In the case of men, there are various coffee shops and bars and apart from that there is a variety of well-known meeting places (*randebū no basho*), and whether it's a professional (*puro*) or semi-professional (*semi-puro*), one can stumble across a hook-up nearly everywhere. But in the case of women, there are no such easy opportunities. How can we open up a space for them?

UESHIMA: That's why women are at a disadvantage. (*laughter*) But, surprisingly enough, there is a path for women. Those who set foot on this path head in one direction after another in search of a partner, from the cabarets to the taverns and from the taverns to the bars. To tell the truth, half of my life was like that. In other cases, there are people who are totally infatuated with famous stars like those from women's theater troupes or films, or with singers. In such cases they are not fans but patrons (*patoron*), loosely speaking. They get fulfillment in entirely devoting their small incomes to this.

SAIJŌ: Well, that's completely a spiritual thing.

UESHIMA: The spiritual satisfies women. There are housewives who like to spoil a spaniel. In erotic novels weird things are written, but I think that it's purely spiritual.

SAIJŌ: That's how women feel fulfilled.

UESHIMA: You certainly couldn't say that that's the case for all women, but I, for one, believe it.

Mr. Ōgiya Afu arrives.

ŌGIYA: I'm so sorry I'm late.

SAIJŌ: Thank you for going to the trouble of coming. We've already begun and we were just talking about the spiritual being very important for female *homo*.

ŌGIYA: Well Saijō, it's like this. Originally, the male-female bond of affection can exist and continue without any spiritual aspect. However, in the case of *homo* this is not possible. A bond without a spiritual aspect is for *homo* like a river without water—it doesn't exist.

UESHIMA: You don't write much about female *homo*, do you, Professor (*sensei*)?

ŌGIYA: It's not one of my strong points, in fact.

SAIJŌ: You investigate male *homo* with passionate devotion but females remain unexplored. . . . At present, who would count as a researcher of female *homo*?

ŌGIYA: Hmm . . . you don't hear much of it. Aren't you number one on this point, Saijō? (*laughter*)

SAIJŌ: Don't make a joke of it. I'm only a rookie.

ŌGIYA: At some point Saijō called male *homo* "the third sex" so perhaps in that sense we can call female *homo* "the fourth sex."

SAIJŌ: Of course. If we call normal men and women the first and the second sexes, then the men we call sodomites (*sodomia*)[7] are sexually entirely independent of those two, and hence the third sex, and, as the women we call lesbians (*resubian*)[8] or sapphists (*safisuto*) are again entirely different from that sex, it makes sense to call them "the fourth sex."

MIWA: Interesting. "The fourth sex" . . . it could be the title of a novel.

SAIJŌ: By the way, Miss Miwa, please tell about us one of your experiences.

MIWA: That would be difficult.

UESHIMA: Don't say that. (*laughter*) If so, I'll start to tell it. Only three years ago this girl came in [to my bar] with a company manager. . . .

MIWA: He was a section chief.

UESHIMA: Yes. . . . Came along with her section chief to my bar. She didn't drink but when I looked into her eyes I was startled. And she says that when she looked into my eyes, she felt as if an electric shock had gone through her, which she thought was because I was the same kind of girl as her. The section chief became terribly drunk and I helped him out the back door.

MIWA: That's right. As I had just entered the company and had not thought that men were so frightening, I had carelessly gone with him on his invitation but it was good that thanks to this I could meet Mama.[9]

SAIJŌ: And so you fell in love with Miss Ueshima?

UESHIMA: Don't be absurd. Miss Miwa is more than someone like me deserves. I acted as a go-between for her. In Yotsuya. . . .

MIWA: Mama!

UESHIMA: Alright, alright, I won't mention her. But that person was very grateful to me over it.

ŌGIYA: So you also engage in matchmaking, Miss Ueshima?

UESHIMA: You ask strange questions, Professor. It sounds like I am a panderer or a pimp. I most definitely do not make a business of being a matchmaker.

SAIJŌ: No, I am sure that Professor Ōgiya did not ask his question with that in mind. He just asked it because it is an important point as a facet of the lives of [male] *homo*.

UESHIMA: I shall explain it plainly. Among the women who come to my bar, there are quite a few who are the same sort of woman as I. Therefore, we sympathize with each other and help each other. We are like a simple neighborhood mutual support group, assisting each other in various ways, such as in finding a counselor (*sōdan aite*) for a person who wants someone to talk to, and finding a lover (*koibito*) for a person who wants someone to love.

ŌGIYA: Now I understand. Can you please just explain things without getting angry.

UESHIMA: I'm not angry. I just became enraged because you said you only investigated boys. (*laughter*)

ŌGIYA: How frightening you are. (*laughter*)

THERE IS NO VULVA ENVY

SAIJŌ: What sort of person is that Miss "Yuki," who was briefly mentioned in relation to Miss Kawakami?

UESHIMA: She's this girl's sweetheart.

SAIJŌ: Please tell us about that romance.

KAWAKAMI: Now I'm in trouble. I can't . . . Mama! I'm leaving. (*laughter*)

SAIJŌ: If you leave, *we're* in trouble.

UESHIMA: This girl is very honest.

SAIJŌ: Well then, another topic. Miss Ueshima, among female *homo* are there also male types (*dansei-kei*) and female types (*josei-kei*) [as there are with male *homo*]?

UESHIMA: Sure, in many cases there are. But it's not always like that. Take for instance the case of this girl (*pointing at Miss Miwa*). As you can see, she is a female type. But "Yocchan" from Yotsuya is really a feminine housewife type.

SAIJŌ: According to Professor Ōgiya, in the case of male *homo* this is called phallus envy (*farusu naido*), as they are uniformly envious of the phallus. . . .

UESHIMA: Phallus?

SAIJŌ: It's a male "down there." (*laughter*) The psychology of this phallus envy is said to be characteristic of modern male *homo*. How would this be in relation to this the psychology of female *homos*? Maybe there is vulva envy (*yoni naido*). . . .

UESHIMA: Please speak Japanese. (*laughter*)

SAIJŌ: Well, the question is whether those who adhere to the female *homo* way envy each other's "down there." . . .

ŌGIYA: That's wrong, Saijō. In the case of male *homo*, they envy others' "down there" because they have an inferiority complex themselves. There the phallus becomes something that is revered as representing the person, separate from sex. However, if you compare women to men, they may have it but I think that, to begin with, they do not have inferiority complexes about their vulvas being larger or smaller than other people's.

UESHIMA: We don't have anything of the sort. After all, unlike men, ours is not visible to other people. However much you bathe together. (*laughter*)

ŌGIYA: That's why I think that there is no psychology reflecting phallus envy among female *homo*.

SAIJŌ: Now a question to all three of you: What part of the female body do you find the most attractive?

UESHIMA: In my case it is definitely the breasts. In American films, if I see those breasts that look like they're about to peek out of the blouse, I start to tremble. (*laughter*)

SAIJŌ: That's like the male psyche.

KAWAKAMI: I'm mostly attracted to the complexion of female skin.

MIWA: Me too. And I love long, slender legs.

ŌGIYA: It appears to be difficult to find common points between the psyches of female and male *homo*.

SAIJŌ: What I always find curious is that in the case of male *homo*, even though they are the type of men that are liked by women, they dislike women. Excuse me for saying this, but the three of you women here—although you are also of the type that is liked by men—you dislike men. From our point of view, I think that really is a waste . . . .

UESHIMA: As a compliment, thank you for your praise. But because of that kind of thinking, we are forced to endure hardships. I think that our lives would be much easier if there were no men.

SAIJŌ: In the case of male *homo*, there are professionals and semi-professionals, like cross-dressing male prostitutes (*danshō* and *kagema*),[10] but in the case of women, there is no evidence of such things.

UESHIMA: I never heard of such a thing. But there are some who move from one partner to another many times.

SAIJŌ: It is what Professor Ōgiya calls the fickleness of sodomites (*sodomia*).

ŌGIYA: This is also true in the case of men, but I think that in the case of women the "ideal" is even more limited. On top of that, in the case of women the secretiveness is more absolute than in the case of men. As a result there are probably many who do not meet their "ideal" partner in their lifetime. I think that the fickleness results from that.

UESHIMA: That's right, Professor, but we are definitely not fickle. On the contrary, we are prepared to die for someone we love. But such a person does not exist, such an ideal partner.

SAIJŌ: You have to make an effort.

UESHIMA: That's why I would like you to create a gathering like FKK for us too. Professor Saijō, would that be so expensive?

SAIJŌ: No, but it is a bit difficult if there is not a person like Mr. Ōgiya who ardently leads the group with clear morals and without straying from its purpose.

UESHIMA: Mr. Saijō, don't you want to become the leader?

SAIJŌ: Certainly not. I would lead it astray from its purpose in no time. (*laughter*)

THERE ARE ALSO FEMALE *HOMO* AMONG FAMOUS PEOPLE

SAIJŌ: However, Mr. Ōgiya, in Japanese history there are various famous female *homo*, aren't there?

ŌGIYA: Not as many as male *homo*. It appears that it has been written that this was practiced in various ways among the shogun's maids in the inner palace during the Tokugawa Era (1603–1868) and in women's prisons.

SAIJŌ: Among male *homo*, that is among sodomites, there are a number of famous people about whom such rumors exist. In particular among entertainers and writers there are many, but it appears that there are only a few famous female *homo*.

UESHIMA: Don't be absurd. There are plenty. All along, the novelist _____ has been living with her lover, and there's Miss _____, there were many rumors about her at one point, although she hasn't been writing lately. She also made quite a few passes at this girl (*pointing at Miss Kawakami*). And then there is the physician Dr. _____, she is a splendid member of our party. The film stars Miss _____ and Miss _____ are also that way.

SAIJŌ: Indeed, we do not hear any rumors that they married.

UESHIMA: Of course they haven't married. Kissing in films is just business and that's why they have to do it.

SAIJŌ: According to the story of someone who researched women's theater troupes in depth, the male types (*dansei taipu*) have successful marriages [with men] but marriage does not work for the female types (*josei taipu*). That is to say, that among female *homo* the stimulation felt by the male type [when she's with a female type] is weak but the stimulation felt by the female type [when she's with a male type] is very strong. Even if female types marry, that stimulation [she would feel from a man] does not compare, and therefore they feel disillusioned upon marrying. What could this be?

MIWA: That's awful.

KAWAKAMI: I wonder if this is true.

SAIJŌ: What do you think, Miss Ueshima?

UESHIMA: I wonder. Among women it may be possible to attain endless bliss, but if you marry a man, I don't think that hell and heaven are an issue.

ŌGIYA: After all there are genuine and false [female *homo*]. In the case of the false ones, it may be that there is a turning point at which they marry a man and have a normal sex life, but genuine ones are from the start members of "the fourth sex" and therefore such a comparison is not possible.

UESHIMA: Professor, do you think that our character in this regard can at all be corrected? There are some who want to have it corrected no matter what. They say that this is because they have to marry due to their family situation.

ŌGIYA: Well, in the case of men there are many who have such worries. Very many of the people who come to me for advice are like that. I think that those who have it by birth cannot be corrected. However much they try to correct it, it's impossible. But for women who started on that path having acquired it, it can be mended. If they marry, they can lead a normal wife's life. Apart from that, among men both cases are also possible.

UESHIMA: How ever much we visit a doctor it is useless, isn't it?

ŌGIYA: For those for whom it's congenital, it's indeed useless.

SAIJŌ: Rather than thinking about marriage, it is a matter of how to consciously live a pleasant life. Based on stories we've heard, there are presently many women who do not marry and live happily.

UESHIMA: I have never even thought about marriage, myself.

MIWA: If you don't marry, there are still many ways to happiness.

SAIJŌ: It is alright if you receive a child [from somewhere] when you get older.

UESHIMA: Yes, indeed. But you can still feel lonely. (*laughter*)

ŌGIYA: Indeed, one can still feel lonely. Even someone like you.

SAIJŌ: It is often said that female *homo* use techniques of *to ichi ha ichi*[11] and have many dildos, but is this true, Miss Ueshima?

UESHIMA: That is all lies! Right?

KAWAKAMI/MIWA: Right!

ŌGIYA: Saijō, you should not ask that sort of question in front of a lady.

UESHIMA: Indeed. (*laughter*)

SAIJŌ: Please forgive me. Well, let's end here. Thank you all so very much.

20 December, Kanda, Kitazawa (Tokyo)

NOTES

1. Ōta Tenrei was a physician who also researched and wrote about sexuality. His work focusing on homosexuality among men in Japan, *Daisan no sei* (The third sex), was first published in 1957 and revised in 1981.

2. Ōgiya Afu (Tsuguo) was a minor writer who contributed articles on male homosexuality to popular sexology magazines and penned *Sodomia banka* (Elegy to homosexuality; 1958).

3. Among the best known of these texts is Ihara Saikaku's *Nanshoku ōkagami* (The great mirror of male love) ([1687] 1990). For an English history of such texts, see Leupp (1995) and Pflugfelder (1999).

4. Ueshima is apparently referring to all-female musical theater troupes such as Takarazuka Kagekidan and Shōchiku Kagekidan (SKD). For more on Takarazuka and rumors of homosexuality, see Robertson (1998). See also Toyama (chapter 9) in this volume.

5. The "cabaret" (*kyabarē*) falls under the category of *mizu shōbai* (literally, the "water trade"), along with the better known hostess bars (*hosutesu bā*). By definition, "cabarets" have some sort of stage show. An English explanation of the many permutations of *mizu shōbai* can be found in the glossary in Louis (1992).

6. After prostitution was criminalized following World War II, brothels continued to operate under the guise of being "special tea shops"; police used red lines to delineate on the map of Tokyo the areas where these "tea shops" could be found. One zone in the Shinjuku area of Tokyo had a number of such establishments set up as restaurants, which was indicated with a blue line (Takemura 2004).

7. McLelland observes that, in the popular sexology magazines of the time, *sodomia* was "a general label designating men interested in a range of same-sex

sexual interactions" rather than corresponding directly to the word "sodomite" (McLelland 2005: 8–9).

8. Since the early 1970s, upon the import of American lesbian feminist discourse as well as androcentric pornography, *rezubian* has been used as a transliteration of "lesbian," but in the 1950s and 1960s, *resubian*—as a transliteration from the French *lesbien* and *lesbienne*—was sometimes used, alongside other terms such as *resubosu ai* (Lesbos love). See McLelland (2005: 84–86).

9. Mama is sometimes used to refer to the proprietress of a bar.

10. In the original Saijō refers to both *danshō* and *kagema*. The former term was a contemporary reference to male prostitutes and the latter a term more closely associated with the Tokugawa Era (1603–1868).

11. This slang reference to female-female sexual activity plays off the shape of the *katakana* letters *to* and *ha* and implies that one (*ichi*) woman is the inserter (*to*) and one the insertee (*ha*).

THE ERA OF DANDY BEAUTIES

Toyama Hitomi

A PROFILE OF MIZUNO MAKIYO, AGE FIFTY-SEVEN

On page one of the photo album is a picture of girl singing on a stage. She's wearing an elaborate, frilly dress, her hair is tied up in a pony-tail with a large ribbon, and she has a cool, clever expression on her face. This is the only girlhood picture of Mizuno Makiyo, owner of bar Kikōshi (young nobleman).

He[1] was the youngest of three siblings, born in Hokkaido, in north Japan, and at the age of ten moved together with his family to Tokyo in 1950. This girl, who was quite good at singing, entered the then well-known Otowa Yurikago Kai (Otowa cradle club) children's choir. In this photo in an album he recently discovered, he's wearing a cute, Barbie doll-like dress. While appearing a little embarrassed, looking at the photo now he seems rather nostalgic: "My sister, who's ten years older than me, and my mother sure tried to make me into a cute little girl." This one photo really makes him feel the passage of time.

Translated and reproduced with permission from "*Dansō no reijin no jidai*," in Toyama Hitomi, *MISS dandi—otoko toshite ikiru joseitachi* (Miss dandy: women living as men), Tokyo: Shinchōsha, 1999: 209–221. Toyama Hitomi maintains the copyright to both the original article and the translation. All inquiries regarding reproduction should be directed to her at <http://web.parknet.co.jp/hitomi/>. Translated by James Welker.

Quite a brat when he was small, Makiyo always used to wear knee-length pants and gather together some boys to play with. Even after he entered the choir, there was not a hint of him becoming more feminine, so—worried about his appearance—his parents threw him into a very strict private girls' school, thinking it might turn him into a gentle and meek girl. That was a trick of fate.

As soon as he entered middle school, he developed a crush on a *senpai* (older student), a second-year high-school student on the basketball team. It was his first love. Even though her hair was short, she was very feminine and cute, and he started in earnest to gain her interest.

"That *senpai* is really attractive," he whispered softly into his team-mates' ears.

Soon enough, a rumor had spread: "That person and that person are S, aren't they?"

At that time there was no expression for *rezubian* (lesbian); instead, they used the word "S," for "sister love," a relationship in which two girls considered each other *onēsama* (older sister) and *imōto* (younger sister).[2] Makiyo was athletic and masculine so he didn't use the term *onēsama*, but he always liked older women.

"I 'like' (*suki*) you. Let's be 'friends' (*tomodachi*)."

When he passed on "love letters" to his *senpai*, she would send letters back in reply.

"Let's eat lunch together. I'll be waiting for you in front of the music room."

They exchanged "love letters" every day. They left neatly folded notes in each other's shoe cubbyholes by the door or passed them onto each other via classmates.

"Let's meet at Osenchigaoka (Sentimental hill)."

Osenchigaoka was the name given to a traditional place at this school where girls went to get lost in thought.

"She was a really nice person. When I think about it now, it seems that I instinctually picked her to be the *neko* (femme) of the *neko/tachi* pair and I was acting like the *tachi* (butch)," he said, thinking back on that time. This was an era when girls were expected to be more feminine.

Makiyo's first kiss with a girl was when he was in his first year of high school,[3] and his first time was in 1959, at the age of seventeen.

Though immersed in the flowery female world of the girls' school, he used to toss aside his *ojōsama*[4] school uniform, transform himself into a boy (*shōnen*) by putting on pants and a blazer, and, with three boy friends, head out to try to pick up girls.

Once, heart pounding, Makiyo decided to go all by himself to have a look inside a bijin kissa (café of beauties), then a trendy kind of coffee shop. He stood in front and peered in, and when he moved to the door, someone gracefully opened it for him. Inside was a completely different world—there were so many beautiful women who looked like trendy models at the height of fashion. It wasn't the kind of place to do anything flirtatious with the staff, just somewhere they bring you a cup of coffee, but it was there he fell in love with a cute woman.

As he was the kind of person to devote himself to just one woman once he was infatuated with her, he went in every day and stared at her without saying a word. Before long, when he entered the shop she was the one who opened the door for him.

After two weeks, she suddenly disappeared. Very worried but too embarrassed to ask, he just fidgeted. Someone finally said, "She's sick, so why don't you pay a call on her?"

He sat cross-legged in her room quietly watching her eyes as she lay there. He liked her so much, his heart pounded rapidly, his mouth was dry, he was so nervous.

He rambled on for a bit, but soon enough things started to go more naturally. When there was a break in the conversation, he kissed and held her. That night he slept in her room. He was in his final year of high school and, at twenty-three, she was six years older.

Once they found love, things got more difficult. They were still two women, and the sight of the two of them together all the time got them labeled homosexual (*dōseiai*). Things were much more trying than today—homosexuality was considered a sexual perversion and strongly looked down on, and homosexuals were even considered less than human. When word of their relationship got out, Makiyo's girlfriend was fired, and she had to find somewhere else to work. After that, she moved from shop to shop a number of times.

When she got a job at a coffee shop in Shinjuku, to be sure their relationship wouldn't get out again, they decided to say that he was her little sister so he could visit the shop.

However, on the day Makiyo showed up as the little sister, he fell for a pretty, bright girl at first sight. Of course he couldn't tell his girlfriend, so he kept his feelings secret.

"If she's your little sister, introduce her to me!" the new girl asked Makiyo's girlfriend.

"Go and see a movie with her," his girlfriend suggested.

Those seemed to be the words he was waiting to hear, and so he happily took the new girl to a movie and then for a coffee, and promised to take her out again. That went on two or three times, and before long, they were secretly dating.

Soon thereafter, their relationship was found out, and his older girlfriend became mad with jealousy. Makiyo got scared and left the apartment where they had been living together and hid at his family's place. One day she called out to him in a park. Her eyes were bloodshot, and when he saw her standing there with a kitchen knife in her hand, he thought, "I'm going to be killed."

"I like someone else now, so I want you to let me go."

That's all he said and he ran home scared. Afterwards, he heard that after they broke up she was unable to forget him and ended up leading a miserable life, dating and sleeping with others just because they resembled him. This all happened just before he graduated from high school.

"My daughter's behavior is kind of odd. Every day after school she puts on a man's suit and then goes out until very late. Could it be that Makiyo's involved in some strange kind of fooling around?"

Worried about her daughter's behavior, his mother made a calendar in a notebook and kept track of her daughter's daily comings and goings, recording the time she came home every day.

After he graduated from high school, he got a job helping out at a company in Kanda his brother-in-law was managing. It was an office that registered companies and was in the finance business as well, but, because he was bored with the work, he secretly got a job as a bartender.

This was in Ikebukuro, so it got out to his older sister who was running a bar called Bar Seiko. "If you have the energy to work somewhere else on the side, why don't you work for us. Start working here."

There were six girls at his sister's place, and while mixing drinks he secretly fooled around with the girls.

Soon someone from the neighborhood snitched to her sister.

"Little Mā is playing around with hostesses and girls. Little Mā is homosexual."

Hearing this, his mother and older sister cried all night every night from shock.

"You're less than human. You've strayed from the path of normal people. You 'queer' (*hentai*)."

Even after they said all this, he just ignored them.

Once, when his mother was really at a loss, she told him, "I'm going to talk to your father about this."

"Go ahead," was Makiyo's response.

At that time, the patriarchal family structure was much stronger, and his father, a man of the Meiji Era (1868–1912), was a frightening presence. Makiyo sat down on his knees in front of his father.

"I hear from your mother some talk about homosexuality. Is it true?"

"Yes, it's true."

"It can't be cured?"

"Aside from me dying and being born again, it can't be cured."

"You might be happy with this now, but when you get older and don't have any children, you'll be lonely. Will you still be okay with it?"

"This is the path I chose and decided myself, so I will never regret it."

"Ah. . . . I see."

And that was the last word on the subject. From that point, his father never uttered a word about him getting married. Makiyo figured that since his own character was such that once he said something there was no challenging it, once his father heard the words "aside from me dying and being born again" he must have decided once and for all that there was nothing that could be done if his daughter was that resolute.

Makiyo recalled that his mother kept pestering him until he was thirty: "Don't you want to get married?" His big sister, who was ten years older, said nothing, but she was very fond of him, and people made fun of their closeness, calling them incestuous "lezzies" (*rezu*), and since she liked him so much it may well have been true that she didn't want him to be snatched away by somebody.

From the age of nineteen, he started wearing men's briefs.

While he was still tending bar at his sister's Bar Seiko, he found an article in a magazine about a bar called Yume no shiro (castle of dreams), described as a place of *dansō no reijin* (dandy beauties), and he went by himself to check out the Kanda bar. By that point, he had heard there were *burazā gāruzu* (brother girls)—women dressed as men—who were the opposite of *shisutā bōi* (sister boys), and was aware that somewhere there were other people like him.

In 1961, next to the bathhouse Garasu-yu along Kokusai-dōri in Asakusa, a bar opened that was called Gorō, in which its female bartenders wore men's clothes. It was a tiny bar—slightly larger than 30 ft² (9 m²)—and was run by Hagoromo Chinami, an *otokoyaku* (trouser role performer) of middle standing in the all-female SKD (Shōchiku Kagekidan) musical troupe.

At the time, SKD was extolled as the best in the East for its absolutely gorgeous performances, which had audience members coming from all around the world. In front of the *atomikku gāruzu* (atomic girls) kicking and dancing at the back of the stage, danced the *dansō no reijin*, SKD's top stars. The bar was created to take advantage of that popularity, and it thrived with a clientele whose hearts throbbed at the possibility that they might meet a star, as well as with those who were just curious.

After that, in Ueno and Kanda, Yume no shiro bars were set up as a chain.

To set foot in one of these bars was to enter a flamboyant, dreamlike world, where everyone really seemed to enjoy working.

There were three bartenders in white button-down shirts, black vests, and bow-tie drag, and eight beauties in dresses working as hostesses.

"Here we all had the same friends; it was a nice, relaxed atmosphere."

Until that point, he was constantly struggling against the eye of society, accompanied by a permanent feeling of guilt and loneliness—he always lived as if in hiding.

Since Makiyo was in drag, he always strutted around so you couldn't tell he was a woman. Even though he knew that if he got into a fight at the bar, he didn't have the physical strength to win, he couldn't help challenging people. Even when he was punched, he never squealed at his opponent to stop because he was a woman, and he was always alone.

At Yume no shiro, Makiko met people like himself and was able to confirm for himself that such a world exists.

When he started to leave, a hostess near him said, "Wait. Let's have dinner together later." That night, they had sex. He was twenty-one.

A few days later, the three Yume no shiro bartenders came to Bar Seiko to steal him away.

"Don't you want to come work at Yume no shiro?"

"Of course I do."

Since he was the kind of person who never changed his mind once he made it, his sister had no choice but to give her consent.

He lived with his second girlfriend for a year before his heart was broken. As had happened last time, ultimately, when it got out that they were in a relationship, rumors spread that they were queer. She had a hard time of it too.

Things were much more conservative than they are now, so even if he thought they were having fun living together, they kept their life secret, and there was always a feeling of guilt as if they were doing something bad. His girlfriend got really exhausted with the arrangement too.

"I'm tired of this. Let's break up."

Unable to counter what his girlfriend had said, disheartened and lonely, he left the apartment.

However, just as soon as he started to work at Yume no shiro, he got a new girlfriend and he managed to get more girlfriends left and right. He was so popular that rather than him expressing his interest to a girl, she showed her interest in him.

About 80 percent of the customers at Yume no shiro were men who had their eyes on the hostesses, and the remaining 20 percent were women who had their eyes on the *dansō no reijin*. In the kitchen was a male chef, but all the other employees, bartenders and hostesses, were women. However, the hostesses were, in fact, almost all dating the other employees in drag.

At the time he was dating a beautiful girl, but she was using barbital and while high on it tried to commit suicide. Since Makiyo really hated drugs, he decided to break up with her, but his girlfriend's older sister stopped him.

"She really likes—she's always saying how much she likes you—and I'll make her quit drugs, so please stay with her."

Makiyo explains that the people around him accepted their relationship, which was to him like being accepted in society. Since at that time he thought there was no one who would accept them as a couple, he was so happy at her sister's words that he decided he wanted to take on the responsibility. Eventually, she ended up immersed in drugs again, he resolved to break up with her once and for all, and he quit his job at Yume no shiro.

He began working at the *boisshu* (boyish) bar Ramu (rum)[5] in Yokohama. At that time, he was dating a woman who was a magician, and he started getting popular for his talent at playing the guitar and singing while tending bar.

Before long, the mama of the Roppongi bar Meme (budding woman) heard rumors about him and came to meet him.

"Won't you work at Meme as the manager?"

Meme was a well-known bar in Roppongi, and there was a certain appeal to being the boss at work. He was twenty-five.

From the time of Meme, there were no more hostesses in dresses; instead, all the staff were women in drag. There were three bartenders behind the counter and eight people talking to customers in the room, all wearing suits a lot more tacky than today—white or red, blue or purple, and striped like something a "dangerous" person might wear.

Meme was located next to the cemetery behind the restaurant Seryna and had a shady atmosphere like a secret club, and customers always lined up to get in.

The approximately 165 ft² (50 m²) interior was just wide enough to hold a counter that sat fifteen people and four box-type seats that sat ten before the bar filled up, but still it was quite a thriving place. Makiyo's daily schedule involved working from six in the afternoon until two in the morning, after which he spent time with the girl he liked. The bar was open year-round and he got only two days off a month when someone else took his place, but he liked working at Meme so much that even on his days off he came in to hang out.

Spending time with his girlfriend was an escape from reality. That's why, having chosen to avoid word of his relationship leaking out to his customers, they hid away in a hotel in Yokohama, far away from Roppongi.

Eighty to ninety percent of the customers at the time were drawn to women in drag. The upper echelon included mamas and hostesses from Ginza clubs, geishas and models, female pro-wrestlers, people from Takarazuka and SKD, and rich married women, who all decked themselves out in their finest and came to the bar ready to compete for attention.

On Friday, when the staff wore tuxedos, customers in kimono or evening dresses adorned in furs were quite a sight. It was a much more extravagant time than today. According to Makiyo, being able to befriend such high-class customers was a high-class pleasure. There were many customers enamored with him who brought him flowers, giving him a real star existence.

This was a time when such bartenders were offered bars by their wealthy customers on a daily basis, leading to the birth of a number of *dansō* bars in Roppongi including Don Juan, Sharotto pike (shallot piquet), Hoshi no ōjisama (The Little Prince), Hakusakan (white-sand building), Paru paru, Noa no hakobune (Noah's ark), and Gin no kishi (silver knight). And customers were able to enjoy an extravagant evening of hopping from bar to bar.

Makiyo's goal was to "get and have my own place with my own two hands."

He was the manager at Meme for two-and-a-half years, all the while secretly living with his girlfriend. At a time when the average salaryman was making 30,000 yen[6] a month, he took in 70,000 yen, and by the time he quit, his monthly income had reached 170,000 yen.

After about two years, Makiyo realized that things had been wearing down on his nerves, and he started to want to get away from this world.

"Is this world the only place I can live? Is there no other place I can be accepted?"

After fretting for a while, he decided to quit the bar and start performing in Ginza. "I wanted to see another world, and I wanted to see if I could be accepted in it."

He got an audition at a Ginza club and sang chanson, canzone, and so on. He had experience singing in a choir, and he had practiced singing a lot at Meme with many customers coming to hear him, so he was confident in his ability.

He was given a green light, but it came with a sharp jab: "Keep your hands off the girls."

He performed at Ginza's well-known Kurabu Gōdon (Club Gordon), singing thirty-minute sets at 8:00, 9:00, 10:00, and 11:00. After each performance, he grabbed his music and went to another club five minutes away, singing for another twenty to thirty-five minutes. Guitars were waiting for him at various clubs. After finishing his eight performances at 12:00, he headed for Roppongi's Hakusakan.

After a year of this experience, which helped him develop more confidence and a more objective perspective, he returned to Roppongi. He and his friend Mie together opened Kikōshi. He was thirty-one.

Mie was someone whom he had found working at a cosmetics counter, and while she resembled an *otokoyaku* of Takarazuka, she was a gorgeous person with a feminine flirtatiousness. They ran Kikōshi together for ten years.

"At the age of thirty-three, I experienced the love of my life—I felt so in love every day."

Makiyo's partner was a stage actress six years younger than he was. When he first went to see her on stage, he felt a strong desire to sleep with her. She came into Kikōshi out of the blue.

"It was what I'd been waiting for!"

The real person was even nicer and more attractive than on stage, and while attempting to restrain himself, he tried hard to seduce her, and the two of them got together.

"Sex is something you should really only do with someone you love. A spiritual connection is important."

When they first had sex, the actress wasn't a skillful lover, but she enveloped him in a marvelous, spiritual love. He felt great pleasure at being able to hold such a loving person.

When being with partners who were sexually skilled, glimmers of men they'd been with in the past quickly brought him to reality, spoiling the experience for him. He wanted to be with women as if lost in a fantasy.

Since meeting her was like a dream, he became so nice to her that he actually became aware of how nice he was being to a woman.

When he finished work on Wednesday mornings, he jumped on an airplane and took it to wherever she was, and then took the last plane of the day back to Tokyo again. She also used whatever free time she had and, in disguise, secretly came to meet him.

These rendezvous continued for a year and a half; they spent a splendid time.

Their break-up came without warning—she just suddenly stopped calling. Makiyo was worried there was something wrong so he continued calling her until at last she answered. Her attitude on the phone was so cold it shocked him, and he felt a real separation between their hearts. He never called her again.

Five years later he found out that the reason she left him was that the time they spent together turned her schedule upside down. Going on stage without having slept was a hindrance in her work, and people around her started criticizing her performance so she made up her mind to break up with him.

His pride was too strong for him to pursue her, but he was in an extremely depressed state for a long time. His heartache lingered, and he didn't sleep with another woman for three years.

The word *onabe*[7] appeared first around 1973 in a Roppongi crowded with bars.

Yet, around the same time, this lively era was drawing to a close, the lights went out at one bar after another, and the only bar left from this time in Tokyo was Kikōshi.

"Kids today are taller and cooler, and—more than anything—freer, which is great. Times really have changed, haven't they?"[8] While this world started out with *rezu bā* (lesbian bars),[8] the younger generation identify themselves as *onabe*. They are not *rezubian* (lesbian), but, rather, they assert their desire to love women as men. In contrast, the women who worked at *rezu bā* talk about thinking it was natural to love women with the body they were born with and are prejudiced against those who inject male hormones to make themselves more masculine.

A pioneer in this world of *dansō no reijin*, a sincere Makiyo explains quietly, "The word *onabe* comes as the opposite of *okama* referring to men. Recently, *onabe* who want to change their bodies to male in order to love women, like *nyūhāfu* (new half)[9] *okama*, have been increasing. Things have become freer and more diverse, I suppose. I guess women are thirty years behind *okama* in this regard."

And after a pause, he whispered, "But I didn't need my breasts. In fact, more than twenty years ago, I went to a plastic surgeon to see about having my breasts removed. But I was told that the surgery would be at the Tokyo Metropolitan Police Hospital and it would take two weeks, so I gave up on the idea."

NOTES

1. The use of gender pronouns in this translation replicates their use in the original.
2. A detailed explanation of *S* can be found in Honda (1991).
3. In Japan, elementary school lasts six years (ages 6–12), middle school three years (12–15), and high school three years (15–18).
4. An *ojōsama* is a girl from a rich family.
5. Every attempt was made to verify the intended meaning behind Japanese transliterations of apparently English words in bar names, but in some cases, they represent the translator's speculation.
6. The exchange rate in the 1960s was fixed at 360 yen to US$1, so 30,000 was approximately $83.
7. *Nabe* is a pan and *o* an honorific prefix. *Onabe* is styled on *okama*, or "pot," used of passive male homosexuals since the Tokugawa period, and a reference

to the receptive role in anal sex. *Okama* were considered to be effeminate in nature, and *onabe*, their inverse, that is, butch-acting women.

8. While this implies that the 1960s bars were called *rezu bā*, I have not encountered contemporary references to the bars using this term. The terms *resubosu ai* (Lesbos love) and *resubian* (lesbian), rather than *rezubian* and *rezu*, were most widely used in the 1960s, at least in magazines focused on sexuality. See McLelland (2005: 88, 93).

9. "Half" in Japanese refers to persons of mixed race. A "newhalf" is a person of mixed gender. On the history of the term, see McLelland (2005: 198–99).

⑩

WAKAKUSA NO KAI

The First Fifteen Years of Japan's Original
Lesbian Organization

Sawabe Hitomi[1]

Fifteen years ago one woman started Japan's first lesbian club. Its
history of ups and downs comes as a marvelous response to changes
in women's consciousness.

Near the south exit of Shinjuku Station in Tokyo was an adult toy store
called Paradaisu hokuō (Scandinavian paradise), in a corner of which
lay a notebook through which those into *"homo, rezu, suwappingu,* SM"
([male] homosexuality, lesbianism, swapping, and sadomasochism) could
contact each other. Mixed up among the crowd of men going in and out
was "Komaya Michiko,"[2] just twenty-one years old, who wrote that she
was "seeking to contact people who are 'lez' *(rezu)"* and provided her
newly created post office box address and the telephone number of the
boarding house where she was staying. This message was the beginning
of Japan's first "lesbian" *(rezubian)* organization, Wakakusa no Kai.[3] It
was December 1971.

Translated and reproduced with permission from *"Nihon hatsu no rezubian sākuru—
'Wakakusa no Kai' sono jūgonen no rekishi to genzai,"* which was published under the
penname Hirosawa Yumi in *Onna wo ai suru onnatachi no monogatari* (Stories of
women who love women), *Bessatsu takarajima,* no. 64, Tokyo: JICC shuppankyoku,
1987: 111–19. Translated by James Welker.

IT BEGAN AT PARADAISU HOKUŌ

It had been four years since she arrived in Tokyo. She didn't want the
people who came after her to experience the suffering she had felt ever
since she could remember because she could only love others of the
same sex. She also wanted to do something to make friends. Relying on
the single word *rezu* she had found in a tiny ad in a magazine, she felt
she had no choice but to go to that shop.

From the following day, the phone at her residence rang nonstop for
a week. "Komaya-san, telephone!" the landlord would shout each time.
And each time, the voice she was trembling with anticipation to hear
ended up being a man's. Worse still, the conversation started with questions like, "How do two women do it?" And then the man would say
something like, "Hook up with me—I'll make you satisfied," or, "Once
you get a taste of me, you'll never forget it." Invariably, they wanted to
know whether lesbians had been raped as young women or something
like that, or ran to other women because of bad experiences with men—
such "poor" women who didn't know the goodness of men. If that's the
case—these "kind" men offered—"I'll comfort you."

"This is not what I was looking for," a flustered Komaya thought, and
the next week, she hurried down and erased her phone number.

> Damn, that was a time when I wasn't scared of anything, you know. In one
> weekly magazine, I used my picture, my real name. . . . When I went back
> home for a visit, my father said, "What the hell is this?" showing me the
> article with my picture. It wasn't like my family read that magazine—or so
> I thought when I let my picture get published—but apparently some nice
> person took a copy to my family. At that time, my father told me, "You're
> doing what you think is okay, but this involves your parents too. Just stop
> using your real name." And in a panic I contacted the publisher and asked
> them to use a penname for me.

And that's how the leader of Wakakusa no Kai, "Suzuki Michiko," was
born.

Well, a week after that, finally there was a phone call a little different from the previous ones. Frustrated at yet another man, Suzuki was
about to hang up the receiver, but the man said, "I'm serious here, so
please give me a minute. The truth is, my wife is like that—will you

meet her to talk?" The next Sunday, with her husband and toddler in
tow, this woman showed up. She said it was the first time she had ever in
her life met another lesbian besides herself. A short while later, Suzuki
traced down the only woman to write her address in the notebook at
Paradaisu hokuō, a woman who at the time lived in [neighboring] Kana-
gawa Prefecture. And in this way, with just two members, Wakakusa no
Kai took off.

Since then, fifteen years have passed. The August meeting last year
was the final meeting for Suzuki, who, after the meeting, packed up
her things at her Kamata, Tokyo, residence and set off for a new life in
her hometown of Takasaki [Gunma Prefecture]. "For the time being,
I'm taking a break from the group," she explains. The woman I met at
a coffee shop in front of Takasaki Station is a thin woman with a small
build. So much so that it's amazing to think that she had enough energy
to support Wakakusa no Kai for fifteen years.

Well then, what kind of organization was Wakakusa no Kai in the beginning, and how has it changed up to this point?

A DELUGE OF INQUIRIES

> Women with women. We're the only national organization [for you]. Not
> just a club (kai) to find a friend, etc. . . . but a place where many people
> walking down the same road can open their hearts and talk freely with
> each other. . . . In the hope that we can all feel at ease and live enjoyable
> lives, we currently hold regular teas (sawakai) in Tokyo and Osaka. Write
> your age and occupation, and send 1,000 yen [US$10].[4] (No men.)

This was Wakakusa no Kai's ad, and while it might seem logical that
as a lesbian group it would advertise in women's magazines, this ad
only went into somewhat smutty manga (comic) magazines like *Purei
komikku* (Play comics), *Yangu komikku* (Young comics), and *Manga
tengoku* (Manga paradise). Of course they also wanted to advertise in
Josei jishin (Women ourselves) but not only was the advertisement rate
100,000 yen (US$1,000), their advertising ethics committee controlled
the content of the ads, and while ads about male-female relations were
accepted with no problem, they were not so lenient about female relations and thus would not permit the ad. Feeling there was no other

choice, they settled on advertising in the manga magazines they thought women were likely to read. To earn the 40,000 yen that it cost them to advertise, Suzuki took on a part-time job that started after she finished work at her regular job. Basically, she did whatever it took to let people know about the existence of the group. She appeared on *O-hiru no waidoshō* (Lunchtime talk show) and the evening program *Tunaito* (Tonight) and left fliers in public restrooms in train stations.

As a result of the promotion of the group, in came a deluge of inquiries. However, as the group's leader, she felt that keeping out "strange people" was absolutely essential, in order to protect the other members. So, according to her cautious method, she held face-to-face interviews with each person who contacted her, to size them up, and she only allowed people who passed the test to join the group. About sixty to seventy people joined Wakakusa no Kai in this manner each year. Even at a very conservative estimate, more than five hundred people, ranging from high school students in their teens to housewives in their fifties, have become members. Add in all the people she just talked with and the figure reaches no less than several thousand, Suzuki says.

So, after meeting directly with the leader and passing the interview, then paying the enrollment fee and annual dues, you could officially participate in a regular meeting. At the time, Suzuki lived in a tiny two-room apartment, but once a month she offered it up as a space for members to gather together for a cup of tea or sometimes something stronger. Twenty to thirty members attended each regular meeting. There were, however, quite a large number of people who kept up their memberships but never came to any meetings. C (twenty-six years old) joined the group three years ago and took all of four months before she went to her first meeting. She reflects back:

> Anyhow, I was scared. I wondered what I would do if I saw someone I knew? It wasn't like it is today when, if you are heading out to a bar in Shinjuku ni-chōme[5] and you run into someone, you can get away with saying something like "I'm just out for a good time." But going there, well, of course it's the same as saying I am one [a lesbian]. If I show this weakness, afterwards someone will try to intimidate me, right? Or, I bet the *yakuza* [Japanese mafia] are running it? With fears like that in mind, heart pounding, I went to a meeting.

Both fear about what would happen if their being a lesbian was found out by others and desire to make friends were especially strong among the group's earliest members.

I (thirty-eight), who has been running the Osaka chapter for nearly ten years, explains:

> At the time, two or three times a year, when we'd rent a hall at a hotel in Osaka to gather for a party, Suzuki-san always came down on the *shinkansen* (bullet train). We all met up outside the main ticket gates at Osaka Station. That day at the time we were to meet up, I'd stand there holding a handkerchief in my left hand as a sign. Sometimes it would be red, sometimes white, or whatever. But they would never come up to me. But it wasn't like I could walk up and talk to someone I thought might be one of us—it was really tough. If you were a lez and you felt deep down that you had to hide it, you just couldn't bring yourself to go out. So you couldn't trust people. If ten people came, half of them wouldn't use their real names. They'd lie about their ages. That's why it was really difficult for us to keep in touch with each other after the meetings.

A LIBERATED SPACE WITH A FAMILY FEELING FROM A "CARING MOM"

However, because it had required overcoming so many hurdles to get there, joining Wakakusa no Kai was a happy occasion all the more.

A (thirty-three), who joined the group after learning about Wakakusa no Kai in the *yurizoku* (lily tribe) column in the gay magazine *Barazoku* (Rose tribe)[6] in 1980, describes her situation:

> I tried to stop being attracted to women, but I just couldn't change. I was convinced I had to change myself in order to live in this society, so among my family, at work there was nothing I could do, I felt driven into a corner, always alone. After all, for many years, I was convinced that I was abnormal (*ijō*). Suzuki was the first lesbian I met besides myself. At the time, from the bottom of my heart I felt, "I'm rescued!"

Things you couldn't usually talk about, you could talk about with other members—the bitterness of being alone, of breaking up with your lover (*koibito*), of listening to talk about marriage from your parents.

The love-hate drama of love between women, that's exactly what you could bring out in the open here. That's why Wakakusa no Kai became the sole "liberated space" for lesbians who were living isolated lives. The post office box was always full of letters, at the beginning crammed with sheets of stationery on which the writer had poured her heart out. Suzuki is said to have stayed up until 1:00 or 2:00 a.m. answering these letters. These personal letters, along with the newsletters, were all sent out with the name "Suzuki Michiko," written by hand along with the return address. All this effort was to make the mail look like a personal letter to avoid someone in a member's family opening the mail by mistake, leading to a lot of problems for that member.

The thing that made members happier than anything else was going to meetings and getting introduced to someone who might become their lover. When they joined, members made a card on which, in addition to their name, age, occupation, address, height, and weight, they wrote down a simple self-introduction and a description of their desired partner and attached a photo. At meetings they were able to look at the other cards and choose people they thought they might connect with. Sometimes Suzuki would approach someone to make an introduction, saying something like, "What do you think about her?" Innumerable couples met each other this way.

Older women and women from rural areas were especially fond of Suzuki-san. At whatever party you went to, if you weren't enthusiastic you couldn't get to know others, of course. But when you went there, you somehow met someone thanks to Suzuki-san's introduction no matter how passive you were. Without fail, Suzuki-san would go up to the shy women, sitting timidly in the corner. She was like an *omiai* (arranged marriage) matchmaker. When you're told, "She's quiet, but she's really a smart, warm person," what are you going to do but think, well, maybe she is. Suzuki-san is like "Mom," who really seems to enjoy taking care of everybody. On meeting days, Suzuki-san always made a ton of food for everyone, which we all ate while we chatted with each other. When getting to know a new lesbian, making small talk among couples, or whatever, there was always this warm, family-like feeling. I feel that over the past fifteen years, Wakakusa no Kai has become established in Japan because of the firmly entrenched sense of obligation toward each other that's such a part of this society.

So explains Y (forty-one), who was in the group for nearly ten years, having joined at the very beginning.

AN ERUPTION OF CRITICISM FROM LESBIAN WOMEN'S LIB ACTIVISTS

However, even this small group was influenced by the passage of time. The first wave was in the second half of the 1970s. It started when lesbians enlightened by the women's liberation movement joined and began to criticize the way the group operated, centered around the leader.

The gist of their criticism was mainly five points:

1. The leader coded each member's introduction card with "O for feminine, Δ for boyish (bōisshu), □ for willing to take the lead or be the passive partner depending on their partner," solidifying the male-female sex role-playing in the group. Lesbians are born in a male society that discriminates against women so they should stop using a system based on male values.
2. The leader collects and uses the enrollment fee and membership dues so she should issue financial statements.
3. The leader shouldn't control the information on members' cards but rather should make it more public.
4. Lesbian does not solely indicate "liking women" but is one way of resisting male society so it is "odd" (okashii) to allow members who are housewives taking advantage of the security offered by the marriage system to join the group.
5. Gathering together people who "like women" solves nothing. The group must change into a group that has some sort of purpose.

These women tried to take the theory they got from the lib movement and apply it to the group, which valued the very Japanese feelings of sympathy and affection. Certainly the sense that the group was just a place to meet a partner was fading, and given the group's character, which was getting into a rut, that criticism hit them in a sensitive area.

However, their demands were so impatient and confrontational that rather than being understood, they were met with an emotional rejection, and they were unable to get support from Wakakusa no Kai's members or its leader.

Y, who under the strong influence of American lesbian feminism at the time attempted to create a space for lesbians to meet each other, explains about the circumstances then.

> First, N-san and her friends probed Suzuki-san about how membership dues were being spent. So Suzuki-san started making frequent financial reports. She was running the whole thing all by herself, and doing so out of kindness, so where did they get off criticizing her like that? It seemed like a real surprise to Suzuki-san. She seemed to figure that if she worked herself to the bone, everyone would trust her—she had a naïve faith in everyone. She wrote the club's monthly newsletter by hand every month. Whatever it was—taking care of mail, forwarding letters from *Wakakusa tsūshin* (Wakakusa communications)[7] personal ads, taking care of fixing people up with *homo* men to marry, dealing with the media—she did it all, by herself. So everyone was able to just relax and come to meetings. As a fee for being able to not have to worry about all of that, I think 10,000 yen (US$100) as the annual membership fee was cheap. Even if she made a profit off of it, that would've been fine, but she didn't have enough time to work [to make a living] for herself. That must have been really tough. To do something for women, to sacrifice yourself like that, you can't do it if you don't think you are doing it as a volunteer.

According to I, things were like this:

> Those people who said Wakakusa no Kai was just a dating club, that we didn't know anything, that it was just a stupid club—you know, things didn't go well from the start. When someone asked for help, Suzuki-san flew down to Shikoku or Kyushu at her own expense. Just her phone bill alone must have been horrible. It's a shame that there were so many people who didn't know how hard she worked. She used to say, "When I come to Osaka, it's such a relief. Nobody criticizes me like they do in Tokyo."

It may seem like nothing, but the reason the group was able to come this far was because she carried its burdens on her back. However, some came later and criticized her, picking out a few points to justify what they believed. For Suzuki, who, from her early twenties, gave up her youth for other lesbians, it's not surprising that she accepted criticism from the lesbian liberationists in such a way. But a person's drive and kindheartedness has its limits. And the people around her got used to things as they were, forgot their sense of gratitude, and continued to increase their demands on her.

THE ARRIVAL OF CHEEKY LESBIANS

The lesbian liberationists left the group to start their own, and in came the next wave of Wakakusa no Kai. This time it was the young people raised in the city who didn't think it was a big deal to be a lesbian.

> For the club, over the passage of ten years, times had changed, or rather young people had reached the point where they just wanted to be much more practical about everything. They came looking for a partner, without really being serious about anything, and when they found one, they'd stop coming. They'd be with that person for a while and when the passion ended, they'd break up and come back to the group. But the person they dumped would stop coming. This coming and going was pretty intense. Whatever it was, these members were rather irresponsible. We'd plan a trip and when the time came, they didn't show up. Suzuki-san seemed really disappointed.

This is according to U (fifty-five), who joined the group in its second year and was a member until last year. For lesbians, finding a partner is a keenly felt problem. Particularly as you get older, or if you live away from a major city, finding a lover is really difficult. Among the group's members are people who confessed to a coworker their attraction to her, where the coworker proceeded to tell the boss, and they lost their job. So when you know from the start that the person you're talking with is of the same "sexuality" (*sekushuariti*),[8] all the anxiety about possible negative reactions is gone.

However, young people raised in the city were really knowledgeable about personal ads and lesbian bars, and that anxiety was never as much of a problem for them. Because for these young people things had reached this point, they had no idea of the hardships that the founding members had faced. So an increasing number of prospective members sent return postage and a note with nothing more than "send me some info" written in it, or just that and the type of woman they were in to. A cheerfulness drifted into the meetings like a breath of fresh air. But lost was the feeling of camaraderie felt sitting around the *kotatsu* (heated table) and chatting about life. In addition, in place of members who felt a sense of guilt about being lesbian, those who married and became housewives for financial reasons, and those who were living as men, were an increasing number of members who consciously chose to be lesbian, who planned from a young age to be independent, and who had full-time jobs.

Behind these changes was a society in which women were increasingly visible and a growing number of single women were living on their own in larger cities. Besides which, in Shinjuku ni-chōme and elsewhere, there were bars now opening where young people could go and drink cheaply,[9] meaning that there were more chances for people to meet each other outside the group and fewer women who had to deal with not knowing any other lesbians. Through these changes, you could say there was a change in lesbian consciousness.

EVE & EVE WOULDN'T SELL

Well, in addition to these changes, the third wave of the group reared its head. This was the failure of *Ibu & Ibu* (Eve & Eve),[10] Japan's first lesbian magazine, published in 1984. At first, Daini shobō, the publisher of the commercial gay magazine *Barazoku*, had promised to publish it, but three or four months after the manuscript was passed on to them, they went back on their word. The ostensible reason for this was that the "designer only wanted to do something aimed at men," but in fact, Suzuki explains, "I think it was because the content wasn't porn aimed at men, and they didn't think it would sell."

The manuscript was all written by members or professional writers who were acquainted with members. Of course they couldn't just forget about it. For Suzuki, it was a longstanding dream to sell lots of lesbian books at bookstores, so she borrowed 5,000,000 yen (US$50,000) to finance the launch of the magazine, publishing two thousand copies of the first issue. In the first issue, they had announced plans to publish the second issue six months later, but unfortunately Tōhan, Nippan, and other distribution routes were essentially closed to self-financed publications. They were able to sell off some magazines through the mail and others by visiting bookstores, but before she was able to pay off even half the loan, they published issue two, and in a flash, the loan had grown. She asked members to lend her money but there were few who could loan her very much.

As Suzuki recalls,

Yep, we were amateurs after all. In spite of the fact that we hadn't yet been able to open up distribution routes, we thought things would some-how work out in six months—we were really naïve in our expectations. So having put together the manuscript for the second issue already, it seemed a shame to just shelve it. Basically, we made it because we wanted to. But we had no financing, and no one knew whole the sad story behind it.

"If you let us take some photos of one of your parties, we'll introduce your book [in our magazine]," offered a major photography magazine. But when we asked for details, they expected "scenes of women holding each other, women all over each other." They thought that we took off our clothes and had sex at the meetings, and they wanted to put those scenes in their magazine! It's not as if we'd do *anything* to sell our magazine, so of course we turned down the offer.

Ultimately, the loan was a big blow to Wakakusa no Kai, which was sustained by this singular force. Suzuki became busy trying to pay off the loan and thus devoted little time to running the group. I talked to ten different Wakakusa no Kai members to research this article, and those who joined the group before *Ibu & Ibu* and those who joined after have very different impressions about Suzuki and Wakakusa no Kai. And generally speaking, those who joined after are more critical of the group and its leader.

H (forty-four), who was a member for just one year in 1984, says, "It's just a club loosely organized for people who 'like women' so it could take any direction depending on what kind of people joined the group." She has bitter memories of getting wrapped up in the financial trouble of a woman she met through the personal ads in *Wakakusa tsūshin*. Even if they use the word "lesbian," there are lots of different people, just because someone says she is a lesbian doesn't mean you can trust them, and to make a group just around that is really difficult, she explains.

M (twenty-five), who joined the same year, adds, "After seven years of suffering and worrying, I finally joined the group, but I didn't feel comfortable being in the group because it was all just vulgar sex talk and chat."

A member who joined two years ago, O (thirty-five), describes the weaknesses of the group:

> Coming and going, in and out—a lot of people joined and left the group, but in the end I didn't feel a connection with anyone. Only Suzuki-san has a personal connection with members, but the other members just periodically gathered like a "salon"—at that time, in that place—then just faded, so it's not a place to cultivate friendships. There are many people who come just to find a partner, and if you aren't careful you'll find yourself with a rival, so you don't find yourself sharing your phone number or address. And on top of that, it feels like the housewives are always asking, "Why do you ostracize us?" And there were a lot of people who were afraid to speak out. When it comes down to it, it seems like there were an awful lot of people who were only concerned with their own relationships and had very little social awareness. So when they found a lover, they stopped coming and just went off into their own world.

You can't shut yourself off and be fulfilled by just being aware of the communal existence of lesbians. You want to throw caution to the wind and go out in the world to stretch your wings. People who came to this not through logic but with their hearts have started to appear.

SO WE CAN OPEN OUR HEARTS TO EACH OTHER

> My parents are old now so I decided to go back to my hometown, and well, I guess my passion is gone anyway. I suppose it's what you call getting tired of people. But now there are all these bars, and you can meet one person after another, and lesbians are looking much brighter. Now there is no need for me to give advice to someone one-on-one. In that sense, Wakakusa no Kai has accomplished something.

This is Suzuki's explanation of why she's "taking a break from the group."

But even so, what was it that kept Suzuki working just for other lesbians for all of fifteen years?

Whatever I might say, I like women—that isn't rational. But that's the basic standard for joining our group. That irritates some people, but everyone has their own way. There are some people in formal marriages with *homo* men, and others who say, "Why, I'd never!" but in this society, people who are married and divorced and who say they can't remarry are more accepted than those who never married. I want to protect what these people want to hold on to. It's sad but in this world there are many people who have to carry the burden of these kinds of bonds. It's not as if there are mainly people who are blessed in being strong enough to be open and indifferent to what others think. But, I hope that one at a time we become stronger, and our hearts become brighter.

There may be a day when homosexuals will be accepted in Japanese society in the same way that heterosexuals are. But we can't wait for someone else to make that day come. If even after we, as individuals, try to make compromises with heterosexual society we still can't stop loving women, we have to at least hang on to the feeling.

That's the "help" Suzuki Michiko, who should rightly be called the "lesbian founder," gave to Wakakusa no Kai members, one at a time.

NOTES

1. The article was originally published under Sawabe's penname Hirosawa Yumi. In 1983, an article describing Wakakusa no Kai written by Suzuki Michiko, the subject of this interview, appeared in the women's magazine *Fujin kōron* (Women's debate). See Suzuki (1983). Another description of Wakakusa no Kai also based on an interview with Suzuki and written in the same time period can be found in Fukunaga (1982: 98–106).

2. This is a pseudonym.

3. *Wakakusa no kai* literally means "young grass club." *Wakakusa* (young grass) is an old expression used to indicate young woman. Louisa May Alcott's *Little Women*, in Japanese translation, has been given the title *Wakakusa monogatari*, which is best translated as "tales of young women."

4. All monetary conversions in this article are approximate and are based on the current, rather than historic, exchange rate.

5. The district in Tokyo with the most gay bars and lesbian bars. While Shinjuku ni-chōme is almost synonymous with gay nightlife, the area does have numerous establishments not aimed at gays or lesbians.

6. At least since the early 1960s, *bara* (rose) has been used as a symbol of homosexual men, hence *Barazoku* (Rose tribe) as the title of the magazine aimed at homosexual men. *Yuri* (lily) has been used as a symbol of homosexual women since at least the early 1970s. In November 1976, "Yurizoku no heya" (Lily tribe's room), aimed at *Barazoku*'s female readers, first appeared in its pages (*Barazoku* November 1976: 66-70) and was included sporadically after that through the mid-1980s.

7. This was the group's newsletter, which contained personal ads.

8. In the original text, the word *sekushuariti* is parenthetically glossed as meaning *seishikō* (sexual orientation), indicating the word's lack of widespread currency at the time the article was originally published.

9. Most of the bars where lesbians could go and feel relatively at ease were quite expensive in the early years. See the interview with lesbian bar owner Sunny in *Aniisu* (2001: 42–45).

10. There has been another "lesbian" magazine called *Eve & Eve*, published by San shuppan, which contains pornography aimed at male readers.

⑪

THEY'VE GOT THEIR
HAPPY FACES ON

The Birth of Regumi no Gomame

Hisada Megumi

Plotted out here is the story of a group born of native lesbians and the women's lib movement, a place where lesbians came together, fought, and groped for words their own.

Feeling a bit drunk, I climb into satin pink clown pants and don a silvery Moghul hat, and—totally out of character for me—start frolicking and dancing around. Swaying my body to the music, I feel free—right down to the very tips of my fingers. I'm like a tiny bird, and I look up toward the sky. This is the very pleasant sensation of being liberated.

The reason I'm in such high spirits is probably that I usually feel so constricted by social norms or common sense that it's hard to even breathe. I look around while thinking this and I see women, women, and more women. There are seventy or eighty women, Japanese and foreign, and everyone has such ecstatic smiles on their faces as they jostle up against each other in this narrow basement room. It's as if we've all

Translated and reproduced with permission from *"Genki jirushi no rezubian 'Regumi no Gomame' tōjō!"* which appeared in *Onna wo ai suru onnatachi no monogatari* (Stories of women who love women), *Bessatsu takarajima* no. 64, Tokyo: JICC shuppankyoku, 1987: 120–29. Translated by James Welker.

unconsciously given into the music as we eat, drink, rub shoulders, and chat with each other.

Within this crowd of women, out of the blue I see someone I know and give her a sign. She looks over at a friend from work who's wearing the same getup I have on. She taps me on the shoulder and smiles, "Is she your partner? So, you're a part of this, huh?"

She's a lesbian? Or maybe not. . . . And suddenly this all-too-familiar thought pops into my head. But my heart gets back into the groovy music, and before long I've succumbed to a new mindset—what does it matter if she is a lesbian or she isn't, if I'm a lesbian or I'm not? And I start dancing like crazy again.

Dancing over in the corner, dressed up like a black cat, is "Hazuki Inaho,"[1] smiling from behind her glasses. "Hirosawa Yumi,"[2] decked out as the white rabbit from *Alice in Wonderland* and dangling a giant watch, is bouncing around the party shaking her white tail. Looking very much like a bartender, the petite "Kagura Jamu" is wearing a black waistcoat and a narrow purple necktie.

The ever rough and boyish "Mochizuki Tao" is wearing a gorgeous *furisode* (hanging-sleeve) kimono and has a large ribbon in her very short hair. Her *obi* (belt) is tightly wound around her, squeezing her chest. "This is *really* tight. . . . So this is what being a woman is like, huh?" she grouses.

"Kusama Kei" is hanging out in an Indian sari, with a quiet expression on her face, and in a long lamé skirt, "Kawahara Karido" is circulating around the room, making introductions.

These are the faces of the lesbian group Regumi no Gomame,[3] a group that I did an interview with just three weeks ago.

On 1 March, 1987, this costume party was held to celebrate the opening of the first lesbian office, Regumi Studio Tokyo (Regumi sutajio Tōkyō), in the rented basement floor of an apartment building in the city.

These lesbians support themselves with various jobs in the "common" world of "straight" (*sutorēto*)[4] society, where it is "hard to breathe." In this "uncommon" women-only space, these women can all feel relaxed and let their hair down.

And after the party is over, in the room where people are casting off their costumes, a long-haired woman with a crestfallen look on her face grumbles, "Yuck. It's back to work tomorrow, back to 'normal' (*futsū*). . . ."

I feel the same. Why is it that in a space with no men, a space that's only women, we can feel so at ease? Yeah, I could really get addicted to this. . . .

JUST WHO ARE THESE LESBIANS LIVING INDEPENDENTLY?

I first encountered Regumi no Gomame when I was doing work collecting surveys from women's groups all around the country. I was looking over a bundle of surveys when I was suddenly drawn in by the words "lesbians living independently" (*shutaiteki ni ikiru rezubian*). These are not mere lesbians. They are lesbians living *independently*. Just what kind of people are these women? As I continued, I came across the following description, and I thought then that I really wanted to meet a member of this group.

> *Gomame* are small fish used in *osechi* dishes at New Year's.[5] It may well be that no matter how hard we lesbians try, under the current circumstances we are nothing more than "*gomame* grinding our teeth" [protesting in vain]. But when many small fish come together, we can take the form of a large fish, and like Swimmy,[6] we'll have the ability to fight against other big fish. We *gomame* take the wisdom and power we get from meeting each other, and swim off again into many other seas. Indeed, with our Regumi (lesbian)[7] *hachimaki* [head bands] wrapped around our heads, we are a powerful school of *gomame*.

I waited two weeks after sending a letter to their post office box asking if I could do an interview about the group. And finally, I heard back, and at the day and time we agreed upon, Hirosawa Yumi came to my office. She was the first woman I met who called herself a lesbian.

She was wearing a polo shirt and jeans. Standing there with a shiny gold chain dangling around her neck, she had a very boyish air about her.

If truth be told, as thoroughly immersed in the values of straight society as I was, just meeting a lesbian made me nervous. As someone who

had been unconsciously imprinted with the idea that men are the opposite sex and women are the same sex, it was hard to figure out where
to position myself relative to-her. My sense of balance was gone, and I
was overwhelmed by a feeling of anxiety.

But as we talked, my armor came down. And before I had a clue what
was happening, I started to feel really comfortable with the sort of sexy
energy she was giving off.

The sexiness, of a woman as a woman, seemed to rise out of the fact
that she was a woman at ease with her own sexuality. Later, when I met
other lesbians, I always sensed this sexy energy emanating from them,
which made me think, "how fantastic (*suteki*)"!

Plus, meeting Hirosawa Yumi was my ticket to the other side of a high
wall where the lesbian world could be found. This was a world that I
thought had nothing to do with me but which had now transformed into
a space I felt so close to.

And through these women's perspectives as lesbians, I came a little
closer to cracking the riddle of the shape of love between two people, a
riddle that can't be solved just by looking at the oppositional relationship
between women and men.

THEY MET FIFTEEN YEARS AGO

Turning to the past, Regumi no Gomame was established at the end of
1984. Upon seeing a slide show called "Women Loving Women," which
had been produced by American lesbians, Hazuki Inaho and Kagura
Jamu called for Japanese lesbians to themselves create the same sort
of slide show. And that's how it all started. "Women Loving Women"
was created to correct prejudice against lesbians and introduce the lives
and endeavors of American lesbian feminists who are active in various
fields.

Upon hearing the call to create a slide show, three others, Kawahara
Karido, Hirosawa Yumi, and Kusama Kei, joined those two, and the five
lesbians immediately formed a group, Regumi no Gomame, and set to
work. However, due to people's anxiety over making public the fact that
they were lesbians, the group couldn't get anyone to consent to being in
the show, so the slide production was temporarily caught in a snag.

In any case, as the slide show was going to take some time, they continued to work on *Regumi tsūshin* (Regumi journal), a lesbian *mini-komi* (zine) that was first published in May 1985.

In Japanese society, lesbian lives resemble the isolated lives of deep sea fish. And as the water pressure of heterosexual society is so high, they just can't rise to the surface. Finding each other is difficult too. American lesbians insist that they probably make up 10 percent of the female population, but most Japanese lesbians remain submerged beneath the surface, unaware of such a figure.

Given this situation, what sort of process did each of the members of Regumi no Gomame go through in order to find each other? The story can be traced back to around fifteen years ago, at the beginning of the 1970s.

At the time, there was a women's collective known as Ribusen, the nickname given to Lib Shinjuku Center (Ribu Shinjuku sentā), in Tokyo's Shinjuku district. This was the base of the women's lib group led by [prominent feminist] Tanaka Mitsu.[8] Among its members were Hazuki Inaho and Kawahara Karido, and the two had already met there. But at the time, lesbians had not yet appeared as a part of the women's lib movement in Japan, and the two hadn't even dreamed yet of a future in which they would live as lesbians.

However, after around 1974, information about American lesbians started to arrive at Ribusen and an announcement was put in *Ribu nyūsu* (Lib news) calling for translation staff. A student at the time, Hirosawa Yumi first visited Ribusen during that period. According to Hazuki Inaho, when the two met, Hirosawa was the first lesbian she had ever set her eyes on. But Hirosawa didn't find anything she could relate to in the movement. And later, she and some lesbian friends from university put out the lesbian *mini-komi* (zine) *Hikari guruma* (Shining wheel), among other activities, and she remained all the while inclined toward doing things her own way.

LESBIANS APPEAR ON THE WOMEN'S LIB MOVEMENT SCENE

It was just the time.

Kagura Jamu was enrolled at a university in Kyoto. She heard the far-off voices of the lib women in Tokyo. However, at the time, the lib movement was fighting to prevent the Eugenic Protection Law (Yūsei hogo hō) from being changed for the worse,[9] and all Kagura heard about was "unmarried mothers" and "abortion"—problems that stem from relations with men. Strongly attracted to women herself, Kagura didn't feel any sort of connection. These women's energy appealed to her, but she didn't move any closer.

> At the place I was living, the woman next door had a copy of the lib theory magazine *Onna erosu* (Women eros) in which there was an article about American lesbians.[10] But one look at the word "lesbian" gave me a start, and I slammed the magazine shut.

Even though around her were some old-style lesbians who wore men's clothes, there were no lesbians who lived true to themselves, dancing to their own tune. She felt a real sense of isolation in heterosexual society. How was she going to find a way to affirm her lesbian sexuality? In a bold move, she left Japan to wander around India for six months. However, "I went to a chaotic country and I, myself, was in a state of chaos. So I returned to Japan even more mixed up," she explains.

During the same period, in 1975 Hazuki Inaho went over to the United States and, in a women's clinic in California, underwent training to be a counselor. After that she worked in a women's clinic in Oakland, but almost all the staff were lesbians, and thus she was strongly influenced by lesbian feminist thought. A year later she returned to Japan.

> Originally, I was extremely resistant to accepting my own sexuality, and even when I was in a relationship with a man, there was no communication. And so, with no respect for a god that had nothing to do with me, I stayed away from men and just lived my life. However, through meeting self-identified lesbians—precisely because they were the same gender as me and we experienced the same gender discrimination—I discovered the joy of being able to create love with someone who was an equal.

To the extent that you become sensitive to gender discrimination, when you come face-to-face with men in this male-dominated society, you become aware that somehow your true self gets twisted out of shape. It seems that this is a feeling many feminists have experienced for themselves.

Yet from that time even within the Japanese lib movement, lesbians began to appear on the scene. In the *mini-komi* (zine) *Subarashii on-natachi* (Wonderful women; 1976) appeared the following declaration: "Since women have the potential to foster a trusting relationship based on mutual equality, it is wonderful to form a loving relationship that includes sex with other women. Women's lifestyles that reject men are the final and strongest means of reforming androcentric society, which treats women as slaves."

In the middle of that vortex, Kawahara Karido—who was, however, bisexual at the time—suddenly opened her heart to a lesbian she met. But afterwards things didn't go well. She wrote the following about the experience in issue 9 of *Regumi tsūshin*:

> I had so many things I was holding inside—like a Pandora's box. When I opened my eyes to loving women, and I met a part of myself I hadn't known before—and I tried very hard to cling [to the woman I was dating]. But she was more surprised than I [by the change in me] and she jumped ship in a heartbeat and found another woman.

What remained in Kawahara Karido was the "sparkling, dazzling, shining idea that 'lesbians are wonderful' and the memory of the warm feeling of being at ease." And she resolved that "since loving that woman caused me so much anxiety, I decided to live my life cherishing the ideas that she left me with."

That's the way that, at the age of twenty-eight, as both an ideological and a political choice, she came to live as a lesbian.

"I'M GOING TO TOKYO!"

At the same time, Kagura Jamu, who was working in Osaka after having graduated from a university in Kyoto, was still greatly troubled by her own sexuality. By chance, at the women's cafeteria Morimori, she picked up a *mini-komi* and got a great shock reading it.

"'What's this?' I thought. Right in the *mini-komi* it said, 'At a meeting in Tokyo there were people who unabashedly declared they were lesbians (*rezubian sengen wo shita*).' These women were so wonderful you'd want to throw your arms around them, it said. It was my first experience reading about lesbians who were described as wonderful women, so I was really moved," she recalls.

"I'm going to Tokyo, and then I'll be able to meet those wonderful lesbians!" And with the sun cutting its way through the fog, Kagura Jamu went off to Tokyo. She thinks back later about starting to live with Hazuki Inaho: "Through meeting her, I came to be able to trust people again."

On the other hand, having graduated from university in 1978, Hirosawa Yumi found a position at a company, and her job started to push her to withdraw from lesbian activism.

Yet, in the spring of 1980 Kusama Kei showed up as Hirosawa's co-worker.

The two became close friends—a lesbian and a straight woman—and a year later, after Hirosawa suddenly confessed her love for Kusama, the two became lovers. When I heard the details their story,[11] frankly speaking, I felt my own sexual identity waver. That's because it's the first time I understood the fact that all women have lesbian sexuality inside of them, and when it is triggered, their lesbian sexuality can rise to the surface.

"When she confessed her feelings for me it was truly the first time I realized that I was in love with her. But for a long time, I wasn't able to feel proud about saying I was a lesbian. I love a woman so now I'm a lesbian, but if I don't like her any more does that mean I'm not I lesbian anymore? That was something that I really questioned myself about. Now, I think that I've conquered that lesbian complex. I can say it out-right—I'm a lesbian!" Kusama Kei says with a laugh.

Around the same time in Kyushu, Mochizuki Tao felt profoundly alone from a young age when she realized that she was only able to like women. She was casually thumbing through an issue of the gay magazine *Barazoku* (Rose tribe), and in the classified ads she learned about the existence of the Tokyo lesbian group Wakakusa no Kai. And she made a decision—I'm going to Tokyo! She had had enough of day after painful day in Kyushu—I'm going to find some friends. I'm going to find some freedom. In 1981, the summer of her twenty-fourth year, she climbed aboard the *shinkansen* (bullet train).

"It was August 15th—a day I'll never forget. That was the day I set off for my new life, but there was a big earthquake and I was stuck inside the *shinkansen* for thirteen hours. It was a pretty ominous sign," Mochizuki Tao recalls.

A PRICELESS SPACE TO MEET OTHERS—*REGUMI TSŪSHIN*

Among lesbians, there are those we call the old type. Modeling their relationships after heterosexual society, they have fixed roles—male roles (*otokoyaku*) and female roles (*onnayaku*)—from which they derive their identities. In Wakakusa no Kai, there were many of these women. Among them, Mochizuki Tao was confused about just how to form a relationship between two women. This confusion led to a feeling of hopelessness.

She wanted to get rid of the whole male-female framework so she could be a lesbian and just be herself. So, Mochizuki very gradually became involved in lesbian activism from a feminist perspective.

Then in 1980, at the fifth of a series of gatherings jointly organized by Japanese and foreign resident lesbians, she met the other Regumi no Gomame members who were already involved in activism.

The members of Regumi no Gomame had many experiences and made many choices in life that led them to each other. And through the wisdom and power they had obtained just in meeting each other, they created spaces in which they were able to express themselves as lesbians. One priceless space they created was *Regumi tsūshin*.

In the pages of *Regumi tsūshin* could be found all sorts of personal histories, family histories, tales of falling in love and breaking up, anecdotes about work, travel memories, interviews, reports, film and book reviews, short stories, poetry, etc.—which were often reader contributions. Freely expressed in these pages were thoughts and discoveries that arose out of women's experiences living as lesbians.

When you think about it, in straight society these women must have been hindered from saying things openly as lesbians. To get a space in which to be able to say things freely, things you want to say, things you want to write, things you want to express . . . it was positively overflowing.

"Just what kind of people are we lesbians? No one will tell me. What's more, we have to discover the value by ourselves and affirm ourselves." And what of the women who wrote things like that? In order to affirm themselves as lesbians, these women had to put into words the truth inside themselves—it was a necessary step they had to go through.

And, to the extent that *Regumi tsūshin* contained announcements about spaces where lesbians could meet each other—bars, concerts, parties, camps, meetings—and, in addition, information about lesbian life and activism abroad, it served the role of expanding the network connecting solitary lesbians.

When it was first published, its readership didn't even reach 30 people, but two years later, its readership had quadrupled, increasing to around 120 people.

QUARRELS AND COMPROMISES

Each issue of *Regumi tsūshin* was edited and put out by a staff of six. The head editor of a given month did everything—wrote the copy, did the printing, and sent it out. For women already busy with other things, this prevented the need for multiple meetings to carry out a cooperative activity. It further allowed them to avoid solidifying roles—such as *I*, the person doing the writing, and *you*, the person doing the printing—or specifying someone who always has to push others to do something—meaning there was no vertical relationship, which would destroy the equality in the group.

"That was the rationale, but what it came down to was that the Regumi lesbians' self-assertion was strong and obstinate. Even though we all decided what to do, people who didn't agree with something wouldn't do it. So the way to protect the right of the person responsible to do what they wanted [meant that] each person's natural characteristics came out, and in the end a unique magazine was produced—I suppose," reflects Kawahara Karido.

People were free to do what they wanted, but it wasn't as if they could do what they wanted with the personal ads column.

At a monthly meeting, the draft issue was brought out, and each staff member rather earnestly gave her impressions and opinions.

"You're not sticking with the facts, so I can't really tell what you want to say." Such harsh criticisms were sometimes spoken, including, at times, calls for the whole thing to be redone.

"To take what was your own experience and neatly put that into words is really hard. But we wouldn't let go of writing about our experiences.

The kind of groundless prejudice and discrimination we've encountered as lesbians—it's all connected with what's happened to us and what we're troubled about." Kawahara Karido continues, "To draw intersections is a matter of tracing the conditions of a universal problem which happens to each individual lesbian."

While the Regumi members are all lesbians, as is explained above, the process by which each one got there was quite different. There are three women who were troubled about their sexuality from an early age, so-called "native lesbians" (*nekkara no rezubian*).[12] Two women are "ideological lesbians" (*shisōteki rezubian*), who chose to identify themselves as lesbian within the lib movement, and one is a straight woman who became a lesbian. The problems that each of them has to deal with is somewhat different from those of the others, and as these differences are felt or thought about from various perspectives the gap becomes apparent.

For example, a recurrent debate is that of the "butch" (*bucchi* or *oto-koyaku*) and "femme" (*femu* or *onnayaku*) issue. "Ideological lesbians" Hazuki and Kawahara's relatively negative and sensitive response is that such relationships are modeled after the oppositional relationships in straight society and contradict the equality of lesbian relationships. The "native lesbians," including Hirosawa, give more leeway to that kind of relationship and are occasionally offended by the former opinion, bemoaning that "the way they talk, they one-sidedly cut down other lesbians."

In addition, the issue of polygamy versus monogamy is also a point of debate. While some insist that the inclination toward monogamy gives rise to the feeling that your partner is your possession, and such relationships become exclusive, shutting off the possibility of relationships with other lesbians, others assert such excessive denials are hard to take and that deeply loving someone on an individual level is the essence of love.

Of course, given that I haven't known lesbians for very long, it isn't as if I fully understand these issues. However, listening in as a bystander, it seems that these women's debate reflects the oppositional male-female relationship of straight society—like a mirror shedding light on a deep place.

Be that as it may, through various problems and the process of bumping heads, fighting, and pushing individual opinions on each problem, it becomes a means of affirming each woman's self and a process whereby together they can more deeply understand each other.

Then in February 1986, Regumi no Gomame ended its role and was absorbed into a new organization.

THE ESTABLISHMENT OF REGUMI STUDIO TOKYO

After a short while, five of the six Regumi no Gomame members (Kawahara Karido was concentrating on work and night classes at a university and decided to offer support from the sidelines) joined with ten staff members to establish a new base of lesbian activism, Regumi Studio Tokyo.

The group's main activities would be to produce *Regumi tsūshin*, throw parties, hold events, plan gatherings, hold lectures, collect and preserve lesbian-related materials, and so on and so on. The purposes for opening the office were

1. to create a network to consult with and support solitary lesbians around the country and create a sense of solidarity
2. to reflect on just who "women who love women" are and find out their value
3. to provide accurate, fact-based information about society in order to eliminate discrimination and prejudice against lesbians

Nationwide lesbian campaigns and membership dues are used to maintain the office and fund the activities, and in order to move beyond being just a place to talk, their telephone number has been made public so people can call in for advice.

After hearing from an effusive Hirosawa Yumi how "everyone is really enthusiastic—really excited!" about the project, I was a little uneasy.

Just what kind of bold thing are these women starting? It's hard to imagine that this conservative, male-centered, straight society will accept lesbians so smoothly. Didn't even Hirosawa Yumi herself say something like that before?

The existence of lesbians is a threat for men given that their own lover might leave them for a woman. So even though they are also homosexuals, unlike *homo*, lesbians are the object of male animosity. A society in which women form such bonds with each other is a society in which men don't know when they might get axed in their beds.

Couldn't some unseen power, with a single thought, crush these women in its fingers?
"Yeah, but. . . ," Hirosawa interjects.

If someone were to curl up into a ball because she was a lesbian, whoever it was would become very warped in the heart. What's frightening about prejudice is not that stones might be thrown at you or that you might be the target of discrimination. What's most frightening is that in restricting yourself you get caged up in your own world, and you lose your psychological freedom and end up believing you can't do anything, living as if you had already died. As proof that you are alive, you really have to muster up the courage to express yourself. And what we have discovered, we have to express it in such a way that it reaches the hearts of others.

Psychologically, in our daily lives, in the choices about our way of living, and in the way we love others sexually, culture and norms coerce us into following a certain path. For the members of minorities who must diverge from that coerced path, this society is difficult to live in. However, if they stop being so resolute, they will simply be erased.

Now, lesbians have wrapped around their heads a *hachimaki* with the word "Regumi" imprinted on it, and they are out swimming in the big sea. I hope this idea can reach the hearts of many women.

NOTES

1. Hazuki Inaho was the name used at the time by activist Wakabayashi Naeko.

2. This was the penname used at the time by Sawabe Hitomi. Sawabe contributed chapters 1, 10, and 13 to this volume.

3. "Regumi" is a contraction of *rezubian* (lesbian) and *kumi* (group). The meaning of "gomame" is explained below.

4. This term appears in the original text as the loan word *sutorēto*, but, acknowledging that a number of readers might be unfamiliar with the intended

meaning of this term, it is parenthetically glossed as meaning *iseiai* (hetero-sexual).

5. More specifically, *gomame* are a type of dried anchovy. *Osechi ryōri* (*os-echi* cuisine) is the name given to the special dishes served only at New Year's.

6. As glossed in the original text, *Swimmy* is a children's picture book by Leo Lionni (1969). Swimmy got other small fish to gather together so they looked like a big fish.

7. The original text parenthetically glossed "Regumi" as *rezubian*.

8. For details on Tanaka's activism and writing, see Mackie (2003: 144–45, 157–59).

9. See Mackie (2003: 166–67).

10. An abridged translation of chapter 9, "In Amerika, They Call Us Dykes," from *Our Bodies, Ourselves* (Boston Women's Health Book Collective 1973) appeared in two parts, in the April and September 1974 issues of *Onna erosu* (Women eros); see Boston Women's Health Book Collective (1974b, 1974c). While the 1974 Japanese translation of *Our Bodies, Ourselves* does not include this particular chapter, it does include a brief section on homosexuality; see Boston Women's Health Book Collective (1974a).

11. A more detailed telling of this tale can be found in Kusama (1987), which is contained in the same volume as this story originally appeared.

12. I base my translation of the term *nekkara no rezubian* (literally, "a lesbian from the root") as "native" lesbian on Izumo Marou's use of the term *nētivu* (native). See Izumo et al., chapter 12, in this volume.

⑫

JAPAN'S LESBIAN MOVEMENT

Looking Back on Where We Came From

Izumo Marou (writer), Tsuzura Yoshiko (language teacher), Hara Minako (translator), and Ochiya Kumiko[1] (high school teacher)

IzUMO: [. . .] Today I'd like to talk about the history of Japan's lesbian movement on the activism scene, focusing on what was actually happening at the time, as well as how some of that history might connect with the present. While there are others with whom I hope to have the opportunity to hear from as well, I've decided to hold today's discussion with the women assembled here.

I'd like to devote the first part of this discussion to an explanation of the kinds of activities each of you have been involved in, and then give the latter part over to an exchange of opinions if not debate.

First of all, prior to 1975, Wakakusa no Kai (Young grass club) had a large number of members and held tea parties at its leader's apartment.[3] I believe that at the time Wakakusa no Kai was Japan's only lesbian organization. However, in that era it was quite difficult even to learn about the existence of the group. [. . .]

Lesbian liberationist activism arose from women's liberationism, which itself grew out of [the left-wing student organization] the All-Campus Action Committee (Zenkyōtō).[4] There were lesbians among

---

Abridged, translated and reproduced with permission from "*Nihon no rezubian mūvumento*," in *Gendai shisō* (Contemporary thought), special issue on lesbian and gay studies, vol. 25 no. 6, May 1997: 58–83.[2] Translated by James Welker.

the liberationists, who together rallied against [feminist activist] Tanaka Mitsu and developed their criticism of Wakakusa no Kai—and thinking that there must be more lesbians around, they created a survey. That was the "Wonderful Women" (*Subarashii onnatachi*) survey about lesbians.

They received a large number of responses and held a "panel discussion" (*zadankai*). I happened to respond to the survey, which was given to me by a friend, and was asked to join the discussion—that served as the first time I met lesbians other than myself. And that's also how I learned about Wakakusa no Kai. The discussion, itself, was held at Lib Shinjuku Center (Ribu Shinjuku Sentā), which was strongly influenced by Tanaka Mitsu. Ribusen, as it was generally called, was based on cooperative activity.

During the panel discussion, it was decided to reach out to many more lesbians, which is how the *mini-komi* (zine) *Wonderful Women* was created. [. . .] Having grown out of the All-Campus Action Committee and the women's lib movement, we were connected to an underground culture. And so in order to circulate our materials well, we placed our books at a number of different bookstores [and other places] through an underground network. [. . .]

At the time, partly due to American influence, Japan saw the first appearance of lesbians by political choice. There were quite a number of people within the lib movement who read *Wonderful Women* and became interested in lesbians. And that led to a number of debates.

For instance, what I wrote in *Wonderful Women* included dark things. Having grown up in a society based on "compulsory heterosexuality" (*kyōseiteki iseiai*) and then living as a lesbian, of course I was wounded and I thought something was wrong with me—but I decided, *so what?* this way is fine too, I'm going to live—and I finally dared to write about all this. And in came the reaction: What the hell is this dark piece included in the *mini-komi?* Lesbians are "wonderful women," aren't they? Basically, the direction the lesbians by choice wanted to take the movement meant that anything that wasn't supporting the idea that lesbians were wonderful was meaningless.

But [. . .] unless you thought about the wounds you'd suffered, there was no way you could solve lesbian problems. It bothered me to be used like that by the political lesbians, so I didn't associate with them.

And after the split in 1977, the group Mainichi Daiku (Everyday dyke) was formed, and started a publication, *The Dyke* (*Za daiku*), using a word play based on the Japanese word "carpenter" (*daiku*) and the English word "dyke."[5]

[. . .] During that period, I started going to more women's lib gatherings, and I told them I was a lesbian. The reason it was necessary to say this was that at the feminist gatherings all women ever talked about was in relation to men. In order to address the fact that there were also women who weren't like that, at a meeting on January 28th at Yamanote Church, I first declared publicly that I am a lesbian.

At the time in addition to *The Dyke* there was *Hikari guruma* (Shining wheel). This publication came about due to a conflict that arose among members of Mainichi Daiku at one of the group's meetings. There was a woman who said that some lesbians wanted children even though they were lesbians. But women can't make children together, so that's why on that issue we lose to straights. The lesbian liberationists criticized them for having an ideology that idealized heredity. Wanting your own children itself is based on this ideology and the root of all evil, they said. It led to a huge quarrel and those who left Mainichi Daiku and some volunteers started a group called Hikari Guruma, issuing a group publication with the same name. But the positions of *The Dyke* and *Hikari guruma* weren't especially different. And with time, the two groups started to cooperate [holding parties and a lecture series].[6] [. . .]

And in 1978, both Mainichi Daiku and Hikari Guruma disbanded. What led to this development was the Lesbian Feminist (LF) Center and "consciousness-raising" (CR) workshops. In fact, when Mainichi Daiku and Hikari Guruma broke up, I distanced myself from lesbian activism.

Just ideals and criticism . . . at the time the state of the community was just factious groups, nothing that would lead to a real rights movement. But behind the factions were oppositional feelings. More than searching for what kind of identity made a lesbian, or the theoretical weapon that lesbians are wonderful, I thought, lesbians really exist, so isn't it necessary to get rights for us. But I decided that things weren't moving toward a rights movement at the time.

And when you're talking about lesbian issues, naturally this also involves women's issues, minority issues, and at that time, the Sanrizuka standoff.[7] Of course I think there are ways for joint struggle, but I saw women's issues as always at the center of their activities. Later, there was something that I just couldn't accept—the gap between homosexuality as desire and "sisterhood" (*shisutāfūdo*). And within that, what I couldn't put up with was the tendency to look down on having respect for one's partner.

And again, I came to write *Love upon the Chopping Board* (*Manaita no ue no koi*; 1993),[8] and somehow I'm in this panel discussion . . . that's how things happened.

AMERICAN LESBIANS AND LESBIAN WEEKENDS

HARA: What I'm here to talk about today is the Lesbian Weekends (*rezubian uiikuendo*), which began in 1985. And I was involved with them from the first one until 1992 or '93. I would like to talk today about how I felt when I was involved in group activities. Therefore, first of all, I hope you'll understand that my comments are based on my own personal analysis.

I came out to people around me around 1983, but I'll begin before then, with my truly individual history.

In the mid-seventies, not knowing anyone at all, I was active on my own. This was at places like Mosakusha, and [the women's "free space"] Hōkiboshi [both in Shinjuku]. I went to bars in [Shinjuku] Ni-chōme as well, but at this time there were hardly any women, so I always went home disappointed, not having run into any lesbians—the seventies were like that. After that I was out of Japan, and when I came back in '82, there were a lot of women's groups. It was through one of these that I was first invited to a lesbian party, and it was the very first time I talked to a lesbian in Japan.

Then I started going to a monthly women's party at a bar in Shinjuku called Mako, made some friends there, and from that point, everyone was always saying, "they're having a party over at such-and-such a place," so I went to that one too—and on and on like that, I made my way around. At the time, a lot of the parties at private homes were held by women from the American military bases. Having learned about the lesbian weekend retreat from one of those women, I decided to go.

Lesbian Weekends sprang out of the International Feminist Meeting (Kokusai feminisuto kaigi), which was jointly sponsored by IFJ (International Feminists of Japan) and Japanese Feminist Group (Nihon no Feminisuto Gurūpu). There, Hazuki Inaho and some other people held a lesbian session, and an incredible number of people showed up. And well, it was pretty clear it was possible to have a meeting just of lesbians . . . and the "Weekends" were born.

In the beginning, most of the workshops were in English. I wondered what these workshops might be, so I went to see, and the discussion was all about lesbian sexuality—how to make relationships with women, feeling hurt because you were always treated as an "asexual old maid"—really familiar talk. Well, that was something we could do in Japanese too . . . and from the second time, there were an increasing number of Japanese workshops.

Among the Weekend participants, the majority were white women working as English teachers. On the other hand, coming out (*kamu auto*) seemed to be quite a problem for lesbians in the American military community, since there were background checks and problems like that. In *Odd Girls and Twilight Lovers*, which I recently translated into Japanese [as *Lesbian History* (*Resubian no rekishi*); 1991/1996] as well, Lillian Faderman writes in great detail about the lesbian community in the military, and I heard exactly the same thing from women on American military bases in Japan.

We got to know each other at the parties, and when we went to the Weekends we were called the "party lesbians." And that's where I met women who were involved in Mainichi Daiku, Hikari Guruma, and Lib Center. It was like an encounter with the unknown. And two or three years later, I joined those women in creating Regumi Studio (Regumi sutajio).

In the beginning, there were around fifty women attending the Weekends, but there was also a period when that number was over a hundred, and they're still being held today. They're held around three times a year, so there've been more than forty in total, I suppose—held at public educational facilities. And there has been a problem about whether we could use the word "lesbian" (*rezubian*). There were people who couldn't say "I'm participating in a lesbian retreat," and even for those who *could* come out, there was a problem on the side of the facilities themselves which made it so you couldn't write "lesbian" on the publicity materials. So, ultimately it was decided to consistently use a name that wouldn't reveal that it was a lesbian group, but in reality, the lesbian gatherings went on as before. Even then, sometimes a facility wouldn't let us make a reservation [. . .]. Still now, the problem with public facilities is the same as the OCCUR (Akā) court case over use of the Fuchū Youth Hostel (Fuchū seinen no ie), but to this day, we haven't made a formal issue of this as OCCUR did.[9]

Originally IFJ was a feminist gathering, and some lesbian feminists felt strongly that no matter what they tried, lesbian issues just didn't come up, so "separatism" (separetizumu), which means creating a lesbian-only gathering, was proposed. Japanese lesbians jumped on board. Along with it went the stance that even if you were both women, if she wasn't a lesbian, you shouldn't be associating with her. The number of women who called themselves "separatists" (separetisuto) was quite small, but a lot of women, myself included, understood what they wanted. We're lesbians so let's take part as lesbians—a lot of women seemed to feel that way.

But recently, there have been problems in organizing the Weekends. For example, when some women called to say they want to attend, they were asked, "Are you a lesbian?" which came as quite a shock for them—why should women be forced to say whether or not they are a lesbian? They also asked me this question in order to attend. So, saying whether or not you are a lesbian has become a kind of shibboleth. When we heard this, a huge debate ensued over how a person's qualifications for attending should be evaluated. [. . .]

The good point was that there were no longer any experts. Since there was no one lecturing "what kind of a person is lesbian," everyone could work it out together. If you compare it with women's studies today, it really seems like we listened more to each other. There were a lot of first accounts of the problems we were facing, and we felt like we could do something to support each other. That's how Regumi Studio came to be.

THE FOUNDING OF REGUMI STUDIO[10]

HARA: Regumi Studio had twelve members to start with, and I'm sure they all had different motives for forming the group. In my personal case, what motivated me to participate in the founding was that I got a threatening phone call at my home from the father of someone I met at a Lesbian Weekend. At the time, I was living with my partner and my daughter was small, so I found it really threatening. I thought there ought to be a place outside the home [for people to call and to go]. I was worried that if something happened, someone could find out where I live and harm my family, so I wanted to form Regumi Studio to protect myself.

The group Regumi no Gomame had been formed after Hikari Guruma dissolved. It was a political feminist group whose approach was too theoretical in my view. So, why did we join forces? One of the reasons was because these threatening phone calls couldn't be solved individually and the resulting sense of crisis made us band together. The name of the *mini-komi Regumi tsūshin* (Regumi journal) was carried over but the content was changed. [. . .] Later, there was a problem over privacy [and . . .] Regumi Studio split up. Hirosawa Yumi, a founder of Regumi Studio and editor of the book *Stories of Women Who Love Women* (*Onna wo ai suru onnatachi no monogatari, Bessatsu takarajima* [1987]), left the group, along with some other women.[11]

Looking back, Regumi Studio was created in coordination with the publishing of the *Bessatsu takarajima* book. Hirosawa really threw a lot of energy into *Stories of Women Who Love Women*, and a lot of people—myself included—also helped with the project and later became involved in the formation of Regumi Studio. Gathering together women who wanted to write for the book at the Weekends, Hirosawa really shouldered the total responsibility for the project, and, at the same time, decided there should be an office. So I see the Weekends, *Bessatsu takarajima*, and Regumi Studio as a set. [. . .]

Another cause [of the break up of Regumi] was the conflict between the lesbian "by choice" (*sentaku*) and "native-born" (*nekkara*) lesbian factions. There were some people who made the political choice to be a lesbian precisely because of the compulsion to be heterosexual, and they ran up against strong feelings that they weren't really lesbians. Since Hirosawa left as a result, it might seem that it was the lesbians by choice who remained, but in fact there were only a handful of people who outright *chose* to be a lesbian. But if one person said she was a lesbian by choice, from the outside it just seemed like everyone else was the same. [. . .]

Still another cause was the lack of willingness to acknowledge the feelings of hurt that were still festering for some people. [. . .] Gloomy topics and any topics related to mental illness were all seen as undesirable. It was the flip side of fear—I can understand it now, but at the time, having experienced a long period of depression when I was a teenager, I too thought that somehow we had to be out there as cheerful, healthy lesbians. On the one hand, some people were critical about having fun at parties, and, on the other, criticism came from elsewhere about being studious. We couldn't affirm each other at all. [. . .]

TSUZURA: But everyone was trying to take a unified path, weren't they? All trying to do something?

HARA: Exactly. Trying to do something. In the meantime, Hirosawa and some others created the magazine, *Hyōkoma Life: Seeking New Ways of Living* (*Hyōkoma raifu—atarashii sei no yōshiki wo motomete*). This was after the breakup. It was along the lines of a literary magazine. I think around seven issues of it were published [between 1990 and 1992].

One of the activities of Regumi Studio was going to places like the Tōhoku region and Kyoto, and answering letters from all over the country—and slowly, small groups began appearing here and there, in the Tōkai region and Tōhoku.[12] I think the role of the *Regumi tsūshin* [in building lesbian communities] was huge.

Also, since most women's groups had lesbians in them, we circulated our information through those lesbians. For instance, at a gathering called "From the Body Retreat" (*Karada kara gasshuku*), organized by the Group against Counter-Reform of the Eugenic Protection Law (*Yūseihogohō Kaiaku Soshi Renrakukai*)—which was a considerably large gathering—we held discussions on lesbians and sexuality. Periodically we did things like that with other groups.

There was also activism against the AIDS Prevention Bill (*Eizu yobō hōan*). There was a pamphlet titled "AIDS as a Women's Issue" (*Onnatachi no eizu mondai*), and among the women's groups the most passionately involved, I would say, was Regumi Studio's Hazuki Inaho. At the time there was interaction with the [Japan chapter of] ILGA (International Lesbian and Gay Association), OCCUR, and the Hemophiliacs' Association (*Ketsuyūbyō no Kai*). However, the issue of women working as prostitutes was abandoned.

An alternative bill proposed by the Tokyo Bar Association (Tokyo Bengoshi Kai) basically said that while women working in the sex trade couldn't avoid getting blood tests, the same not be asked of gays and hemophiliacs. When we complained about discrimination, things got rather sticky. And so it seemed that we just couldn't join forces. Though each of us could understand our own position, we weren't able to understand the positions of others. [. . .]

LESBIANS AND ETHNICITY

IZUMO: The issues around ALN (Asian Lesbian Network) have to do with the reason you left Regumi Studio, don't they?

HARA: The original impetus for the '92 ALN meeting was an international lesbian meeting held in Geneva in '86. Among the Asian lesbians at the meeting, there was talk about the lack of space for them among the predominantly white women. So, in 1990 five or so Thai women called together around sixty women from all over Asia and held the First Asian Lesbian Network Conference. And we decided to hold the next one in Tokyo, so in '91 we starting preparing, but no sooner had we started, we ran up against varying degrees of political motivation and generational conflicts, and all the problems that had happened before came back.

So, younger lesbians held a workshop at a Weekend called "Just What Is ALN?" (*ALN tte nanzansho?*) at which a series of criticisms were leveled at the planners of ALN. [. . .] That was the young people's first formal expression of their views.

TSUZURA: But when you look at the situation, there was a conflict between those who wanted to have a conference and those who wanted to have a celebration, which is troubling.

HARA: Exactly. And ultimately that's how the name changed from "ALN Meeting" (*kaigi*) to "ALN Festival" (*matsuri*).

IZUMO: There was also a problem about not allowing white women in, wasn't there?

HARA: Yes. That was discussed a lot especially at the first meeting in Thailand. This is because among the sixty women invited to the conference were several white women living in Thailand. The ethnic Asian lesbians who came from America, Canada, and Australia protested: Why are there white women in this space?

Eventually, it was decided that Asian means it's done by Asians, from which came one of the big problems. That came from Zainichi (Resident) Korean[13] participants. The fact was that while calling it an international or Asian meeting, we organizers had ignored the presence of the Zainichi Koreans.

Tsuzura: At the first general meeting, there was an introduction of lesbians from each country, and at the very end when Japan was introduced, the words used were "Japanese lesbians in Japan" (*nihon ni iru nihonjin no rezubian no kata.*) That was when the existence of foreign residents, particularly Zainichi Koreans, was ignored. Well, perhaps rather than that they were ignored, a mistake was made—but it was a fundamental mistake.

Hara: And during the initial registration, there was friction over pronouncing Korean names in the Japanese way or the Korean way, which was *not* just due to a lack of awareness.

Tsuzura: It was like, even though Zainichi Koreans insisted that this is the way the names are supposed to be written in [phonetic] *kana* letters, at some stage the names were all written according to the Japanese pronunciation of the characters.

Hara: I thought we should have officially responded to this claim, but we couldn't respond sufficiently during the meeting. Afterwards, the organizers received a formal statement of protest.

At the point we received the statement at the ALN office, we were sharply divided between those who could agree with the protest and those who could not, and ultimately a statement of apology was issued, but it took a very long time to get there. In spite of all the sharp criticism against the racial discrimination on the part of the white lesbians, [. . .] we couldn't acknowledge the wounds [we'd inflicted on others] and can't acknowledge that we discriminate, too. It was then that I decided the group wasn't going the way I wanted it to. The reason I left ALN and the reason I left Regumi are slightly different, but in both cases it was for things that were really important to me. Now I keep my distance from groups and limit myself to activism on an individual level, translating lesbian books and things like that.

Now I think we need a space where can talk more about our true feelings about various wounds, not just limited to lesbians. And we need to really reflect on the ways in which the legal and other systems operate. If we don't do something about this, we won't be able to solve the problem of the denial of lesbian wounds. It's from that perspective that I am currently involved in a self-help group for survivors of sexual violence. I think this is something along the lines of LF Center members running a rape support center.

"WHAT IS SEXUALITY?"—THE MOVEMENT IN KANSAI

TSUZURA: I'm here today to talk about the development of activism in the Kansai region [in south-central Japan, surrounding Osaka, Kyoto, and Kobe] from around 1987 or '88 to the present. While focusing on YLP (Yancha Lesbian Power),[14] I'll also touch a little upon things that happened before that.

First of all, before YLP in '77 there was Shambala, a woman's space that opened in a former "snack bar" (*sunakku*) in Kyoto, where they held a lesbian meeting once a month. Copies of "*Wonderful Women*" were available there too.

Shambala closed in '82 but after that, well, since the seventies, there was a coffee shop called Freak (Furiiku) in Osaka that was a woman's lib space and they held gatherings there once a month. This place is still operating, and the lesbian night is too, with a different organizer each time.

In '86, when Wakakusa no Kai ceased, people who were in it started a club called Sophia (Sofia) and put out a newsletter. That group continued until around '89.

Now I'd like to move on to YLP, which started around '87. Why was this group started? One reason was to make lesbian issues more visible within women's activism. That's why they held a discussion group every year at the Women's Festival (Onna no fesutibaru) in Kyoto. In the Japanese Women's Studies Research Society (Nihon Joseigaku Kenkyūkai), there was a special interest group, Considering the Choice of Women's Sexuality (Onna no sekushuariti no sentaku wo kangaeru kai), which was the YLP's actual predecessor, and it was clearly connected with the "native lesbian"/"lesbian by choice" issue.

IZUMO: Did this turn into a debate?

TSUZURA: No—there was nothing confrontational about it. Kansai YLP was started as that kind of group, so in that sense, I don't see it as an ordinary organization.

First of all, there were no membership cards, and no membership list. Second, there was an understanding that if you wanted to do something, you could go ahead and use YLP's name, that anyone who felt that they belonged to YLP could use the group's name. There were very few members really running it, and everything was basically done on an individual basis, so there weren't any formal decisions being made as a group.

HARA: In YLP have there been decisions like, when will we gather again, things like that?

TSUZURA: Not very often, but, yes, occasionally there were. YLP participated in the Women's Festival from '89 to '94, but they were most active surrounding the '90 workshop "So What Is Sexuality?" (*Sekushuariti tte nan darō*). While thinking about women's subjectivity with regard to sexuality, they put a lot of thought into what a lesbian is. In addition, they also considered the image of lesbians in society, but I'd say there were changes in that image due to the publication of Kakefuda Hiroko and Sasano Michiru's books.[15] Kakefuda in particular worked hard to push for the nationwide recognition of lesbians, starting in 1988 when she became the first lesbian in Japan to come out in the mass media. And then in 1992 she published her *On Being "Lesbian"* (*"Rezubian" de aru to iu koto*), and in spite of her anxieties she faced a double-edged sword by appearing on TV to proclaim lesbian existence to the whole of Japan.

OCHIYA: Kakefuda's book was huge, wasn't it? After that what we call the "the *Labrys* generation" really started growing.

TSUZURA: We're not talking today about *Labrys* [a magazine first published in 1992 by Kakefuda and others], are we? The people involved with *Labrys* were involved in all sorts of activism, but the primary thing was connecting with the lesbian masses by widening their range. After that came the commercial magazines *Phryné* (*Furiine*; 1995) and *Anise* (*Aniisu*; 1996–1997, 2001–2003).

What's been really important for YLP has been the use of the word "lesbian" within women's groups and as a part of women's activism.

One example of that was the Asian Women's Conference (Ajia josei kaigi), which was the same year as ALN. During the conference a lesbian group discussion was held, centered around YLP. What happened was that YLP was approached by women's groups who thought that lesbian issues should be included since it was a conference about women.

HARA: There were a lot of people invited from abroad for that one, weren't there?

TSUZURA: That's right. But wasn't the Osaka region group the only one to use the word "lesbian"? The Tokyo group did the sexuality discussion group. When you frame the discussion around sexuality, sexual violence and prostitution come to the fore very easily [at the expense of lesbian issues].

HARA: About that point, it did seem like it was about women's sexuality [in general]—and the organizers didn't use the word "lesbian."

TSUZURA: YLP's activism pretty much ended with that. Around that time at the Women's Festival—and YLP wasn't directly involved with this but— Lesbian Mothers' Club (Rezubian Mazā no Kai) was started. I think there's one in the Kantō region [surrounding Tokyo] as well.

Well, then, around 1994 OLP (Open Lesbian Power) [16] was started. As more and more people joined YLP, there was the opinion that there was the need for some kind of organizational consciousness, for it to somehow be run as a "formal group" (kai). And there was also the need for a debate on whether we could involve bisexual women or married women. YLP was never able to make a space for that kind of debate, so first came the move toward organization, and coming from a completely different space, OLP was created.

At the time there was a debate over who should be able to join, and it was decided that as long as someone supported our aims, anyone could join regardless of their sexuality or whatever. In the beginning it was women only, not limited, however, to women who were biologically female but open to people who identified as women. At the time there was already a problem over what to do about transsexual people, but it was decided that they would be very welcome, and we've been working together since the beginning. Of course heterosexual and bisexual women participate as well, and recently there have been men involved too.

OCHIYA: There was quite a big membership change when the group changed from YLP to OLP, wouldn't you say?

IZUMO: What was the basic reason for the change from YLP to OLP?

OCHIYA: There was no consensus that YLP was lesbian only, but inevitably it was done by people who could be said to identify as lesbian. When it was said that we should allow anyone who supported our aims to participate in OLP, people who wanted to do it as a lesbian-only group left. But as for actual opposition, I didn't hear any. There were people who couldn't stand people who were married, but since they never said anything publicly, there was no direct confrontation.

HARA: How about the opposite? Were there no attacks on lesbians by heterosexuals or bisexuals?

OCHIYA: No, there were no confrontations. After all, they joined OLP because they were intrigued by it.

TSUZURA: Actually, there was. One thing was that in OLP, the thinking was that the meaning of "lesbian" was, broadly, "women who love women," but L didn't clearly represent the word "bisexual." At the beginning, a name like Labia, Lesbians, and Bisexuals was put forth, but, in the end, it became OLP. I think it wasn't that the bisexual issue was made light of, but rather that it wasn't problematized. Where the bisexual issue was taken up and the movement continued was in *Labrys*, of course.

Finally, in OLP for the sake of "lesbian studies" (*rezubian sutadi*), a connection was established with women's studies researchers. OLP very first began lesbian studies in '95, and at the time the family system was the issue. At that year's Japanese Women's Studies Association Conference (Nihon josei gakkai taikai), the theme of which was "Various Feminisms and Me" (*Tayō na feminizumu to watashi*), there were lesbian presentations. That year OLP also organized a workshop at which to take up the issue of how sexual orientation got taken out of the Platform for Action [at the United Nations Fourth World Conference on Women] in Beijing.

In addition, there was also a connection with AIDS activism. There was some joint activism with APP (AIDS Poster Project [Eizu posutā purojekuto]), a group that was involved in education activism about safer sex for male-female, male-male, and female-female couples.

Basically, OLP is involved with the Women's Diary (Ūmanzu daiari) project that sprang out of that.

HARA: Have there been other lesbian groups in Kansai besides YLP and OLP?

TSUZURA: This is where *Labrys* is a critical gap in today's discussion. There's also a club scene that's something approaching activism that I'm not able to talk about this time. And, while it's not a lesbian group, there's Project P (Purojekuto P).

OCHIYA: That's the "Lesbian? Gay? Bi? Hetero? In life and sexuality anything's possible!" group.

LIVING TOGETHER IN SOCIETY—COMING OUT AT THE WORKPLACE

OCHIYA: Well, this has all been food for thought—listening to this talk about the past. Ultimately, while you can really see how things have changed shape, it's still all the same issues today.

What I'm here to talk about is pretty much all personal, but I became involved in the community from November of '88. If I had to say one way or the other, I've been mainly involved with events—planning cherry blossom viewing parties, autumn leaf viewing parties, and the like.

I kind of became involved with activism in 1995, around the time that Sasano Michiru's *Coming OUT!* was published. When I saw how Sasano spoke so freely and directly about herself, I thought, y'know, I can be like that too, which was the impetus for me getting involved.

OLP is a very open group so heterosexual women can participate too. One of them, who was involved in Seikyōkyō (The Council for Education and Study on Human Sexuality),[17] asked if I wouldn't address the group, and in November I spoke to a study meeting of the Hyōgo [Prefecture] chapter of Seikyōkyō on the topic of "things seen from a lesbian perspective"—and I included my own personal experience. The gist of what I said was put into a pamphlet that went on sale the following August. Attached to it was the catchphrase "unhappy about not being able to say how happy you are." And in my explanation of lesbians, I said there are very many kinds of lesbians—much like the fact that you can't really explain a [typical] heterosexual—and what they have in common is the fact that they love women, and society compels women to love men. These women carry wounds and deal with oppression in this society, where heterosexuality is compulsory. And that's about it, or so I said. Asking why people become "homosexuals" (dōseiaisha) is meaningless, I asserted, and focused on the oppression and injuries inflicted in a compulsory heterosexuality society. And after that, I finished up with some grandiose talk about how if lesbians and [male] homosexuals are liberated, Japan will be liberated too.

In '96, at a seminar in the Kinki region[18] that I participated in through Seikyōkyō, I met transsexuals and hermaphrodites, and I came to realize that it wasn't just about sexuality, that we needed to include the perspectives of transsexuals and hermaphrodites. That June, at the Japanese Women's Studies Research Society, as part of the discussion on allowing married couples to have different surnames,[19] I was asked if I would talk about the partnership law called for by homosexuals.

In July, I went to a planning meeting for the national meeting of Seikyōkyō, and I complained that if I am going to be speaking about homosexuality as a member of OLP, this is what I want to do. Since the image of homosexuals who were troubled because they were discriminated against was so strong, I said I wanted to combine that with a focus on how, being liberated, I was able to live my life my own way.

That same month, at work I participated in a forum called "The Korean Minority in Japan" (Korian mainoriti in Japan), which was focused on Zainichi Koreans, and there I encountered the group Matsubara Apuro, which is focused on cooperation between Zainichi Koreans and Japanese. [. . .] Apuro is Korean for "moving forward." The members of Matsubara Apuro want to cooperate with people involved with other issues, and anyway they said they enjoy meeting other people. If that's the case, I thought, maybe they would want to take up lesbian issues more, and after the discussion finished, I went over and talked with them on an individual level and came out as a lesbian, which is how I ended up speaking at Matsubara Apuro that November.

About Matsubara Apuro's study group, they passed out one thousand fliers in front of Matsubara Station, and about fifty people came for the first time—people who saw the flier or something, including local high school students.

[. . .] At that time I took the stance that I should just talk about my personal history. When Matsubara Apuro planned it, based on what I would say, they designed the flyer to explain that although I want to live in a way that's "true to myself" (*jibun rashiku*), I'm suffering because of the pervasiveness of the notion—generally taken for granted—that men and women like each other. And there are a lot of people suffering from straying from this taken-for-granted sense of values. Hmm, "ordinary" (*ippan no*) people will be able to accept this way of explaining things, I guess. More so than if I were using feminist discourse, I thought that maybe listeners could feel the contrast between what's ordinary and being true to oneself, so I really pushed that point.

Matsubara Apuro is a fun group—so much so you wonder if it's really an activist group, and they take a stance that doesn't divide people into those who discriminate and those who are discriminated against, but that we're all living together so when someone is facing a barrier we must work together to remove it. [. . .] And that's how they got involved with lesbian issues.

Since I encountered Matsubara Apuro, [. . .] a discussion group has been created to think about living in cooperation with homosexuals. In that sense, isn't being able to formally say it at the workplace a part of *dōwa kyōiku* (anti-discrimination education)? [20] Since Matsubara Apuro is based on the idea that if you try to change things locally or with your friends, I also thought that I wanted to do something like that—seeping myself into my own local environment.

I thought that, well, of course it has to begin at work, and on January 16th I ran for chair of the *dōwa kyōiku* research committee, and then I came out, and I promoted the idea of a cooperative society. For me, being open at work might cost me my career, and I thought that if something happened I'd take it to court or something like that, but I was able to come out in a very positive manner, so much so that I'm quite satisfied with the whole thing.

HARA: And did you win the election?

OCHIYA: I did indeed. At work, I had already come out to a handful of people and made some allies, and in the end it was fine. For two or three days I got a stern expression from the principal, but I think she realized that it wasn't as if I was going to start handing out fliers the next day or start a movement or something. But something might happen if I appear in magazines or anything—that's something I need to do little by little, two steps forward, one step back, and I think they'll gradually get used to it.

IZUMO: I'd like to move on to the second half with an exchange of opinions and even debate. I've got the impression that what you've all shared is the same problem, one that has taken on various forms at different times. But the kind of activism seems to have been quite different in the 1970s and the 1980s. In particular, the tendency toward members' sexuality being unrestricted. . . .

HARA: Speaking as an "individual who deals with her own issues" (*tōjisha*), I feel that if there were no longer any lesbian members in OLP, that would be a problem. People can get grounded with issues around lesbians precisely because they're surrounded by lesbians, so we have to hang on tight to the core.

TSUZURA: I think it's really important how much heterosexuals who comprise the majority feel this is their problem too—in fact, I think that even if there weren't a single lesbian in some group it would be okay. [. . .]

OCHIYA: Of course OLP has a mission statement. "This is a woman's group whose activism is aimed at [creating] a society without discrimination, prejudice or oppression [that would lead] women-loving women to lie about themselves." Agreeing with this statement is a requirement of joining. [. . .]

HARA: Think about this—in OLP's mission, there's no word "lesbian," is there? "Understanding various experiences of women-loving women"—it's "women-loving women" (*onna wo ai suru onnatachi*).

TSUZURA: There's no clear distinction being made between a psychological connection and physical desire. It's all bound together in the broad meaning of women who love women. In OLP there are people who don't identify with any of the words/categories, "lesbian," "bisexual," or "heterosexual." [. . .]

TSUZURA: Having an identity based on a word is different from choosing a lifestyle, wouldn't you say?

[. . .]

HARA: The times I come out to say "I'm a lesbian," is when I'm compelled to talk about my lifestyle. I have a child, as you know, and so when my child was small and we were walking around together, of course 120 percent of the time people thought I was hetero. When some people I met thought I was hetero, I would feel compelled to come out. Sometimes I wanted to come out but couldn't. When it comes down to it, deciding when to come out or not may have been the most difficult thing for everyone, not just me.

IZUMO: I definitely say something if it seems people will think otherwise.

[. . .]

OCHIYA: When I came out at work, I didn't use the word "lesbian"—I said things like, I live with a woman, she's my "lover" (*koibito*), she's my "domestic partner" (*seikatsujō no patonā*). So there wasn't really anything else to say, and I didn't think about lesbians so much.

If I said it, I'd be labeling myself—that's the way I'd be seen at work, as some people have told me. On the contrary, since I've stopped worrying over whether I should say it or not, I feel like I've become free.

DO "LEGITIMATE LESBIANS" EXIST?

IZUMO: Before you said you are opposed to the whole idea of male and female role-playing—is this something that's being debated anymore?

TSUZURA: In OLP that isn't talked about. What we've come to see in the eighties and nineties is, of course, the transsexual issue, wouldn't you say? We've come to see sexual identity and sexual orientation as different things. But in the past they were conflated.

IZUMO: One of the criticisms of Wakakusa no Kai was against *onabe* (stone butches)[21] and lesbian *otokoyaku* (male-role players), which is lumped together as "butch bashing" (*bucchi hihan*). But rather than criticism of butches, it was really criticism leveled at their "maleness" (*otoko-sei*). There was always contempt for butches who acted like they were men and tried to be domineering, which became linked with criticism of *onabe* as well as of role-playing, and everything got all mixed up.

About that, I'd say it wasn't until the import of the word "gender" (*jendā*) or as long as transsexuals didn't make their existence known, it wasn't going to clear up—it was just all mixed up. Because there didn't used to be a word for "gender" [as distinct from "sex"], there was criticism against male/female role-playing—it seemed so much more simple to everyone then. [. . .]

Ochiya: We don't really pay that much attention to men's existence now, do we? We've stopped thinking about judging a butch on whether she thinks from a man's perspective anymore, haven't we? There isn't any criticism of butch/femme. People act based on their own preferences, all the more so because the number of people who haven't really come into contact with the feminist movement has been increasing.

Hara: [. . .] So what happened was that their saying "no butch/femme" was just like saying "you'd better think of yourself as a woman." It's not that I thought of myself as a man or anything like that, but I didn't particularly think of myself as a woman either. I mean, I went so far as to give birth. I had an awareness that I, personally, liked women, but I couldn't feel my femaleness very well so I had a child. I think there are a lot of women who've had a child for that reason. But of course that didn't change anything. The gist of it is that there's a big gap between me and what is generally called "femaleness." But however much I might ignore the image of femaleness, it still exists as a social fact—you know, it's really curious. [. . .]

Izumo: Well . . . but in my case, in whatever way, I'm a "woman" (*onna*), aren't I? It's better to direct any gripes I have at society.

Tsuzura: However I look or whatever I do, I can say once and for all I am a woman.

Hara: Have you always felt strongly that you are a woman—from the beginning?

Izumo: No, I haven't . . . no. Basically, being a '70s woman was really tough. There was no way for me to be a part of it—I thought women had nothing to do with me then. So then, out of the blue, lesbian liberationists popped up and said, you're a woman, aren't you? Hmm . . . . oh, that's right, I am—is that okay?, I asked. I think that, ultimately, it was a good thing.

And, when I talk to people in this group, there are a lot of people who say that lesbians are really wonderful, and that they've really been displeased with being hetero up to this point. Um, then I thought, right, there are people who've been hetero because of society's compulsory heterosexuality. I think that under these circumstances, for me to have held on to my desire—no matter how strange people may have thought me to be—for me to maintain my consciousness that I like women is proof of my health.

Hara: In my case, it was really tough when I had to say which "sex" (*sei*) I was.

Tsuzura: It's no problem for me to say I like women. But I had to say clearly whether I was a woman or not. If both weren't so, I couldn't have become a "lesbian."

[. . .]

LESBIAN SEXUALITY

Tsuzura: This was written about in 1970s *mini-komi*—what really bothered people was when they told a man or a woman that they were a lesbian, the response was, so how do you *do* it? For straights, they ask, do you have a lover? What kind of person are they? And even though this is what they ask of straight people, for lesbians it always comes down to sex. We have interpersonal relationships as well—you can't explain them just by talking about sexual activity.

Ochiya: I've never been asked something like that.

Izumo: They ask me.

Tsuzura: The way sexuality is regulated is a problem that needs to be rethought starting from what counts as sexual activity—plus which, it's not possible to limit the discussion to sexual activity. Even when YLP was problematizing women's sexual subjectivity, when they redefined the clitoris or talked about orgasms, some lesbians objected strongly, questioning whether this kind of talk was making sexual activity too central. If two people have a good relationship, even without having sex, whether heterosexual or homosexual, it's a good thing, It's the same as heterosexual married couples who don't have sexual intercourse.

Izumo: I think that it's good to push the physical, bodily aspects of being a lesbian. What I don't like is the inevitability that these discussions contrast lesbian and gay sexuality. [When they say] for gays, desire is an incredibly strong presence, but for women it's hard to see—things like that.

TSUZURA: Perhaps Japanese lesbians might be pushing the sisterhood thing a little too much to the fore, while overstressing that it's not a physical thing.

IZUMO: That's why when people talk about sisterhood with me, I somehow disagree. Usually it's talk for women who have a hard time understanding desire. [. . .] Are you kidding? I have strong sensations that I understand very well. I get irked when the discussion omits physical desire. [. . .] I think that now the range of who is a lesbian has widened, and if someone says they're a lesbian, doesn't that make them one? But there needs to be an awareness on both sides that people who say that they are not the same kind of lesbian as I am.

HARA: For me, it's pornography that's the most critical. At a conference on violence against women I attended in England, there were numerous lesbian-only workshops at which this was discussed. And again and again it came up that just the fact that you are with another woman makes you a sexual target. Especially from men. [. . .]

And then I came out, of course. And there were times when I was really pestered by men saying they really wanted to sleep with two women, and things like that, and there were times when work relationships became really unpleasant. I think that images from pornography have really become lodged in the minds of both men and women. Some women have told me they want to see what it's like to sleep with me too. But from women, it's never felt threatening—not as if any of this was coming from my boss. [. . .]

IZUMO: In the seventies, instead of denying desires, it seems like people really affirmed it too much. Things escalated from free sex (*furiisekusu*)—the world in the Barbara Hammer film where everyone got naked in a field and started rolling around on top of each other. (*laughs*) As for affirmation of desire, that era was definitely strongest and it seemed like we just talked about sex to our hearts' content. When I read some things from the nineties, I thought, what's the deal with the desire being so watered down? I was really shocked reading so many lesbians writing about how they weren't sure if they were lesbian or hetero, but now at long last they know.

HARA: In the '80s, from the beginning *Regumi tsūshin* did a number of special sex issues, but slowly they stopped. The reason I translated Pat Califia's *Sapphistry: The Book of Lesbian Sexuality* (1980/1993) was that everyone stopped talking about sex, especially sexual desires—I thought there just wasn't enough. [. . .]

TOWARD THE ACQUISITION OF RIGHTS

IZUMO: What do you think? Do you suppose the same problems that ran through the seventies and eighties have continued on to today? As for me, I met my partner, put out a book, and somehow ended up back out in the community—and a number of years have passed since then. (*laughs*) Not a thing has changed. Even now, the same problems are being talked about as they always have been. . . .

The field has gotten much wider. I mean, separatism was so oppressive but now the walls have been torn down. Of course, groups where working together isn't a burden have appeared, like OLP. I think it's a good thing, but. . . I came back to Japan [after a year in Australia] in '93, and I thought, yep, we still don't have any rights.

That's why we asked Nakagawa Shigenori, the lawyer involved in OCCUR's court case, to help us make an official legal document, a Joint Living Agreement (*Kyōdō seikatsu keiyakusho*) that would conform to Japanese law.[22] I think in the future there will be a debate in Japan over the creation of a partnership law to legally protect the rights of partners. In the American lesbian scene there's currently a debate raging over whether to recognize same-sex marriage. There's a group that wants to know why on earth, in the face of all the effort on the part of lesbians to quash the family system—the patriarchy, the importance of heredity—would lesbians want to have this stupid marriage. And there's another group who just want to get married, who want to hold a wedding ceremony. Regardless, it's a problem that's bound to emerge in Japan too, and what I keep thinking is that now we don't have a choice one way or the other. I wonder why—when we can't choose the right—are we arguing over whether or not to choose. It's just so stupid. [. . .]

That's why, for the past twenty years what I've been wondering about is, why—in spite of not choosing anything, not having anything—are we always talking about ideals? That's why I really think hard about how each group—gays, lesbians—can come together and what direction they should focus their activity on.

TSUZURA: I think we can really collaborate with gay men to fight the family law system, which prevents us from fitting into hetero society. However, as far as problems like economic independence and discrimination at the workplace are concerned, we're quite different.

IZUMO: It's like, that's women's problem.

OCHIYA: Can't we just work together on some issues and not others?

TSUZURA: [. . .] I think we should spell out what kind of rights are necessary.

IZUMO: Well, at the very least, we need a partnership law. Things like the rights of inheritance, to nurse an ill partner, the right to be the beneficiary of your partner's insurance. That's not about heredity, or even about the idea of a couple, it's something you choose. It should be okay even between friends.

OCHIYA: There really isn't much debate over heredity or anything like that, and there are a lot of people who don't think about inheritance. I think it'll just take a little more time. Women in their twenties haven't really gotten themselves established yet, for them what's essential is finding a girlfriend and things like that. More women are worried about how to get along with their parents than how to rework the family system, at least in OLP. [. . .]

TSUZURA: When you talk about family in Japan, the image of the family system is quite strong, so you can't think about making a family or having children without thinking of it as a duty. At present, I believe the reality is that you can't think of family as something you actively choose. [. . .]

IZUMO: Lesbian couples and gay couples can't produce children, but you can't talk about that as being on the same level as hetero couples who can't have children. I think we should be able to talk about it as being the same. That it's the same as infertile hetero couples.

HOMOSEXUAL EDUCATION

HARA: In the end, it's a problem unless the numbers increase in absolute terms. There are really few lesbians with children. A Lesbian Mothers' Club (Rezubian Mazā no Kai) was created but it disappeared almost immediately. Children with lesbian mothers can't get together and talk about things—"My mother has a new girlfriend, *again*." Even if they get together, unless the parents of both kids have come out to their children, it's impossible. [. . .]

A while back, I went to talk to Seikyōkyō—did you know they made quite a questionnaire? First of all, they asked children what they think about gays and lesbians. And of course, when they did this, lots of discriminatory words came out. They should have talked with the children about where these ideas came from and who is hurt when you talk like this, but instead they used the answers to make the questionnaire, which was then widely distributed. This thing included a list of items like, "they make me sick" (*kimochi ga warui*) or "I think they're not good" (*yokunai to omou*). Worse, they didn't show the questionnaire to us.

And I was really angry. It's like teaching about bullying or human rights—I want them to teach about what happens when you say those kinds of things to people.

OCHIYA: In fact, Seikyōkyō complained [about our reaction]. They told us, don't stress that it isn't abnormal. My complaint is that if there's a girl among the students who realizes she's a lesbian, she'll feel like she can't tell her friends, there's no way. [. . .]

HARA: That kind of talk assumes that there aren't any [lesbians or gays] in the classroom, but there are—after all, we were all students once.

COMING OUT

IZUMO: In addition, there needs to be some legal response or assistance to counter negative treatment of people due to their sexuality.

TSUZURA: Sweden has various laws we can consider as a model. There's a law prohibiting discrimination against homosexuals, and, as I recall, there's even a fine for doing so. It's imposed for dismissing someone from their job for being homosexual, for example.

HARA: I feel there's a big gender difference in terms of access to the power of the police and the legal system. As the system is overwhelmingly run by men, that's to be expected. If this isn't changed, even if rights for gays and lesbians are accepted—I don't know about gays, but for lesbians, they'll be treated like other women or beneath them. That's why if we're demanding rights, we have to clear that hurdle too. Even in America, while women now exercise their rights, for example, the rate of lawsuits is very low. That's related to economic circumstances, and awareness, and, culturally, the level of trust is a large factor.

IZUMO: I think the level of trust is a huge factor. You don't want to sue using a lawyer who can't understand you, since you think it could just make matters much worse. That's why it's necessary to foster lawyers who specialize in gay and lesbian issues. The existence of even one lawyer who really knows gay and lesbian issues or has studied transsexuals would make a huge difference. [. . .]

OCHIYA: I'm reassured by the appearance, little by little, of commercial lesbian magazines. If there are people for whom [the magazine] *Anise*[23] has existed for as long as they can remember, maybe there'll be people who are already out when they get a job. After all, it's exhausting to be a forty-year-old with a degree of status and to get the courage to come out and start taking part in activism. It's better if, from the start, people get a job and come out just like that. It'll be hard if people like that don't start increasing. I think, when talking about what you want legally, if you're not out, it's quite a struggle. [. . .]

HARA: [. . .] Why don't the people in the generation a little older than that come out—life is almost over, so why not? And in various groups fighting violence against women, there are lots of women who live with other women. Whether they think of themselves as lesbians or not, I don't know, but I think that, at least using OLP's broad definition of "women who love women," these numbers are increasing, I think, and more people are entering that age group.
[. . .]

IZUMO: I would say that the activism of the seventies is showing its age about now.

HARA: I really wish more people from that generation would show their faces.

IZUMO: If that happened, it would be easy to see all kinds of people from various perspectives.

HARA: Indeed. But what of the generation before YLP—do you have any connection with them? These people are in the closet or something, aren't they?

TSUZURA: Well, not very many of them join us. We haven't got a connection, but we have to make one somehow. Well, rather, what I think is important is a recognition that we're connected when we judge the past. We can say, please come join us, but these people from the past aren't just going to come. Some of these people are taking a break, so we don't need to go digging them up, do we? Rather than the previous generation saying to the next generation that we did things like this so your generation is following on, it's easier for the later generation to just search and keep going. [. . .]

IZUMO: With these steps, at least we're making progress. With these steps, we'll be able to have our partners protected within the legal system, and we can expand on that. I think we've accomplished things, and if we don't study what we've done already, we won't be able to start.

NOTES

1. Ikeda Kumiko used the penname Ochiya Kumiko at the time this article was published and has asked that the name Ochiya remain in the translation. She began publicly using her real surname upon the publication of her book, *Sensei no rezubian sengen* (A teacher's lesbian declaration; 1999).

2. In the process of translation, a limited number of corrections and clarifications of the original publication have been made in consultation with the participants.

3. The history of Wakakusa no Kai can be found in Sawabe, chapter 10 in this volume.

4. Zenkyōtō, an abbreviation of Zengaku Kyōtō Kaigi (All-Campus Action Committee), was a left-wing student group that emerged from the student uprisings at the end of the 1960s.

5. Two issues of *The Dyke* were published. In Japanese, the expression *nichiyō daiku* (Sunday carpenter) refers to do-it-yourselfers. *Mainichi daiku*, with *daiku* written in *kanji* (Chinese characters), ostensibly means "everyday carpenter," but *za daiku*, which was written in the *katakana* script generally used for writing loan words, could mean "the (*za*) carpenter" or it could be a transliteration of "the dyke."

6. Lecture topics included practical discussions on becoming a "self-assertive woman" and running a women's company, as well as the lives of lesbian foresisters, translator Yuasa Yoshiko and her one-time lover, writer Miyamoto Yuriko.

7. Sanrizuka is an area of farmland in Narita, Chiba Prefecture, that the government tried to take control of to construct Narita Airport, outside of Tokyo. A protracted battle ensued and the airport was built around a few plots of land that farmers refused to sell.

8. Izumo later coauthored a revised English-language version of this book with her partner, Claire Maree; see Izumo and Maree (2000).

9. For a discussion of this incident see Lunsing (2005).

10. For a more detailed discussion of Regumi, see Hisada, chapter 11 in this volume.

11. Hirosawa Yumi was a penname used at the time by Sawabe Hitomi, who under that and other pennames wrote a number of the articles appearing in "Stories of women who love women" (*Bessatsu takarajima* 1987), three of which are reproduced in chapters 1, 10, and 13 in this volume.

12. Tōkai refers to the central and Tōhoku the northern part of the main island of Honshū.

13. Zainichi Koreans (*zainichi Kankoku Chōsen jin*, literally "South and North Koreans in Japan") are the residents of Japan who are of Korean ethnicity. Some Zainichi Koreans have adopted Japanese names and have taken Japanese nationality, while others strive to maintain a distinct identity. Discrimination against Zainichi Koreans remains a deep-rooted problem in Japanese society.

14. The group was formally known as Kansai YLP. *Yancha* means mischievous.

15. Kakefuda's *"Rezubian" de aru to iu koto* (On being "lesbian"; 1992) and Sasano's *Coming OUT!* (1995), along with Izumo's *Manaita no ue no koi* (*Love Upon the Chopping Board* 1993), were perhaps the most influential books by and about Japanese lesbians in the 1990s.

16. An alternative meaning of OLP is *Ōkikunatta* (increased in size) Lesbian Power.

17. The group's formal Japanese name is "Ningen to sei" kyōiku kenkyū kyōgikai.

18. Kinki is a region that overlaps with Kansai and contains the cities of Kobe, Osaka, and Kyoto.

19. While there has been a movement to change this, according to current Japanese law, married couples must both legally be known by the surname of

one or the other spouse, and in the vast majority of cases it is the husband's name that is adopted by the wife.

20. A term meaning social integration—literally "being peaceful together"—*dōwa* is strongly associated with the integration of Japan's traditional low caste, the *burakumin*; *dōwa kyoiku* is generally used to mean education aimed at eliminating discrimination against *burakumin*, though it can be interpreted more broadly.

21. *Onabe*, which literally means "pan," is the female equivalent of the older term *okama* (pot), used to refer to homosexual men. While *okama* often points to particularly effeminate men, *onabe* is used to refer to very masculine women, particularly those who cross-dress. See chapter 9 in this volume for more on the emergence of the term.

22. See Izumo and Maree (2000: 97–103); Maree (2004).

23. *Anise* (*Aniisu*) was published between 1996 and 1997, and again between 2001 and 2003.

⑬

LESBIANS LIVING IN THE MOUNTAINS

Sawabe Hitomi[1]

Is lesbian sexuality unnatural? Ōzaki Harumi, who lives off the land with her lover, talks about issues of lesbians and nature.

It's been five years since thirty-year-old "Ōzaki Harumi"[2] moved to the mountains. Ever since she was a student she had loved the countryside, and it had been her dream to live off the land. The spring when she was twenty-five, she abruptly quit her job of three years and, together with a friend, moved to a depopulated village around three hours by car from Osaka. They rented land from an elderly couple whose sons had been taken away by the city and who were themselves making a meager living from farming. It was a wild plot of land roughly 100 *tsubo* (1,080 ft² or 330 m²) in size. They cleared the land, and with 350,000 yen (US$3,500)[3] built a small house with a galvanized steel roof. Five years later, they are growing enough rice and vegetables to feed themselves, and, once in a while, when they need to earn some cash, they go off to work [in a nearby town].

Translated and reproduced with permission from *"Yama ni sumu rezubian no hanashi,"* which was published under the penname Ōgura Yūko in *Onna wo ai suru onnatachi no monogatari* (Stories of women who love women), *Bessatsu takarajima* no. 64, Tokyo: JICC Shuppankyoku, 1987: 56–63. Translated by James Welker.

At the end of last year, I made my first visit to the mountain where Harumi lives with her thirty-three-year-old lover (*koibito*), "Miyamoto Sachiyo." She and I had been acquainted for about a year but this was the first time for us to really be able to talk.

When I got off the train at a little station in the valley, Harumi was there waiting in a small pick-up truck. "*Yōkoso!*" she welcomed me, her white teeth gleaming in stark contrast to her suntanned face. She was wearing a quilted cotton jacket and had a towel wrapped around her neck. With her powerful hands, she tossed my bag in the back of the truck—what a cute lumberjack! I happily climbed into the passenger seat. She told me her house was another three miles (5 km) out past the village here at the foot of the mountain. After we had driven about fifteen minutes from the station, the asphalt ended and we were suddenly on a gravelly, weed-covered mountain road. The sun had already gone down, and against the pale blue of the twilight sky I could see the dark silhouette of the mountains. Through the windshield, the ridge pressed in closer and closer.

"We're just a little ways in but even so, the people from the village have never come out here," she said as she turned the steering wheel left and right to avoid the puddles produced by yesterday's rain.

Then there we were at the house. Just inside the door was a long, narrow kitchen about four *tatami* mats[4] in size. Underneath a light bulb hanging from the ceiling were a gas stove and a sink. Through a door on the left was a six-*tatami*-mat room that doubled as a living room and bedroom.[5] The only electrical goods in the room were a *kotatsu* (heated table)[6] and a cassette player—essential for listening to the music they love. When they built the house, she explained, they put the most money into the bath. Of course—the bathroom they put in at the end of the kitchen was about the same size and held a marvelous *goemonburo* (old-fashioned bathtub).[7]

Sachiyo was unfortunately away working that day. Dinner was tempura made from heaps of vegetables harvested from the garden behind the house. Those organically raised vegetables—carrots, onions, and the like—had an aroma and a sweetness I had forgotten. We chatted late into the night, all the while drinking Kenbishi sake, which Harumi was kind enough to open.

WON'T YOU COME OVER AND HANG OUT?

Harumi first met Sachiyo four years ago. This was when, having re-claimed one strip of land in the mountains, Harumi went to Tokyo to listen to chansons with a friend. When she entered the Roppongi (To-kyo) bar her friend took her to, among the beautifully dressed women in the dim light, there was one woman in jeans. At the beginning of the performance, that woman got on stage and began singing. She sang with such feeling—her voice, enveloped in sorrow, penetrated Harumi's heart. That person was Sachiyo.

"In the beginning, there were all these lesbians around her, but she didn't notice. A person named Masumi-san who worked there was also a lesbian and lived with her lover and the two of them ate together and took good care of her, but Sachiyo didn't have a clue. Basically, she had no experience in male-female relationships either," Harumi laughed. "Masumi wore a suit and lived with a woman, but Sachiyo never made the connection. Well, that evening, I felt that meeting her was somehow fate, so I knew I had to go up to her and tell her about myself, and Ma-sumi-san and I started telling her about lesbians. And was that girl ever surprised! Well, there she was, sitting alone with a kind of puzzled look on her face, like it was the first she'd ever heard of this. I guess it was a bit of shock for her," Harumi chuckled.

That evening, absorbed in conversation, Harumi missed the last train, and Sachiyo offered, "Well, then why don't you stay at my place?" She had no suspicion about this person who she met for the first time, and she was going to let Harumi stay at her place! What a beautiful heart! Harumi says she fell in love with Sachiyo upon hearing those words.

"When we got up the next morning, she let me listen to her practice singing. I was enraptured. That evening, I go back to the bar—of course. And then I ask, 'Will you let me listen to you sing tomorrow?' and she goes, 'Sure. . . . I'll give you a call at 12.' And the next day I got up early and waited at my friend's house, hoping she'd call. And *she* said she was all nervous *too* for some reason, even though it was just a phone call," Harumi recalled with a laugh.

"And so, when I go to her apartment I confess my feelings to her. 'I like (*suki*) you a whole lot,' I say. And she goes, 'I really like (*daisuki*) you too!' So I say, 'Um. . . . I like you romantically (*ren'aiteki ni*).'[8] 'Huh?'

she goes, and then just sits there in thought for a few minutes. 'It makes me happy to hear you say that, but . . . if only you were a man,' she says. And I tell her, 'I don't want to make you worry or anything like that. See, I just wanted to tell you, that's all. It's nothing to feel bad about or anything. If you aren't interested in me like that, we can just be friends. . . . Well, I don't know when we can meet again either,' I say. 'I'm going home tomorrow.' And I guess she thought it would be pretty tough not to be able to meet me again. And she runs over to me and goes, 'Me too, I like (*suki*) you!' Of course I'm immediately thinking, *yes!!* The clincher was when I ask, 'So, do you wanna come over and hang out?'" Harumi bursts out laughing.

"I tell you, that girl really was cheerful. I've never before met someone who was so relaxed from the very beginning. 'Okay, hold on a minute,' she says as she pulls closed the storm shutters," Harumi chuckled. "At the time she was thirty, and she had never slept with anyone, or so she says—but she didn't seem at all uptight about it. I guess it was because she didn't have any prejudice against lesbians or something. She'd never read any of the tabloids,[9] she says. So it's like whatever she feels, she just expresses it with her body. Up to that point, the people I'd slept with, in the beginning they were like dolls—just lying there. She was . . . well, she squealed, she moved her body, her legs were all over the place, she thrust her hips—she was so wild. She was just so amazingly free. It was like she even surprised herself. And it felt great for me too. She goes, 'Sex is really great! *Wow*—I'm so glad to find out about something this good—imagine never knowing this—what a waste!' And I was flabbergasted. . . . What a funny thing to say. 'Well then, it's a good thing you know now,' I say," Harumi laughed.

After that, they had a long-distance relationship for a year, meeting in Tokyo and Osaka once in a while, but they just couldn't take it any longer and, for the past three years, they've been living together.

NATURE HAS A STRONG WILL

These two young women living together is the focus of attention in the village. At the place outside the mountains where they sometimes go to work, occasionally a gaggle of middle-aged women will tease them:

"You two—you're lezzies (*rezu*), aren't you?" In which case, Harumi invariably replies with a grin, "Sure are—two women together is just plain easier." Taken aback by how matter-of-fact the two of them are, the women burst out laughing. And then one of them will say, "Must be nice. You're so comfortable with each other, being two women. When we were young, we didn't have any idea that was an option. If we had only known, we'd have been like that too."

"We're really close," Harumi says with a smile. "When we're with those ladies, we're always grinning, you see. When they see how much fun the two of us are having, they seem a little jealous." On top of their dresser sits a photo of the two of them working hard in a field. When there's a break in our conversation, the darkness creeps in.

I ask her what her biggest discovery has been since coming to the mountains. "Well . . . it's that after spending a few months here all by yourself, you really feel the importance of nature. Nature has a will of its own. This teeny little seed will become that great big cedar tree—who decided that? Are there stupid cedar trees that turn into pine trees by mistake. Nah—it'd never happen. It's a mystery."

Since she brought up the word "nature" (*shizen*), I decided to ask about something I'd been vexed by for a while. In heterosexual society—where only love between a man and a woman is considered proper—homosexuality is dismissed with a single word: "unnatural" (*fushizen*). So how does she take this kind of attitude? In 1975, at a meeting of the American Psychological Association, it was resolved that homosexuality is not an illness, nor is it something to be cured.[10] In psychological terms, there's an awareness that rather than "abnormal" (*ijō*) with its implication of "illness," it's nothing more than "atypical" (*heikinteki dewa nai*), and on the way to becoming the general consensus. But I think the meaning of the Japanese word "unnatural" goes beyond the word "abnormal"—it carries the connotation of some kind of absolute conflict that goes against nature, and thus this word gnaws at the hearts of homosexuals.

"There's no difference between us and animals if we think it's natural for the male and female of a species to reproduce and leave offspring, going on and on forever. But animals and people are completely different. Animals live their lives being satisfied with the ways that were given by God. They are content living as the creatures God

made them to be. Humans are also God's creation, but they can also
become creators. Our flesh is animal, but our souls are the same as
God's. Humans are the only creatures that can gaze upon nature and
think, 'Isn't that beautiful.'

"And nature doesn't stagnate. Things are always changing or dying
out. Human cells all regenerate, don't they? And take stars, for example,
they have billions of lives—and if one dies, another star is born. Looking
at it from the vastness of space, things are evolving for eternity. Everything has the will to evolve, but human memory—seen from the length
of eternity, it's just an instant. When I look up at the night sky, this is
what I feel.

"When it comes down to it, the purpose of our lives, as humans, is
always to elevate our selves, our essence, our true character—we're
all working to make ourselves into something close to God's image.
To do that, we have to accumulate a lot of experiences in this world,
through which we advance ourselves. But we forget our own lofty mission: People just think we're born, we get married, we have and raise
children, and then our role is done—we're not defying nature. But it's
a big mistake to reassure ourselves thinking this is all just fine. Nature
has deeper, more wonderful wisdom, it's got a powerful will, it's always
moving forward. So, if we live our lives according to nature's will, that's
quite sufficiently natural.

"However, if perhaps, among lesbians there may be some who think
they are just imitating male-female couples, especially the sex part. But,
men and women, c'mon, it's not as if every time they have sex it's really
a meeting of soul and soul. That's the ideal, of course. Sex takes a lot of
physical energy, and it sometimes becomes animalistic, it's wrapped up
in all the knowledge we've gained and our subconscious, but we don't
need to worry about it at all. To be in love with that person is really
pure (*junsui*), and if through that we can live confidently, soon enough,
we stop worrying about it. It's such a small thing we don't have to worry
about it. If you think you're a little bit masculine (*otokoteki*), you should
just think, *nah*, it's no big deal.

"I feel like I have a direct connection with God, you know. I'm not
praising myself or anything, I'm doing the best I can in this life, but
if God still sees me as unnatural—what about others [who aren't doing their best]? Of course such inequality can't exist. God doesn't do

inequality. I'm strongly opposed to the kind of God who would do such inequality—I'll have no part of it! I have my own God."

Her God isn't the God of any established religion. It reminds me of [Alice Walker's] *The Color Purple*, a novel about the liberation of black women, when Celie's lover Shug Avery tells her, "Your god is inside of you."

IT'S ENOUGH TO DO THE BEST YOU CAN IN LIFE—EVEN IF YOU DON'T HAVE CHILDREN

"So. . . ," I ask, "what exactly is life (*inochi*)?"

"Life—it's an individual will, with or without the physical element. Call it life, call it a soul. . . . It's something you keep acquiring as you live. When a soul is born here on earth, it needs flesh as a vessel to shelter it. It has to receive a physical body or it can't be born, and being born into this world is serious training for a soul. So I'm really grateful to my parents for giving me my physical body. But our lives do not belong to the fathers and mothers of our physical bodies. Because our souls come from God, we are all—parents, siblings, everyone—on the same level. The parent of the soul is God—who is our parent much more so than the parents of our physical bodies. The physical system just means having ancestors."

Women who live as lesbians, for the most part, don't have children. Those who become lesbians after having children and those who have children through artificial insemination are known as "lesbian mothers" (*rezubian mazā*). Among the lesbians I know, there are some lesbian mothers, but not very many, and as for the latter kind, I've not yet encountered any in Japan. Women just need seed to bear children. But without considerable financial resources, in contemporary Japanese society it's still very difficult to raise children outside the marriage system. So there are a lot of women who say they've given up on the idea of having children. However much they may love each other, two women cannot make a child. There are some women who, describing love between women as "fruitless," chose to marry men. For lesbians who choose to live their lives together with other women, this is a difficult problem.

"Not to have children—isn't that a minus in life?" I continue with my questions.

"Not at all. Bearing children. It's giving a physical body to a soul, so it's a really good thing, but it's also a good thing to be a person who doesn't have children, who does something else. If not, there'd be no hope for married couples who can't have children. If it were God's law for men and women to get married and have children, it wouldn't be possible for there to be people who couldn't have children or who didn't want to have children. The kind of God who would make those people suffer doesn't exist. God is love, after all. So God gives humans absolute freedom."

Her words really moved me.

BEING BORN A LESBIAN IS BEST!

"Being human can be really tough—for example, being in a maze that's like—suicide once you go in, you're basically stuck in it, but if you can jump out of it, you can find real freedom. The gist is, it's about going with your feelings. If you end up in a daze and don't look up, you look over here and you look over there, you go crazy. If you close those eyes and quietly look inside, you'll know how blessed your existence is.

"You shouldn't let some puny commandments and rules made by humans take away from the vigorous mind that you possess as an individual. Just in being devoted to love, lesbians are marvelous. Well, I suppose we've come to know "love" (aijō) through a less calculated, purer bond than men and women, something we need to expand. If you really love your lover, that love spreads to other people. Through feeling pain themselves, people understand the pain of others, which is why people want to be nice to others. Lesbians—most of them understand this wonderful experience, right? They get all the way there, and it's just another push. When they see how wonderful that can be, their lives change. To think that's a misfortune—that's ridiculous. Something worth punishing? No—it's something you should be thankful for—for you to gripe about it, God would be really surprised," Harumi laughs.

"In these changing times, being born a lesbian is best. I really mean it. If God appeared before me, I would say, 'Thank you very much. You were the one who let me be born a woman and have all sorts of experiences as a lesbian, weren't you? To carry out my duties living out the life I was given—I'm trying really hard to polish myself, and live a good life!'"

In the *Tannishō*[11] there's the adage, "If good people can go to heaven, so too can the bad." Even in what she says, there's a real paradox. Living within social norms, to flip this around is to only be able to live the same way as the masses of others. If you see a minus as a minus, that's that, but if you think the bigger that minus gets, the more energy that you have stored up to transform it to a plus, then the reality gets connected to a completely different situation, which is mysterious.

"To the extent that science is progressing, humans need to become closer to God—otherwise, humans are on the road to ruin. If humans live however they want, like they are now, they distinguish between themselves and others, the gap between them widens. And this expands to an international level: If your country prospers, it doesn't matter if other countries are knocked down in the process. If things continue like this, we will have either World War III or a giant natural disaster. That can't be allowed to happen. If, on an individual level, we don't put out positive ideas, there's no hope for the earth. If the humans living on earth continue on with such anxiety in their hearts, well, one could say, lack of faith in God, how can they get the power to live? However grandly we dress things up with a theory, if it doesn't ease your own heart, you haven't been helped. First, we have to be truly bright and honest individually. Without doing this, we won't be able to connect our powerful hearts, we won't be able to carry out powerful activism. There's no future. It's up to the lesbians!"

The next day, we went into the mountains and I helped her gather firewood to light the fire for the bath. Her landlord cut some large trees into logs two and a half feet long and a foot and a half (80x50 cm) in diameter. After she drove in three by six inch (8x15 cm) steel wedges with a mallet to cleave the logs in two, she chopped them into smaller pieces with a hatchet. She raised the hatchet over her head and swung it down at the heart of a log. Without strong stomach muscles the tip of the hatchet will be deflected by the log. Harumi heaved the hatchet time after time, with sweat running down her forehead all the while. With each chop, a pleasant cracking sound echoed through the mountains. Occasionally I took her place and swung the hatchet. Before long, there was a nice pile of firewood under the eaves of the shed.

"It feels good to work up a sweat, doesn't it? Do this and lunch tastes really good."

On the way back, we gathered up a bunch of shiitake mushrooms that must have been six inches (15 cm) across. They were so thick even their stems were almost an inch (2 cm) wide. When you turned them over, the white gills were springier than I'd ever seen before. All of a sudden Taro, the brown-colored puppy of a dog who was around this area in the year when Harumi moved in and who had gotten used to her by now, darted out in front of us and behind us and followed along. When we reached the housecat who, true to its nocturnal habits, last night was nowhere to be found, it came up and rubbed against her ankles, I felt for a moment how Harumi's life was bathed in sparkling brightness.

NOTES

1. This article was originally published under the name Ōgura Yūko. Sawabe used several pennames in *Onna wo ai suru onnatachi no monogatari* (*Bessatsu takarajima* 1987), the collection in which this article first appeared, in order to create the appearance of a larger number of contributors (Sawabe, personal communication 2005). See chapters 1 and 10 in this volume.

2. This is a pseudonym. Throughout this conversation, Ōzaki alternates in her choice of self-referents between *watashi* (I) and *atashi* (I), the former of which is used by both women and men in formal situations but primarily by women in more casual situations, and the latter of which is significantly more feminine.

3. Monetary conversions are approximate and based on the current, rather than historical, exchange rate.

4. Room size in Japan is often measured in terms of a standard-sized *tatami* (straw mat), which varies from eastern to western Japan but is roughly 6 ft. (180 cm) by 3 ft. (90 cm).

5. Using rooms as both a living room and a bedroom is typical for traditional-style Japanese homes. The minimal furniture can be pushed aside to make room for the bedding, which is stored in a closet during the day.

6. The *kotatsu* is a table that sits low to the floor and under which hangs a heating element. In the winter, people sit on the floor around the table, often under a heavy quilt to keep in the heat.

7. The *goemonburo* is an old-fashioned bathtub that is essentially a steel pot, underneath which a fire is lit to heat the water.

8. The terms *suki* (like) and *daisuki* (like a lot) can have a stronger meaning than their English equivalents, particularly so as the expression *ai shiteiru*, which means almost literally "I love you," is seldom used outside film and television dialogue. Thus, what Ōzaki said to Miyamoto—*Atashi wa anta no koto sugoku suki nan da* (I like you a whole lot)—can be understood on several levels.

9. The weekly tabloid magazines she might have read contained celebrity gossip and sordid portrayals of sexual activities, including lesbian sex. One particularly influential lesbian scandal, occurring in 1980, around the time these events took place, was when celebrity Kathy (*Kyashii*) Nakajima revealed in a tabloid that she and singer Sagara Naomi were having a lesbian affair (Sei ishiki chōsa gurūpu 1998: 79, n6; Lunsing 1999: 251–52; Yajima 1999: 198).

10. The equivalent body in Japan, The Japanese Society of Psychiatry and Neurology (Nihon Seishin Shinkei Gakkai), came to a similar conclusion in 1995 after prodding from the lesbian and gay rights group OCCUR (Akā).

11. This is a Buddhist text containing the teachings of Shinran (1173–1262).

14

BREAKING GENDER RULES WITHOUT REMORSE

Noriko Kohashi

I was born in a suburb between Osaka and Kobe, and when I was in kindergarten, my family moved to a large city in the southern part of the country, where I spent most of my elementary school days in the mid-1960s. As a little child, I was unwilling to comply with gender codes. For instance, when entering the first grade at school, six-year-olds were required to purchase a specific style of schoolbag for elementary school students. Almost all schoolbags sold at stores were black or red, making it very difficult to find schoolbags of other colors. Generally, boys chose black bags, and girls chose red ones—or rather these colors were chosen for them. But I did not want either, because I thought that black was considered the "boys' color" and red the "girls' color." I didn't understand why I couldn't just have the color I liked most. And I liked yellow, so I decided I wanted a yellow schoolbag. An uncle of mine who wanted to give me a schoolbag to celebrate my entering school had a hard time finding a yellow one, but eventually he did. Out of all the students at my school from the first to the sixth grade, I was the only one who had a schoolbag that was neither red nor black, and I was proud of carrying that bag, a bag which was neither for boys nor for girls.

My parents didn't complain about the color I wanted, nor did I hear my uncle complaining about it. I suppose they didn't have any problems with it. I guess that some of my classmates commented—positively or negatively—about my yellow schoolbag, but the fact that I do not remember this means that their comments were not strong enough to hurt my feelings. As a child, I was confident in myself and strong in quarrels and fights with my friends and classmates. Maybe this is one reason why they did not tease me. Or maybe I was just lucky.

My parents wanted me to become independent. They thought that this was very important for me because I was the only child and had no siblings to help me and whom I could help in return. And that's probably why they did not push me to be girlish. They didn't emphasize to me that girls should be meek, tender, caring, etc., and that boys should be easygoing, strong, positive, etc., though, of course, I was told about those things by neighbors, my friends' parents, and teachers. When I was little, I do not remember that my parents told me what to do and what not to do because I was a girl. I played baseball and imitated TV heroes. My parents never complained about buying me whatever equipment I needed for such so-called boys' games. I suppose that in their eyes I was girlish enough because I also played house and with dolls.

I always thought that I was a girl, and what is more, I felt proud of being a girl. However, I did not like to be told that I was girlish, but I liked to be told that I was like a boy. For example, when I took lessons in calligraphy, I was often told that my calligraphy was strong as well as free-flowing, like a boy's. While this kind of comment made me feel a little uncomfortable because I thought that it belittled girls, at the same time, it pleased me because I thought that I was not perceived as a "second-class citizen" myself. By that time, I had already noticed that women and girls were placed in the position of the second-class citizens in society and were denied many of the rights men had. And I refused to do almost everything that society expected women and girls to do, such as cooking, cleaning, and other household chores. Nor did I want to belong to girls-only groups. One day, when my father asked me if I wanted to join the Girl Scouts, I said no—because it seemed to me that it would be a place to discipline girls into the "good wife and wise mother" (ryōsai kenbo) mold. Plus, joining a girls-only group meant to me that I would be putting myself into the second class.

However, I never wanted to be a boy, either. I was proud of being myself, including the part of me that was a girl. I remember one day in elementary school when one student started asking other students whether they would want to be a girl or a boy if they were born again. I definitely thought that I would want to be born a girl again. Boys never appealed to me, although some of the characteristics that society stereotypically assigned to boys and men—such as independence and magnanimousness—attracted me. I wanted to have them in myself, and liked to be told that I had these characteristics. I noticed, however, that not many boys and men actually had those characteristics themselves.

Even in literature, I couldn't find girl characters I was comfortable with. When I was in fifth or sixth grade, I found an independent and strong girl character in a translated edition of Lucy Maude Montgomery's *Anne of Green Gables*. I liked Anne but was not completely satisfied. She deserted her career and ended up serving her husband and children as a "junior partner." On the other hand, I felt good about boy characters in adventure stories. And when I recall my relationship with my parents, I feel that when I was little I identified more with my father than with my mother. I was very interested in what he was doing and how he was doing those things, though I spent less time with him than with my mother because he worked outside home while she stayed at home. They had no doubt about the gendered division of roles in their marriage, though my father was not authoritarian. Every day I saw my mother doing many things including all housekeeping jobs, but I showed little interest in such work. I was not interested in even how she dressed or put on makeup.

Just before I entered junior high school, in the early 1970s, we moved to a small industrial city in Ehime Prefecture on the island of Shikoku and lived there until I graduated from high school. Even in my teens, I continued refusing to help my mother with the housework. I never went in the kitchen unless I needed something there—even when my mother was cooking dinner. One of my friends said that when her mother was cooking she was usually in the kitchen, talking with her mother while she helped her or even when she wasn't helping. On the other hand, when I was at home while my mother was cooking, I was usually reading the two newspapers my parents subscribed to or watching TV in the living room. As a high school student, I rarely even cracked eggs or peeled fruit, much less anything more complicated.

When I was in high school, I read many books about how human beings should live and what the meaning of their lives should be. The authors of those books usually used the terms "human beings" and "people," rather than "women" or "men," but in the context, "human being" and "person" clearly meant "men." I never saw women included in their arguments. While reading, I always had to translate the writers' use of a "people" that excluded women into a "people" that included them. If I read that kind of book now, I would be too angry to finish it. In my teens, however, I tried hard to convince myself that the books were talking to me minus the part that was a woman, talking to my essential human core, which I believed was neither woman nor man. Before puberty, I just did not want to be seen as a member of the second class, though I was proud of being a girl. During puberty, however, I began to consider it to be very important to think *as a human being*. I started seeing myself as simply a human, and I began to look at others as simply humans, too. I thought that it was odd to emphasize whether people were women or men, and to make sharp distinctions between them. Although society tended to put much stress upon the differences between women and men, I thought that it was wrong because, when you paid attention to the fact that they are all human, only a little difference existed between them.

When I was in junior high school, I found it very strange that people were only supposed to be attracted to the opposite sex. I thought that romantic love between people of the same sex had to exist too. In my view, one person loved another because of her or his personality and character. People loved someone because they loved the inside of that person, her or his heart, regardless of her or his gender. If you felt something wonderful about someone's heart, you could love that person even if she or he was the same sex as you. So, I couldn't understand why people usually thought that if you were a woman you would love a man and never love a woman, and vice versa. I told adults around me how I felt about this, but they always replied that it was natural to be attracted to people of the opposite sex. I remember that a teacher in my junior high school said that boys and girls were attracted to each other just like the positive and negative poles of a magnet. I wondered if we were all really just magnets, and I wasn't convinced at all. I felt that we were being persuaded into thinking that people should be divided into the categories of women and men and that we were being forced to be interested only in the opposite sex.

In spite of these ideas, however, I didn't date other girls then. None of the people I knew had similar ideas to mine, or at least they never told anyone about it. Besides, I didn't see people around me who were attracted to the same sex. Meanwhile, I still shunned anything regarded socially and culturally as related to women and girls. I didn't like flowers, because women were expected to like them. Nor was I interested in fashion and accessories. I never made any effort to dress nicely and didn't care about my appearance. I felt that it was foolish not to eat as much as you wanted just because you feared that you might gain weight. And of course I ate as much as I wanted—even fattening food such as cake and ice cream.

Though I had female friends in high school, when I reflect back on those days, those friendships were sort of superficial. My friends then only talked about boys, fashion, TV programs, and studying. We had few interests in common to talk about. I couldn't talk about things I really wanted to because I felt that my friends would take no interest in what I wanted to talk about—I didn't think they would even understand those things. Other than talking about being a girl, I was interested in talking about political and social problems, and philosophical things such as the meaning of life. And I couldn't find girls who were interested in such issues. Though I was disappointed not to be able to find like-minded girls at school, the idea that I should or could meet such girls somewhere didn't occur to me. I suppose that at the time I just enjoyed being different. Besides, my surroundings in those days didn't encourage me to give much thought to my sexuality. Classmates and friends were talking about boys, but almost no one had boyfriends. At school we were strongly discouraged from doing so and, instead, were encouraged to concentrate on study.

Through my college years in Kyoto in the late 1970s, I resented what women had to face socially during the course of their lives. Friends and I talked a lot about these issues and what was necessary in order to improve conditions for women. But, to me, my friends seemed to be conservative about women's roles in society. They wanted small changes, not fundamental ones. As I studied law as an undergraduate, I found articles in some Japanese laws containing discrimination against women. And I wanted to study focusing more on women's issues from other perspectives, not just from a legal standpoint. I could not find a graduate school in Japan to pursue this, so I decided to go abroad. I found two universities in the United States that had a graduate-level women's studies program, and I chose the one in New York state because its program seemed not just liberal, but radical. Of course my parents felt sad to see me going abroad, but they never tried to interfere because that was what I wanted to do. My father even considered it a good opportunity for me to expand my horizons.

When I entered the women's studies program, I met many students and faculty members who were lesbians. It wasn't something I had been expecting. I felt that at last I found the answer to my struggle with gender and sex, and became friends with some of these women. Given these circumstances, I at long last found myself having a good time among many women. And I could explicitly admit to myself that I liked women. At the same time, I then realized that, up to that point, I had built a barrier inside me against having a relationship with another woman. This was in spite of my resistance since childhood against gender codes and my feeling since junior high that it was strange that people were only supposed to be attracted to the opposite sex. I realized that I had held myself back from developing feelings toward women and that I had subconsciously told myself not to cross the river or I would have to give up having a decent position in society. Although I now enjoyed myself spending time with women, I still felt that there was a high wall in front of me, and it took time to get over it.

In the late 1980s, after two years in that women's studies program, I returned to Japan and joined a women's group in Kyoto whose activities included discussing and studying women's issues in order to create social change and emancipate women. Through the group's activities, I met many women whose basic values in their lives were similar to mine, and I felt very comfortable being among them. However, most women in the group were involved with men, leading heterosexual lives. Some were married, and others lived with men as domestic partners without being legally married. I thought at the time that the group had few or no other lesbians. In the group I met a young woman who I had heard from another member was actually bisexual but wanted to label herself as a lesbian. The woman, herself, never told me anything like that, however, and I hesitated to ask her about it directly. Years later, I found out for sure that she was a lesbian. In spite of having known each other for so long, it took all that time for each of us to learn that the other was also a lesbian.

After several years in Japan, I returned to New York to study anthropology with a professor I had met in the women's studies program. Anthropology, in fact, was the most interesting discipline to me when I was studying women's studies. My main interest then was development and women, not specifically focused on lesbians or same-sex love in cultures. When I completed my master's degree in anthropology, I decided to stay in the United States because I wanted to have a wider range of choices about the kind of job I could get and where I could live. I continue to visit Japan and maintain close friendships with women there. I still think that it was easier for me to pursue an independent lifestyle here in the United States than it would have been if I had returned to Japan. In practice, it is relatively less difficult here to find a job to support yourself if you are a woman and not young. Of course I sometimes have unpleasant experiences, partly because I am Asian and partly because I am a lesbian—factors that work in different ways in mainstream society as well as in the Asian and lesbian communities here.

I don't have a strong sense of gender identity as a woman even now. When I have to go to a public restroom, I enter the door with the sign indicating women. When I am asked to indicate on a form whether I am female or male, I check the female box. It is not because I think of myself as a woman, but because I know that I am assigned to the category of woman. I just act according to the rules. I know that other people see me as a woman. When someone refers to me as "she," or when I feel that I am treated as a woman, I am aware that I appear to be a woman in other people's eyes. However, I don't identify myself with social and cultural norms expected of women by society. Of course, I do not identify myself with male norms, either.

In contemporary Japanese society, I feel that too much emphasis continues to be placed on the division of people into women and men, and too much importance is attached to these categories, categories still viewed as polar opposites. In spite of many changes over the last several decades, members of society are still expected to conform to the gender norms for the category to which they are assigned. Through this system, society deprives people of chances to learn their true selves and to develop according to their own capabilities.

Although I thought since my teens that it was strange that there should be only heterosexuals in society, I only had opportunities to have relationships with men in my young adulthood. In these relationships, I never felt particularly enthused, nor did I experience intense feelings. At the time, I thought that the feeling of loving someone was normally like those experiences I had then, rather than something powerful like in literature. When one person whom I had been dating for a few years used to say to me that he felt he was melting or that I was radiant to him, I always thought that he was just trying to flatter me. I certainly didn't believe that he really felt that way. I couldn't imagine that people actually had such feelings when they were in love with someone because I had never experienced this, even when I thought that I liked a man. Later, when I had similar feelings toward women, I found that his words were actually sincere.

I think the reason why I did not discover my sexuality earlier is not only that I had no nonheterosexual models but also that the society I grew up in discouraged women from exploring their own sexuality. It was and, to a large extent, still is expected that respectable women should not be desiring subjects. Through what women are taught by parents, teachers, and the media, women are disciplined to be passive rather than active when it comes to sexual relations. This prevents women from learning about their own sexuality—what and how they desire, and what kind of people they feel truly attracted to.

I thought that I didn't care about society's expectations for women. I always thought that the best thing for me was to be myself. However, even when I met lesbians, there was a very high hurdle for me to overcome in order to live according to my true inner feelings. That hurdle was something that I, myself, had internalized. And when I finally reached a point where I felt that it would be all right for me to love women, I clearly remember I experienced a strong sense of relief. I thought that at last I was able to become a free person.

When I was younger, heterosexualism held too powerful a sway over me for me to be able to swim freely in the ocean of society. I feel that if I had been able to explore who I was without such constraints, I could have found my true self much earlier and enjoyed my younger years more. I see now that lesbians in Japan have been very active in improving their situations to make their lives better and easier, and that more support groups for lesbians have formed rapidly throughout Japan since I left. We have more places to meet other lesbians in everyday life. Even on my brief visits to Japan or maybe because of them, I feel the air there is freer than before, especially when I meet with lesbian friends. At the same time, I feel that there is still a long way to go before lesbians are accepted as natural beings in the larger society.

⑮

TRUE TALES FROM NI-CHŌME

Ōtsuka Takashi

TRANSLATORS' PREFACE

Ōtsuka Takashi, known to his friends as Taq-san, has been a prominent figure in Tokyo's gay scene since the late 1970s when he appeared
regularly on the radio talk show the *Snake Man Show* as an openly
gay man offering upbeat advice about living a gay life in Japan. In the
1970s he worked as an editor on some of Japan's first commercial gay
publications, including *Barazoku*[1] and *Adon*.[2] In the 1990s, he edited
three important gay-themed volumes of the popular *Bessatsu takarajima* series produced by the magazine *Takarajima*: *Gei no okurimono*
(Gay presents; 1992), *Gei no omochabako* (Gay toy box; 1993), and *Gei
no gakuen tengoku* (Gay campus heaven; 1994),[3] and he has written
numerous essays that have appeared in both the gay and mainstream
press.[4] Taq is also a playwright; his play *Chigau taiko* (Different drum),
which looks at the life of a gay couple in their fifties, was first performed
in Tokyo in 2003 with Taq himself playing the lead.

Abridged, translated, and reproduced with permission from Ōtsuka Takashi, *Ni-chōme
kara uroko: Shinjuku geisutoriito zakkichō* (Ni-chōme rediscovered: notes from Shinjuku's gay street), Tokyo: Shōeisha 1995: 46–51, 66–69, 214–19, 257–63. Translated by
Katsuhiko Suganuma and Mark McLelland.

In 1982 Taq opened Tac's Knot, a bar in the Ni-chōme section of Shinjuku, which has been a popular Tokyo gay area since the late 1950s and is said to house around two hundred bars catering to a wide variety of sexual minorities—including gay men, lesbians, and male and female cross-dressers. His book of memoirs, *Ni-chōme kara uroko* (Ni-chōme rediscovered), was published in 1995. The following extracts are taken from Taq's memoirs and describe his first rather disappointing visit to Japan's preeminent gay area, his debut as Japan's first openly gay radio personality, and his decision to open a gay bar.

Despite housing the world's largest concentration of gay bars, very little is known about the history or the lifestyle of the community that has developed in the Ni-chōme area.[5] Gay rights' activists, in particular, have sometimes been dismissive of Ni-chōme's community—viewing the area as simply a place for drinking and casual sex. However, in the narratives below, Taq explains the important role that Japan's largest gay town plays in the lives of many gay Japanese men, and he tells us a little about his hopes and fears about the future development of the area.

SETTING OFF TO NI-CHŌME

The first time I visited Shinjuku ni-chōme was in 1968. I was a freshman who had just started commuting to the Tama Art University to study design—it was a period before the publication of *Barazoku*.[6] At that time I had a friend known as QP who was in the same school year as me. He was my first-ever gay[7] friend.

In the sketching classroom for first-year students, the instructor had left a small notebook in order to help the new students get to know each other by writing down brief self-introductions. QP had written that "I like Morinaga homogenized milk (*homo gyūnyū*)."[8]

I needed gay friends. Although while attending middle and high school there were several people I could call "best friends," and I had come out to one of them, I got the feeling that I was quite alone and could not share my anxieties with anyone. Right after my first sexual experience in my third year of high school, I came out to my friend who had this to say: "At the moment, we are approaching some very important university entrance examinations. If we succeed in getting into the university, then I will take you along to the hospital, but don't concern yourself with this matter for the time being." For him this was probably an expression of his deep friendship (and in fact he did remain faithful to me even after this). But, since at the time there was no information available that could give me confidence about being gay, I thought that it would be unreasonable to expect more from him. Unfortunately, I felt that there were limits to my straight (*nonke*)[9] friendships (not that I even knew the word "straight" at the time). What on earth did he mean that "the university entrance examinations were more urgent" or that I "should go along to the hospital"? It was just hopeless!

It wasn't so much that I was worrying about being gay, rather I was worried about the fact that I didn't know how to cope with living my life as a gay man in the future. What I really longed for was a friend who both shared and could understand the problem I was grappling with. Soon after I had started my new university life and I had spied the words "I like homos" sandwiched between "Morinaga" and "milk" in the sketch classroom's small notebook, I felt that the future had become a little brighter. Doubtless QP also had the same idea as me. I thought that "homogenized milk" must be his heartfelt cry—and I certainly received his message.

I soon approached QP. Of course, I didn't tell him that I was gay right away, but in the course of our various conversations he must have begun to consider that we were both somehow different from other people. Both of us liked movies and it just so happened that the opportunity to come out was at a movie entitled *The Vixen*. Just about this time the movie based on D. H. Lawrence's novella *The Fox* had been released. The movie is about a lesbian couple living in the midst of a forest covered in deep snow whose lives are changed by a man who arrives from the outside. Because, figuratively speaking, it is the man who is the fox since he threatens the lifestyle of the two lesbians, we began by talking about how the film had been absurdly titled (in Japanese) *The Vixen*, and, while tentatively discussing our opinions about lesbianism, QP asked me something like if by any chance I was also "that way."

And so our mutual coming out was over without incident. We became good friends, not simply because of the fact that we were both gay, but because we also shared many interests, and so I can say that I was extremely lucky to find such a gay friend. Even if we hadn't shared the same interests, it would still have been a blessing, but he and I became best friends. Even today he is still one of my most important friends. My life at university brightened up considerably.

One day QP discovered an article in a weekly magazine that mentioned a place in Shinjuku ni-chōme. According to this article, it seemed that there was a certain "homo establishment" called "The Pioneer" (Pioni-iru) where, "from midday onwards attractive young men gathered." The article also gave the telephone number. Whenever QP and I got together we would always talk positively in a high-spirited manner, but in reality we had both had only one sexual experience and where things relating to being gay were concerned we were absolutely on the timid side. Since this closeted situation would not change otherwise, we decided to go and check out the place and with a map clutched in one hand we set foot in Ni-chōme for the first time in our lives. However, since we thought that going there at night would be a bit scary, and since the article had said that the young men gathered there from midday onwards, we set out while the sun was still high, at about 2:00 pm. In the daytime, Ni-chōme was a dirty and undistinguished place. Whether or not it was due to our preconceptions or not, the whole place seemed very seedy.

Since the article hadn't described the location in detail, we telephoned the number given and explained the situation and the guy who answered the phone kindly came to collect us. The guy who came tripping toward us was dressed in a worn shirt and wore sandals on his bare feet; no matter how you looked at him he wasn't the type who could be described as a "handsome young man." The place that he took us to didn't have the look of a bar but felt like an ordinary house. Actually, the article hadn't said much about the atmosphere of the place, but since it had described a place where "handsome young men" gathered, I had arbitrarily gotten the image into my head of an elegant bar and so I thought the actual room was exceedingly shabby. It had no windows anywhere and it was only by the light of an electric bulb that the inner *tatami* room, about four-and-a-half mats wide,[10] could be seen, in which four or five boys slightly older than us were lounging around watching TV. Needless to say, none of the boys looked like "handsome young men"—there was not even a hint of charm in the atmosphere; there was nothing but rather slovenly looking boys. (I'm sorry if you were one of the boys there at the time!) When I think about it now, it was probably a place for *urisen* (hustlers). They were doubtless waiting there for customers. Since I didn't know about such things at the time, I couldn't understand why such good-for-nothing (I'm sorry!) boys were hanging around watching TV in the daytime. After an uncomfortable silence, one of them asked:

"Are you two homos?"

"Err . . . yes."

"I see. It's only interesting here if you come at night. Next time come at night."

"We see."

Taking those words as an opportunity, we were out of that room in under a second.

On the way back, in order to vent our spleen at this unexpected outcome, we talked things over to our hearts' content. Even if there were only the two of us, at least we were in the best of spirits.

"What was supposed to be charming about that place?"

"I'm feeling so low."

"Instead of handsome young men, they are better described as shifty second-rate boys."

"I wonder if the whole of Ni-chōme is like that?"

"There sure is something disgusting about homosexuals."

(Remember, you yourselves are gay!)

This is how our first glimpse of Ni-chōme ended in failure.

It was a big effort for me to accept a part of myself that society deemed shameful. I needed to be told things like "Leonardo da Vinci and Alexander the Great were gay." Since I had barely managed to accept my own homosexuality, I didn't want to recognize that those boys shared the same desires as I did. If I had done so, it would have demolished the very self-image I was preserving.

Nowadays, I've come to think that guys who only want to give up their virginity to someone they love or those who love to fist-fuck or even guys who like to walk about having inserted enemas are, in the end, members of the same tribe. Yet, at that time I couldn't even forgive those youths who were just lolling around watching TV in the daytime. I don't know whether or not heterosexuals can understand this, since even if they witness some kind of perverse heterosexual sex murder it doesn't make them hate themselves. Ni-chōme taught me an important lesson that went on for many years after—that I shouldn't be perturbed even when I encountered gay people who had different values than I did.

We retreated from the first battle and no opportunity to make up for this loss presented itself for a while. Forgetting all about Ni-chōme, QP and I were seduced in movie theaters, got felt up[11] on the trains, and, deriving some confidence from these trifling encounters, passed our time in a safe if somewhat dull manner. Although, given that I was a bit better looking than QP—it was my confidence that was boosted more. (Sorry, QP!)

THE *SNAKE MAN SHOW*

"Good evening, this is Taq. How are all you gays out there doing?"

This is how the Wednesday edition of the *Snake Man Show*, which was broadcast daily on TBS Radio at 10:45 p.m., used to open. The *Snake Man Show* was the creation of Kobayashi Katsuya, Ibu Masato, and their producer Kuwahara Moichi and was a radio program in which the music was interspersed with black humor and risqué comments launched like Patriot missiles. Kuwahara's music sense, coupled with Kobayashi and Ibu's creation of a "taboo" world, was a big encouragement for the feelings of disaffected young people.

From 1979 to 1980 I appeared on the Wednesday edition of the show as Japan's first gay personality. I was able to choose my own topics, write my own script, and talk about various issues of concern to gay people. Although the young people who made up the listeners were certainly not gay, I adopted a gay style of speaking. I continued to fire out the word "gay" to the extent that even I got tired of hearing it.

I probably ought to explain a little about what I mean by "Japan's first gay personality." Of course, although even at that time there were television and other media personalities who were thought to be gay, they weren't able to publicize the fact. Gay people who were popular with critics and exhibited talent within a given field disliked it when the gay part of themselves became a focus for society, so they wanted other aspects of their lives to be looked at through rose-colored glasses, avoiding the fact that they were gay. On the contrary, I made my gay part my only selling point (of course, the fact that I didn't have any other sales point was a laughing matter).

Not wanting to miss an opportunity, I continued to extract appeal from this one aspect of myself. After all, wasn't it a good thing that there was at least one person in the world who had become a personality through advertising the fact that he was gay? I ended up becoming Japan's first gay personality simply because there was no other person who wanted to do this. [. . .]

As I mentioned, the *Snake Man Show* was a program full of strong humor. When Kuwahara asked me if I would appear on the show, I attached two conditions. If I were to appear on the show stating, "Yes, I'm gay," even if this were to be initially taken as a joke, I wanted to be allowed to stay on the show for as long as possible. And secondly, I definitely wanted to be allowed to continue to emphasize the theme that being gay was a normal part of life. Even with these seemingly egotistical conditions attached, Kuwahara kindly agreed that we should go ahead. So in this way "Taq's Wednesday Special" appeared like a demon child in the midst of the radical *Snake Man Show*. (Taq was the nickname I had used in America where people found it difficult to say "Takashi.")

In the little over a year-and-a-half period before the show was suddenly axed because of trouble with the station's sponsors, I was able to do as I liked, just as Kuwahara had promised. Through this program a small gay liberation group was formed and I was able to meet some gay people who were of a different type than those I had met in Ni-chōme. [. . .] The future no longer seemed so bleak and I was able to start to think more positively about things since a situation came about where I was no longer the only person thinking in this way.

[After the demise of the *Snake Man Show*, Taq went on to open Tac's Knot, his bar in Shinjuku ni-chōme, which he still runs today. Although small, the bar has an extremely friendly ambience, described by some as "like a kitchen," and is a popular place for its regulars—both men and women—to unwind on their way home from work.]

CHANGING NATURE OF NI-CHŌME

One day, a couple called Raku and Shima came to see me to ask my opinion about their plan to start their own bar in Ni-chōme. Raku is an ex-salaryman who quit his job half a year ago and who will soon turn thirty, and Shima is currently a salaryman aged forty-five. It's been about two-and-a-half years since they started to go out together. They said they decided to start their own bar after thinking hard about their future. Making the most of this new opportunity, they are also planning to live together from now on. Both of them were about to turn their life around by 180 degrees.

That day, they seemed to be a little more upbeat than usual. In their minds, however, anxiety about whether they could actually effect such a change in their lives lived alongside the excitement of being able to live their lives in the manner they most wanted.

As far as most couples are concerned, two-and-a-half years seems about the right time to shift the relationship from simply getting to know each other better toward thinking about how to move their lives forward in the same direction. The bar that Raku and Shima are think-ing of starting will play the role of a child in their lives. If they succeed in moving their partnership onto a new level, their bond will be stronger than now. But in order to do this, they must achieve financial security to some extent.

"I certainly wouldn't recommend it if you were planning to make big money, but it is possible to make ends meet as long as you are commit-ted. And I believe you two can make it work because you have lots of friends and they're sure to come. Good luck!" As I said this I suddenly remembered my own experience thirteen years before that. I told them exactly the same thing that Kuro-chan[12] told me when my boyfriend and I went to his bar to ask his advice about starting our own bar. As time passes, I realize that now I stand on the side of giving advice.

After listening to their concrete plans for starting their bar, based on my experience I gave them some advice. When you discuss this kind of thing, you cannot decide anything by being too serious. Sometimes you need something like *nori* (an agreeable attitude without being too concerned). "Instead of thinking too much about whether you will be successful or not, it's better to think of what kind of bar would give you the best sense of relaxation and fun, that will make things work and in turn become the unique atmosphere of your bar." Oh yes, this is also similar to what Kuro-chan told me.

After eventually confirming that "we can do it" through looking in each other's eyes, Raku and Shima left my bar trembling with excitement, and the result is a few more new folks will join us in Ni-chōme. At the same time, this also means the number of people who have decided to live their lives as *gei* (gay) has increased. I truly wish them the best of luck.

Two months after our initial conversation, they opened a bar called Islands. I know that someday some frequent customers at their bar will consult with them about their own plans to start a bar. And it might be that Kuro-chan's words will be repeated once again. Imagining those future conversations, I was smiling from ear to ear.

How will Ni-chōme look ten or twenty years from now? Will we see this district becoming even more successful, filled with thousands of gay folks every weekend? Or will it have fulfilled its function for that era and changed into something else? Ni-chōme is not exceptional to the current social situation where people cannot guarantee anything about their future. Although there might already be some signs of transformation that suggest to us the future of this place, it is easy to fail to see the changes when you live alongside them in Ni-chōme. It's like when you look at your face in a mirror every day, you might even think that you look exactly the same as ten years ago.

There are many occasions when I notice some changes in Ni-chōme only after some people who have come back from working abroad point them out to me. Indeed, every weekend I see more young folks hanging out on Naka-dōri.[13] Also I see more "normal"-looking people these days than so-called scary *onēsan* (queens). On the other hand, some say that there are a growing number of *yarō-kei*[14] folk who have rather muscular bodies and leave their faces consciously unshaved. There are also some who say nowadays more bars tend to attract customers through the concept or atmosphere of the bar itself, instead of solely relying on the unique characteristics of the bar's master and *mise-ko*.[15] And others who say they see fewer and fewer folks with lust in their eyes, or who get drop-dead drunk.

Yet, although these are all the kinds of changes that you can usually observe along with generational shifts, there is one recent change that concerns me—the rent of bars in Ni-chōme is getting higher and higher all the time. I started to realize this when Gen and I were looking for a leasehold for Gen's[16] own bar, and I felt it so much stronger when I heard similar things from Raku and Shima. I think this increase in the rents will affect the way Ni-chōme develops considerably.

At the beginning of this book, I told readers that the system in Ni-chōme that gives the district its distinct character depends on the fact that most of the customers migrate from bar to bar in one night. There is a circular system that goes like this:

"cheap rents" → "cheap prices" → "more possibility for customers to migrate from bar to bar" → "the possibility of the existence of various types of bar" → "more customers gather" → "can manage business even with low prices"

It is easy to guess that this entire system would collapse if the starting point were changed. For individual customers, they will be satisfied as long as there are some four to five of their favorite bars left, otherwise they just won't care about all the other bars disappearing. If the charges at all bars go up, all they have to do is to go out to bars less often. Yet, some parts of Ni-chōme that might just seem like a collection of boring bars to some are actually essential to creating the rich and diverse culture of Ni-chōme as a whole. Various types of people gather in Ni-chōme because there are various types of bars. And people hop from bar to bar taking along with them various news and stories. In this constant flow of people many new and unexpected relations can develop. Yet, once the flow of customers is interrupted, unique but small bars with a limited clientele will find it difficult to make ends meet. When water stagnates, the rot sets in. If the total number of customers in Ni-chōme is reduced, competition will be fiercer and the bars will have no other choice but to become more efficient businesses. In this situation, all bars will become more alike as they will try to get the most customers with the minimum of resources.

Well, I hope this anxiety of mine is just fretting about the future, but it's not impossible that it may come about—just as the flourishing *aka-sen*[17] district in this area came to a sudden end, the world's number one gay town could easily be the victim of similar changes in a new era. It is almost miraculous when you think how this unique town has survived in such a convenient district so close to the central part of the city. One time during the bubble economy, there was a tentative plan to transform this area into a business district. If the bubble economy had not burst, we would be looking at a completely different Ni-chōme now. Thankfully the plan came to nothing, yet it might still be successful next time round. Although I look forward to observing how Ni-chōme will change as the times change, I hope that the characteristic style of Ni-chōme—how many customers move around from bar to bar—will be preserved as long as possible. At present, this town still has much potential. It might not be a bad idea to try many new different things while the town still provides rich soil for new seedlings.

Despite its capacity to gather together a great variety of people, this town is still really a nighttime venue based on the consumption of alcohol. I often think that it would be nice if the town could develop a face of its own in the daytime, too. Sometimes I idly daydream that a group of talented gays will get together to develop new types of business in Ni-chōme. It's odd when we consider that there is no such thing as a festival for the entire Ni-chōme community despite the fact that there are tons of gays who love partying.[18] Why not have a cultural festival, or a sports festival? And there are still no community centers for gays and lesbians in this area.[19] If such centers were to develop, it would be possible to hold different events in the daytime (for instance, holding small-scale movie days or lectures for gays and lesbians), and we could help bring in new people to the town. If we could arrange this, it would be easier for people looking for specific services or information to network (and no doubt new kinds of relations would develop).

Revitalization is a necessary thing and not only for sparsely populated areas. If we think in this manner, there is much that could develop in this town, and it is important to take some risks and try out new things through a process of trial and error before Ni-chōme loses its potential. Otherwise, Ni-chōme's unique system may fall apart due to people delaying positive action, thinking they can do things later. Who knows, someday we might live in a world where *iwashi*[20] is the most expensive kind of fish. If we want to transform Ni-chōme, we have to do it now! (Well, people born during the baby boom do tend to respond to old-fashioned calls to action like this.)

In the future, when Raku and Shima are repeating Kuro-chan's words to the next generation, I hope that Ni-chōme will become an even more diverse place for gays and offer a space where gays can develop new and important roles.

NI-CHŌME AND *GEI RIBU*

There is not much love lost between those who visit Ni-chōme and *gei ribu* (gay liberation) activists. In fact, it seems that the two sides confront each other as if they were the Montagues and the Capulets. Speaking for myself, I can say that I play the roles of both Romeo and Juliet since I appreciate both the cultures of Ni-chōme and of gay lib in Japan. For many people who engage in gay lib, Ni-chōme seems like a place filled with (supposedly) crazed sexual desires and has too hedonistic an atmosphere, so they are not good at dealing with people who enjoy the scene there. Since those who engage in gay lib are usually serious and earnest, they have a tendency to look down on overt expressions of sexual desire.

Through my experience, I can say that it is often the case that a part of this distaste for the image of Ni-chōme comes from internalized homophobia. And what is worse, most of these people really do not realize this at all. The more homophobic they are, the stronger their distaste against Ni-chōme tends to be. As a result, for those who express a strong dislike for Ni-chōme, it seems that the men who hang out in Ni-chōme are enclosed within a very limited circle and are on the constant lookout for sex. It might also seem to them that people in Ni-chōme only care about themselves and never bother about social issues outside their limited world. Since gay libbers don't want to be thought of in this way, they either ignore the existence of Ni-chōme or criticize it.

As I mentioned, people who engage in gay lib tend to possess very serious natures. Thus, for those who are already repressed by the norms of hetero society, it is an extremely difficult task to maintain a positive perspective about sexual desires that are often looked down on negatively by the mainstream. For many gay libbers, they must have a politically noble goal to accomplish, such as social change, if they want to change themselves in order to deal with the social stigma that is attached to their sexual orientation. Yet, once people engaged in gay lib become close and relax together, it is not unusual for people to start having sexual relations with others within their circle. Thus it can be said that in the end they are basically the same as people who hang out and have many different sexual relations with others in Ni-chōme. This is just like the situation in which the thing that you hate the most is actually that which you most desire.

It is true, though, that Ni-chōme does not possess an organized system for critiquing hetero society, or voicing dissent against its norms, so gay lib should be valued as a means for pursuing those goals. However, the tendency of gay lib to deny significant aspects of Ni-chōme just because Ni-chōme lacks organized systems of political critique is unjustified. On the contrary, Ni-chōme is valuable as a place where many gay people can liberate themselves and establish important relationships.

Most people who hang out in Ni-chōme do not wish for social change per se. For many it is enough that their homosexual desires can be satisfied and they can relax with their friends there. It is hard for many men to radically change their lifestyles to that of openly gay men, since they have also internalized social norms to a large extent. What is important for them is not to create any fuss with their family members and colleagues, but to maintain their current lifestyles. Yet, while doing so, they also try to accept some repressed parts of themselves and make incremental changes. From their perspective, people who engage in gay lib seem like people who have nothing to lose and their political demands seem peculiar and annoying.

However, people in Ni-chōme also think how wonderful it would be if they could live their lives in any manner that they want. And indeed they understand the importance of taking action against a repressive society; they just try to live their lives by adjusting the balance between what they hope for and what they can achieve in reality. Yet the existence of gay lib often disturbs the balance that they try to maintain. That is why gay lib is so irritating to them. If they do not respond to gay lib, no matter how loudly gay libbers shout demands right beside them, they just think, "what weirdos."

Yet, the flip side of this irritation against gay lib shows their jealousy toward people who can just embrace the gay lib movement without

any obstacles—this is an unconscious sign of guilt for not doing anything—yet what is problematic is that they do not realize this. Repressed
desire can turn into hatred. This hatred can lead those who oppose gay
lib either to completely ignore the need for gay lib or thoroughly deny
it. In Ni-chōme, scornful opinions such as "gay lib is something that guys
who can't find a partner do as an outlet for their unfulfilled sexual desires" are often heard. We can hear the mockery often used against the
early stage of the feminist movement, comments such as "most women
engaged in *ūman ribu* (women's liberation) are ugly," in this rhetoric.

People who are well-suited to the culture of Ni-chōme often deny
the necessity of gay lib by saying, "We don't need gay lib at all! Without
gay lib, I have already accepted myself and liberated myself. And the
proof is . . . my anus is too loose! . . . just joking!" When people adapt
themselves to any situation well, they tend to feel arrogance toward
those who cannot do the same. There are some people whose sense of
self-justification is well-suited to the atmosphere of Ni-chōme. On the
other hand, there are others who cannot get along in this environment.
Different people have different opinions. Even though Ni-chōme's culture is flexible to some extent, we must not forget that there are many
others that Ni-chōme cannot accommodate. It is hard for those who feel
at home in the culture of Ni-chōme to understand that there are some
people who can only relax in a gay lib environment. These people also
tend to overlook the accomplishments of gay lib in the wider society.

Regardless of the differences between people who engage in gay lib
and those who hang out in Ni-chōme, basically they are all midway on
the road to liberating themselves from social norms. It is also hard for
people who engage in gay lib to understand the important role that Ni-
chōme plays in this process. But it is important to understand that there
are many ways to further the process of self-liberation.

Recently, people who feel a little out of place both in Ni-chōme and
in gay lib circles have started to meet other gay people through volun-
teer activities such as AIDS awareness groups and have begun to participate in gay community activities thanks to the Internet. To me, it is as if
everyone is climbing to the same summit but from different routes.

Everyone thinks that they want to liberate themselves in their own
way. As the degree of self-liberation increases, people will be able to
start challenging themselves to find commonalities in communities that

they had previously rejected. There are an increasing number of people who find it easy to make friends through the Internet while also engaging gay lib activities and enjoying Ni-chōme culture.

Ni-chōme and gay lib. These two things that seem like water and oil are not actually fundamentally opposed to each other, but rather mutually complementary, and surely possess aspects that will help all gays to liberate themselves. Without evaluating each side fairly, just treating the other side as an object and throwing around stereotypes and negative labels is just the same as hetero society's denial of the rich variety of individuals by labeling gays with negative stereotypes. Isn't this something that has already caused us enough suffering? We should not make the same mistakes.

NOTES

1. *Barazoku*, or "Rose Tribe," was Japan's first commercial gay magazine, originally published in 1971, and with a circulation of about forty thousand in its heyday. Due in part to increased competition from more recent and trendier gay magazines, it went on hiatus after the November 2004 issue and was able to resume publication with the April 2005 issue. Its publication has again ceased with the January 2006 issue.

2. *Adon*, more politically radical than *Barazoku*, was published from 1974 until 1996.

3. See *Bessatsu takarajima* no. 159, 1992, and *Bessatsu takarajima EX* 1993, 1994. Note also that one of the earliest and most prominent lesbian-themed books was also part of the *Bessatsu takarajima* series, namely, *Bessatsu takarajima* no. 64, 1987.

4. Details of Taq's writings as well as his artwork can be found on his website: http://www.asahi-net.or.jp/~km5t-ootk/1taq.html (22 July 2003).

5. For a description of the kind of interaction that takes place in gay bars in the area, see Ishida (2006).

6. Although there had been small, privately circulated Japanese magazines aimed at homosexual men since the early 1950s, *Barazoku* was the brainchild of heterosexual publisher Itō Bungaku, who realized that gay men represented a market that was not being catered to by commercial publishers. Its publication meant that information about the gay scene became much more widely available. For a discussion of the founding of *Barazoku*, see Aoki (2006).

7. Ōtsuka's use of the term *gei* (gay) in his memoir does not always reflect contemporary usage. During the period he describes in the first two excerpts contained here, *homo* had far greater currency among those men not a part of the commercial *gei kai*, or gay world.

8. "Homogenized" in Japanese is contracted to *homo*, which is also a common term used to refer to gay men. Morinaga is a brand name.

9. *Nonke* is made up of the English loan-word "non" and the Chinese character *ke/ki* meaning feeling; hence a *nonke* is a person with no homosexual feeling.

10. Room size in Japan is often measured in terms of a standard-sized *tatami* (straw mat), which varies from eastern to western Japan but is roughly 6 ft. (180 cm) by 3 ft. (90 cm).

11. The term here is *chikan*, rather difficult to translate into English, referring to men who take opportunity of Japan's jam-packed trains to sexually molest other passengers—usually women.

12. Famous for his conversation, Kuro-chan was the center of a bar called Pal in Ni-chōme, the first gay bar Taq-san visited after his initial disappointing debut.

13. Naka-dōri is the name of a street that cuts through the central section of Ni-chōme.

14. *Yarō-kei* is a term for gay guys who look tough and masculine, emphasizing their muscles, crew-cut hair style, etc.

15. *Mise-ko* (shop kids) refers to boys or men (usually younger than the masters) who serve customers at gay bars. For a description of interaction in typical gay bars, see Ishida (2006).

16. Gen was Ōtsuka's partner at the time of the publication of his book. Gen opened his own gay bar in Ni-chōme called Gen papa.

17. Shinjuku ni-chōme developed into an important red-light district for licensed brothels in the early postwar period. However, with the prohibition of prostitution taking effect in 1958, the nature of the area rapidly changed, giving way to many more gay-related bars and businesses.

18. This was true when written in 1995; however, since 2000 there have been regular "rainbow" festivals (*reinbō matsuri*) held in the area in the summer.

19. A small community drop-in center named Akta has since been established offering safe-sex advice primarily to gay men. Hustler Akira (see chapter 21 in this volume) has been instrumental in its operation.

20. *Iwashi* is a kind of fish that is reasonably priced in Japanese fish markets. Many Japanese think of *iwashi* as a cheap fish.

16

TŌGŌ KEN, THE LEGENDARY *OKAMA*

Burning with Sexual Desire and Revolt

Oikawa Kenji

On the evening of 27 November 2002 in a lecture hall at Waseda University, a frail figure stood under a pink spotlight in front of a colorful, handmade poster advertising "The Legendary *Okama*—A Speech by Tōgō Ken."

Who, exactly, is Tōgō Ken? When Tōgō's name is mentioned, what comes to most people's minds is his self-proclaimed status as an *okama* (queen, faggot), his many unsuccessful attempts at winning election to the House of Councilors, or his various arrests on obscenity charges. Yet, despite these usual images, Tōgō is much more than a politician, a gay bar owner, or the editor of a gay magazine. For instance, attorney Endō Makoto, who reveres Tōgō as a Buddha figure, once commented, "What's special about Tōgō is that he questions everything that 99 percent of the population takes for granted and he acts on his doubts. His rebellious spirit is his great attraction, and the fact that he constantly challenges authority."

In 1971, Tōgō ran in the election for the House of Councilors for the first time and he continued to run in elections over the next two

Translated, abridged, and reproduced with permission from "*Densetsu no okama Tōgō Ken: Aiyoku to hangyaku ni moetagiru,*" *Shūkan kinyōbi* (Friday weekly) no. 367, 15 June 2001: 34–39. Translated by Katsuhiko Suganuma.

decades, making his last attempt in 1995. Tōgō puts his motivation for engaging in politics this way: "Why on earth are there no representatives from oppressed groups of people in the Diet? Liberty and equality for whom? Why are there no representatives from the bottom of society at all?" Looking at the frail figure on the stage, I was struck by the fact that his slender body would snap like a twig if it were stepped on. Wondering about the source of his tenacious and rebellious spirit, I decided to pursue Tōgō for some answers.

It was already well after midnight when I first visited Tōgō at his bar named Saturday in Shinjuku ni-chōme. He still hadn't arrived and there was only one part-time staff member standing behind the bar. There were only about ten seats in front of the bar counter, and behind them was a bookshelf full of back issues of Tōgō's monthly magazine *The Gay* (*Za gei*). Numerous pictures of naked guys were pasted on the walls. It wasn't until after 4:00 a.m. that Tōgō arrived, dressed in jacket and jeans. Although he said, "No interview today!" he did answer my questions. Due to the weather, I thought that he might have caught a cold. I was worried by his repeated sniffling during our conversation and I asked him, "Tōgō, are you ill?"

"Well, since I was attacked by the right wing, my nose hasn't been so good!" he replied.

The incident referred to occurred back in 1984. The Zatsumin no Kai,[1] an organization run by Tōgō, contributed an opinion piece with an illustration to the August 1984 edition of a monthly magazine called *Shin zasshi X* (New X magazine). The illustration depicted the provocative scene of His Majesty the Showa Emperor being raped by U.S. General Douglas MacArthur. Branding the illustration "disrespectful," a right-wing group protested to the publisher. Parking their sound trucks outside the publisher's offices, they screamed abuse from dawn till dusk and at one point they broke into the publisher's office and trashed it. Tōgō's home was also picketed in the same manner, and he received threatening phone calls.

Then, one day, a member of a right-wing organization was riding his bicycle down the street in Shinjuku when he came across Tōgō by chance. Although he had never met him in person, he recognized Tōgō from his television campaigns when he was running for office. He pedaled close up to him and called out, "Hi Tōgō." But Tōgō denied that it was him and tried to get away. "You liar, you little asshole," shouted the right-winger in a rage and plowed straight into Tōgō with his bicycle, knocking him over and then bashing him. He then rode away without getting caught.

Tōgō remembers the incident this way: "I saw a good looking guy on a bicycle coming toward me from over there, and I was wondering, 'Which bar does he work at? What a handsome man!' and I thought it would be nice to give him a smile. At that moment, all of sudden he crashed into me on his bicycle, and I thought, 'Nooooooo.'" After being attacked, Tōgō reported the matter to the police, and two months later the activist was arrested. But why on earth did Tōgō publish the "disrespectful" drawing even though he knew he'd be attacked by the right wing? The background to his behavior is related to the incredulity that Tōgō feels toward Japan's "emperor system."

Tōgō was born in Kakogawa City in Hyōgo Prefecture. His grandfather was a member of the House of Representatives and his father was a member of the Hyōgo Prefectural Council. According to Tōgō, his mother was a schoolteacher who married into the Tōgō family as a second wife after the divorce of the first wife. Since she was only their stepmother, she was bullied by the children of her husband's ex-wife. After her husband's death in 1941, the first-born son of the husband's ex-wife, who became the household head, treated her as his servant. His treatment of her was so harsh that her teeth fell out. It can be said that Tōgō's hatred of the patriarchal family came from the abuse his mother experienced at the hands of his half-brother.

Tōgō says, "Back then the head of the nation was the God Emperor, and the head of the family was the father, and after his death, the first-born son became the head. The authority of the household head was clearly related to the patriarchal authority embedded in the emperor system." He goes on, "Although after the war, the emperor declared that he was human,[2] he continued to be emperor. He completely avoided accepting responsibility for the suffering of the victims of the war. The declaration of his humanity was just a strategy to deflect attention away from his ultimate responsibility for the war and its consequences."

For years, every time Tōgō has campaigned in the election, in his television broadcasts and in his speeches on the streets, he had continued to proclaim that "if the emperor's '*chin*' (a first-person pronoun used only by the emperor) is a symbol of Japan, I prefer the symbol of a man, his *chin chin* (a slang term for penis)." Tōgō comments, "It is difficult to understand that all people are equal, unless we think of them having sex. Even the emperor has a dick—and he uses it. We are not so different from each other."

Tōgō's outspokenness often gets him into trouble. I asked him how many times he has been arrested so far.

"I don't remember every time," he replied.

Among other offences, Tōgō has repeatedly been arrested on obscenity charges. In 1986, for instance, he was caught by Japanese Customs when he tried to bring in magazines from abroad that depicted uncensored pictures of male genitalia. Since he refused to pay a fine, he was prosecuted by Japanese Customs in a case that went all the way to the Supreme Court, where he was eventually found guilty of contravening Japan's obscenity laws.

About this case, Tōgō comments, "Originally there was no such word as 'obscenity' in Japan. In the Edo Era (1603–1867) there existed male brothels where men rubbed against each other's *chin chin*. I don't understand what obscenity is. What's so obscene about the human body? Why on earth should the act of loving between two people be obscene? Love is a form of free expression and it is not right for the authorities to crack down on it."

By the way, Tōgō once had a wife. She passed away in 1999. They were separated for a long time, and, finally, toward the end of her life, she consented to a divorce. They had one boy and two girls. Deciding that he "had to live an honest life," early in his marriage Tōgō left his family for Tokyo where he began to run a gay bar. Later on, he brought his children to Tokyo and raised them by himself. One wonders how such an unconventional father was looked at through the eyes of his children.

"As far as I'm concerned, my father used to have little meaning for me, but I finally came to a point where I could think about him calmly and objectively. I realized that you should not condemn a person who acts against common sense. Now I am able to look at Tōgō not as my father but as an individual." So says Tōgō's son, who once harbored such rage against his father that he punched him. However, for the last eight years, it has become a New Year's custom for Tōgō and his son to visit the Ana-hachiman shrine to purchase good-luck talismans for the coming year. Tōgō's grandson, who is more than ten years old now, also accompanies them on these shrine visits. "The existence of my grandson works as a cushion in my relationship with my son. When my grandson is around us, I become a so-called *ojiichan* (grandpa) rather than a father to my son," says Tōgō.

When I again visited his bar early one Saturday morning, there were no guests—only Tōgō himself standing alone. Tōgō was telling me about this guy who he'd love to shoot photographs of. The explicit photos that Tōgō takes for his own magazine, *The Gay*, are the magazine's main selling point. Tōgō says that although he hasn't had sex for more than twenty years, he enjoys talking dirty to naked guys who are his type. He loves it when their small shrunken cocks gradually rise up in response to his words. When the models get really hard, pointing up at ceiling— that's his greatest joy. "I want to shoot photos at the exact moment that those men feel sexual ecstasy. But that is a very difficult thing to do. One time, one guy shot his load from here to there. . . ," says Tōgō, pointing at the phone. It seems that it was surprising even for Tōgō to see this guy's load shoot almost ten feet (3 m). But these days he feels lonely because he cannot find any good men.

What he most adores now is his beloved cat named Chin. According to Tōgō, she was abandoned in front of his house covered in her own blood from an accident to her shoulder. Chin was hovering between life and death. Tōgō took her in and raised her like his own daughter. Her name Chin comes from the emperor's use of the pronoun *chin*, a kind of imperial "we." He adores her even more than his own children. Now he lives on just because Chin is with him. "She is a really refined cat," said Tōgō humorously.

Tōgō told me that he wanted to show me something interesting, so we left the bar in the early morning light. *Kan-kon kan-kon*—the dry sound of wooden clogs tapping on the concrete streets was echoing all over the now deserted district of Shinjuku ni-chōme. There was hardly anybody on the streets at this time in the morning. How many people would be able to imagine that Shinjuku ni-chōme is one of the foremost gay areas in the world by just looking at its morning face?

We arrived at a 550-yard-long (500 m) underpass connecting the Shinjuku san-chōme subway station with Japan Rail's Shinjuku Station.

"This is it. This is what I wanted to show you."

We viewed an immense jam-packed crowd of people all dressed in hues of grey or black heaving past us. "Look at all these people rushing to get to work on time, surging past like a big wave. I've watched this scene for more than twenty years. This is like a funeral procession of living people."

Tōgō was lurching into the crowd, taking rhythmic steps right and then left.

"I have been discriminated against by people from this crowd. This drunken old *okama* is walking against the wave of this crowd. Every time I see this, I feel that I must continue to live."

Then and there I asked Tōgō why he continues to use the word *okama*, a word that sounds discriminatory. As the term *okama* is associated with the phrase *kama wo horu* (having anal sex; literally, digging an *okama*), some gays feel uncomfortable with it, saying that it emphasizes anal sex.

"I love the word *okama* very much. . . . I feel free to love this word because of the fact that I have been discriminated against through its use." His face was still red, but his eyes showed sobriety, as if he weren't drunk at all.

"There is no need to justify love between men by adjusting the wording. What's wrong with men loving each other, and women loving each other? What is shameful is to live your life lying to yourself, and not being able to love another person."

Tōgō dares to embrace the word *okama*, a term that symbolizes contempt for homosexuals.

"I believe that *okama* originally comes from the Sanskrit word *kāma*, which means love. Therefore, the origin of *okama* is love."

Saying this, his facial expression softened. His anger and sadness slipped away, leaving a soft and very charming smile on his face.

NOTES

1. Zatsumin no Kai was established by Tōgō in 1977. The group's members consist of "people who live at the bottom" of society. He organized this group

in order to provide opportunities for people who are oppressed by social norms, including sexual minorities, to network with and support each other.

2. After Japan's defeat in World War II, a new constitution was issued under the guidance of the U.S. occupation force in 1946, in which the emperor was defined as a "symbol" of Japan and its people, not as a "god," as in the previous constitution.

⑰

WHO SHOULD BE ASHAMED OF WHOM?

Hirano Hiroaki

TRANSLATOR'S PREFACE: THE BACKGROUND TO THE *OKAMA* DEBATE

Soon after Oikawa Kenji's essay "The Legendary *Okama* Tōgō Ken: Burning with Sexual Desire and Revolt" was published in *Shūkan kinyōbi* (no. 367, 15 June 2001; reproduced in chapter 16 in this volume), it led to a contentious debate among Japanese gay communities over the use of the word *okama* in the media. The representatives of Sukotan Project,[1] Itō Satoru and Yanase Ryūta, protested to the magazine's editors, arguing that there was no need for the magazine to use the word *okama* in the title and, furthermore, that the explanation of the word offered by the writer in the text was incorrect.

Sukotan Project had been invited to give a lecture on issues concerning discrimination against homosexuals in Japanese society to the editors of the magazine as the editors were preparing the fifth part of a series called *Ko ni ikiru* (Living as an individual). In the lecture, they had told the editors that it is "as different as chalk and cheese"

Translated and reproduced with permission from *"Dare ga dare wo hajiru no ka,"* *Shūkan kinyōbi* (Friday weekly) no. 387, 9 November 2001: 49–51. Translated by Katsuhiko Suganuma.

when the word *okama* is used by *tōjisha* (persons directly concerned, i.e., gay men themselves) and non-*tōjisha*. Sukotan Project protested to the magazine's editors because they persisted in using the word *okama* in the essay's title despite the fact Sukotan Project had problematized the word's use in their lecture.[2] Although Itō and Yanase made it clear in their letter of complaint that they took no offense at Tōgō Ken choosing to refer to himself as *okama* based on his own philosophy, they persisted in arguing that the editors should have considered the fact that some readers may have been hurt by the term *okama*.

In response to Sukotan Project's protest, a subsequent issue of *Shūkan kinyōbi* (no. 376, 24 August 2001) featured special discussions about the topic in which Sukotan Project's position on the use of the word *okama* in the media was supportively addressed along with other contributors' comments. Hirano's critical essay translated here was written after he examined that issue of *Shūkan kinyōbi* in order to articulate his own understanding of the word *okama* and to outline the critical issues involved in the debate about gay men's identity and prevailing gender norms. The essay was published in *Shūkan kinyōbi* three months after the issue that covered the debate and five months after the original article.

Shūkan kinyōbi's choice of contributors and commentators in issue no. 376 met with strong dissent from other gay writers and community members who did not necessarily agree with Sukotan Project's stance on this issue. As a consequence, leading Japanese gay writer and critic Fushimi Noriaki, along with other community representatives, held a symposium on this debate titled *"Okama" wa sabetsu ka?* (Is *okama* discriminatory?), inviting the chief editor of *Shūkan kinyōbi* to participate.[3] Many crucial arguments and opinions articulated in the symposium are also outlined in Hirano's essay below.

INTRODUCTION

When conducting a productive discussion on this debate—keeping in mind what the vital perspective might be—I was following the *"okama* debate" triggered by an article on Tōgō Ken (by Oikawa Kenji) in the magazine *Shūkan kinyōbi*. In any case, I should probably say that the fact that the debate has emerged at all is itself a sign of progress. Yet at the same time, I should probably state the fact that the most crucial issue has not yet been discussed.

To be honest, I am not an earnest reader of *Shūkan kinyōbi*. I read the magazine for the first time just because of this incident. But the fact that "that" *Shūkan kinyōbi*[4] addressed Tōgō Ken interests me to some extent. Why an article about Tōgō now? What are they trying to say about Tōgō? When I first read the article, there was nothing in it that I thought was particularly special. For those of us who have known about Tōgō Ken as we were growing up, there wasn't anything new about him in it. And I was left with a feeling that the writer should have written much more on some aspects. However, as far as I am concerned, the intent to write about Tōgō Ken now is itself worthy of notice.

A "TABOO" PERSON

In 1971 Ken-san[5] ran in the election for a seat in the Diet for the first time while proclaiming himself to be "Tōgō Ken, the *okama*." Back then it was a "shocking" moment for me who was still in high school. Probably not so many people can still vividly recall that "shocking" moment. For most gay men under thirty, Tōgō Ken is just a "man of the past." The number of young people around me who don't "know" about Tōgō is growing. And for those gay men who are in their mid-thirties or older, he is a "taboo person," "someone nobody wants to remember."

Such matters are clearly expressed in the essay "The Legendary *Okama* Burning with Sexual Desire and Revolt" by Oikawa. The title is extremely suitable for articulating who Tōgō Ken is. At the same time, the title also evokes an uncertain feeling for many gay men. Tōgō became a "taboo person" because he lived his life in exactly the manner the title literally states. I will not play up to him by saying, "You are my precursor. I admire and respect you." In reality, there must have been many gay men who felt uncomfortable about his existence. Despite this, he put in so much effort for the sake of the Japanese gay community from the 1970s through to the 1990s. Aside from some disagreeable aspects of his personality, without him there would not be a "now" for gay men in this country. Thus, the only way to make sense out of this is to start reflecting our own ambivalent feelings toward him.

He is probably the first gay man who raised his voice to say "society should not discriminate against *okama*." At a time when the number among the younger generation who do not know him is growing, and when Japanese society as a whole is shifting toward favoring a more right-wing sentiment, to try once again to understand this man who revolted against the emperor system would be a meaningful thing to do—especially when considering the ways in which the gradually ingrained gay liberation movement of Japan should be directed. However, the debate came in from a different angle.

Not that I "expected" that from the start, but Itō Satoru (from Sukotan Project) protested over this. He claimed that the word *okama* should not have been used in the title, and the explanation of the term in the text was inadequate, and further "we were hurt by that." I have to raise my eyebrows when considering the fact that the editor's response to Itō's claim was, "[P]lease judge it by reading the actual content." In fact the essay itself was not discriminatory at all. However, in the Japanese mass media, it is a matter of course that a great essay will be distorted by a bent title. So when I write something for publishers, I always make sure that my essay, including title and subheadings, should not be "altered" without my permission. When I was interviewed by two weekly magazines in 1991, I demanded that even small details such as captions for the photos, ads in the newspapers, and the banner advertisements for the issue to be hung on trains must be precise. You have to do this much in order to protect yourself from being used by the commercially oriented Japanese mass media. It is not a rare thing for the trust and goodwill between interviewers and interviewees to be easily trampled upon. Considering such circumstances, it is understandable that Sukotan Project was at pains to protest against the title "The Legendary *Okama*."

However, I do still support this title. In fact, if I were the writer, I would even go so far as to put quotations around "The Legendary *Okama* Tōgō Ken." To me "Tōgō Ken" equates with "The Legendary *Okama*." No matter how hard you try, you cannot separate the two. There is no meaning in debating the usage of *okama* in the title without regard to the "Tōgō Ken phenomenon."

The word *okama* coexists alongside "Tōgō Ken," even though it is a "taboo" term for many gay men. So when the word is put in the title, it means that the title now has a "spark." Yet, the author and the editors decided to put the word at the "top." It can be said that they were honorable as persons who value freedom of speech. And they should have responded to Sukotan Project's criticism with what they themselves believed.

THINGS DEBATED AND NOT DEBATED

In response to the protest from Sukotan Project, *Shūkan kinyōbi* ran the topic "Sexuality and Human Rights" in the issue published on 24 August (no. 376). I do have some issues with it, but the fact that they prepared a special feature on this matter is at least worthy of recognition.

After I read it once, I was intrigued by the point made by Sataka Shin: "[T]he critical issue [in this context] is whether the independent 'individual' has a will to embrace with society, or not."[6] Refraining from expressing disrespect for Ken-san, Sataka problematizes the way in which the essay itself was written and just states that "I do not mean to insist that Mr. Tōgō was an excluded/isolated figure." However, in actual fact, the essay was, although unexpectedly, articulating the "exact" point that he was. I think this is one of the reasons why Tōgō Ken was not supported, not only by many nongays but also by gay men themselves. I don't recall such a perspective having been discussed so far (even within our gay community). But this is a very important point to be considered when examining the "future" path for our gay movement.

In the special feature, apart from Sataka's critical point, all the others were just talking about the rights and wrongs of the use of the word *okama* from start to finish. In other words, I could see only too well how the editors were confused by the protest. On the other hand, crucial questions concerning why the word *okama* was so controversial, why the word functions as a discriminatory slur, were never discussed. I cannot be more sorry about that.

Personally, I don't use the word *okama* to refer either to myself or others. I do know that some Japanese gay activists continue referring to themselves as *okama* whatever their own rationales are, and I don't have much to say about that. But I, myself, do not use the word. The reason is because the word is not only discriminatory toward gay men, but it is also related to misogyny and machismo. Paradoxically, I wonder why some of the "feminists" who are touched upon by Ochiai Keiko[7] in her essay can be so naïve about the word *okama*.[8] The issues surrounding the term should be seriously considered by heterosexuals themselves.

Okama is indeed a vague and irresponsible term. Nobody knows its "true meaning." Its meaning and use vary depending on each individual, place, and circumstance. Roughly counting, I can think of more than ten meanings for it, and one can hardly make a clear distinction between one and another. But a common pattern emerges when it is used in a discriminatory manner. That is to say, the word can be used to discredit someone's *otoko sei* (masculine gender). Within a misogynist and machismo-oriented society in which *onna* (woman) and "feminine traits" are undervalued, and conversely *otoko* and "masculinity" are excessively overvalued, the word *okama* works as a slur. Therefore, in my opinion, the word has more to do with "gender" than sexuality narrowly defined.

As I have repeatedly mentioned, I cannot agree with someone's "interpretation" of the word *okama* that ignores such intersection between gender and sexuality. In this incident, although Itō Satoru criticized Oikawa's explanation of the word, he should have reflected upon his own lack of understanding before complaining about someone else's.

TŌJISHA VERSUS NON-*TŌJISHA* THEORY

In this "'*okama*' debate," Sukotan Project developed the argument that it is "as different as chalk and cheese" when the word *okama* is used by persons who are directly concerned (that is, who are gay) and when it is used by persons who are not. At a glance, this seems like legitimate logic and is often used in various other settings. Yet, in most of those cases, the discussion of who is a *tōjisha*[9] is left untouched. In this instance, the issue of who is a *tōjisha* is about being "gay." But needless to say, not every single gay man can come out—and indeed Itō pointed out that a lot of gay men were still in the "closet."

In this sense, nobody should be able to be so sure who is a *tōjisha* or not among those expressing opinions on "gay" issues. I do not know whether the writer Oikawa is gay or not. I think at least, in part admonishing myself, I would not "insolently" argue that "you should not use the word '*okama*,' because you are not gay," just solely relying on the fact that he hasn't "declared" his sexual orientation in public.

I have to say the argument that "it is as different as chalk and cheese if the word '*okama*' is used by persons who are concerned or persons who are not" is too naïve. In such cases, only "persons who are already out" would be granted a right to express an opinion. That would be a "monopoly of speech." As I always say, my principle is based on the policy that "good ideas are good, bad ones are bad, regardless of the speaker's sexual orientation." Compared with some opinions on the use of *okama* by those who do not consider the aforementioned perspectives, I would rather support other opinions by nongay people who understand the critical intersection of the term *okama* with misogyny and machismo.

Since Oikawa said he himself put forward the title of the essay, it is natural that his own opinion, understanding, and reasoning should be included in the special feature (no. 376). But why is it that a lot of the other responses were only written by the "PTA" (the editors and other writers) of the magazine. Contrary to their claim that they wanted to cherish the voices of the *tōjisha*, they excluded voices other than those of Sukotan Project from the special feature, that resulted in strong criticism from those left unrepresented.

The claim by those who said they were hurt by the title should be acknowledged seriously. However, I cannot just muddle the two things together. That is, by "snuggling up to" the feeling of someone who was hurt, we should not be hindered from seizing the core of the problem. My concern goes one step further. I have to ask, if someone was hurt by reading a *non*-discriminatory essay about gay men, then why did that happen? The person has to look inside his mind to find out the reason why, instead of running away from the problem. I would like to say, that is exactly the problem faced by gay men themselves which needs to be articulated.

I find that the problem is one of "internalized homophobia," which is also apparent in some of the abuse rained down on Ken-san by the gay community, and some internal criticism or even "belittling" comments that pop up every year against the "showy" elements of the Tokyo Lesbian and Gay Parade and the Rainbow March in Sapporo.[10] I do not deny that I myself was also once very embedded in a societal norm that "made" me look upon Ken-san with an unpleasant regard. The reason why a person could say he was hurt by being called an *okama* is that the person himself has internalized the social values of misogyny and machismo. When we internalize homophobia, what we do is "kill ourselves."

Commenting on the special feature, some gay men pointed out that there was also a hypocritical narrative underlying the portrayal of the relation of the two parties involved—that of "abused gay men" and "understanding heterosexuals." I think this is a very legitimate critique. Simply crying over their wounded feelings would not only satisfy the superiority of the majority but also contribute to further heterosexism. This may sound too harsh, yet without dismantling "our inner homophobia," there is no future for "us." We cannot just keep crying now.

NOTES

1. Sukotan Project (Sukotan Kikaku) was established in 1994 by the gay activists Itō Satoru and Yanase Ryūta in order to provide information about homosexuality and homosexuals in Japan and abroad to the general public. For a detailed account for their work, see Itō and Yanase (2000). Their website is at: http://www.sukotan.com/.

2. For details of the claims made by Sukotan Project, see the several essays by Itō Satoru and Yanase Ryūta in *Shūkan kinyōbi* no. 376, 24 August 2001.

3. For details of this symposium and the surrounding discussions, see Fushimi et al. (2000) and Lunsing (2005a). For an English review of the text of the discussion, see Gottleib (2006).

4. Here Hirano is gesturing toward the somewhat notorious nature of the magazine which is well-known for its political, left-leaning editorials and articles.

5. In this essay, Hirano switches between two names "Ken-san" and "Tōgō Ken" (or "Tōgō") from time to time. Hirano uses "Ken-san" when he refers to Tōgō as a person who he personally regards. On the other hand, he uses "Tōgō Ken" when referring to Tōgō as a public figure.

6. Sataka (2001: 22).

7. Ochiai Keiko is a feminist critic and writer. In the essay that she wrote for no. 376 of *Shūkan kinyōbi*, she mentions one of her feminist friends who thought *okama* was not a discriminatory word just because her feminist friend also uses the word. For a detailed account, see Ochiai's essay in *Shūkan kinyōbi*, no. 376.

8. Ochiai (2001: 21).

9. *Tōjisha* is a term meaning "person (directly) concerned." Originally a legal term designating an individual directly involved in a case, it was taken up by feminists and members of disenfranchised groups in the 1970s to stress that it is the people directly concerned with an issue, for example women seeking reproductive rights, disabled seeking public access, or members of sexual minorities seeking citizen's rights, who should decide their fate, not government-appointed bodies or panels of "experts."

10. The Tokyo Lesbian and Gay Parade is discussed in chapter 18 in this volume.

18

REFLECTIONS ON THE TOKYO LESBIAN AND GAY PARADE 2000

Sunagawa Hideki

On 27 August 2000 the Tokyo Lesbian and Gay Parade 2000[1] took place. This was four years after the previous Tokyo parade had been held and as such it was a "revival" of the parade. In addition, the Tokyo Rainbow Festival (Tōkyō reinbō matsuri), in which gay bar owners played a central role, was held later the same day in Shinjuku ni-chōme, an area where many gay and lesbian bars are concentrated. The parade itself, in which two thousand LGBT people and their supporters participated, and the evening festival in which the narrow streets of Ni-chōme were flooded by countless participants, made a deep impact on many people and more than a few shed some tears. In this essay, based on my own experience, I want to record the changes that took place in the Japanese gay scene during the 1990s that led to the revival of the parade in 2000.[2]

THE FLOW OF THE TIMES

The early 1990s was a period when gays began to take a stand against "general society" in support of their own existence. In 1991, for instance,

---

Translated by Wim Lunsing.

OCCUR (Akā)[3] brought the Fuchū Youth Hostel (Fuchū seinen no ie) lawsuit against the Tokyo metropolitan government. This suit arose when OCCUR members who were holding an overnight seminar in a local youth facility were abused by other guests. Rather than take steps to rectify the situation, the hostel management instead refused OCCUR permission to use the facilities a second time, leading to the filing of the discrimination suit against the hostel owner—the Tokyo metropolitan government. This suit ended in 1997 with a decision in favor of OCCUR.[4]

In the same year the court case began, Fushimi Noriaki published his *Private Gay Life* (*Puraib to gei raifu*; 1991), a book that pioneered gay studies in Japan. This book contained a facial picture of Fushimi at a time when it was an epoch-making event for a gay man to have his face displayed in a general publication. In addition, in 1992, the Tokyo Lesbian and Gay Film Festival, which presently draws a large crowd, was held for the first time and a gay-themed issue of the popular *Bessatsu takarajima* series, *Gifts from Gays* (*Gei no okurimono*, *Bessatsu takarajima* 1992), edited by Ōtsuka Takashi[5] and Fushimi Noriaki, was published. This book contained an abundance of gay positive messages and gave many gays the chance to regard themselves in a more supportive manner.

In this way, it can be said that the first Tokyo Lesbian and Gay Parade, which was held in 1994, was a symbol of the increased confidence with which Japan's gay scene had come to express itself in relation to the outside world in the 1990s. This parade was organized by Minami Teishirō, the chief editor of the gay magazine *Adon*, who at that time led the groups International Lesbian and Gay Association (ILGA) Japan and AIDS Action (Eizu Akushon). He should be given great credit for bringing about a parade at a time when many people in Japan thought such an event impossible.

Although the number of people participating in this parade grew annually for the second and third events, during the third parade in 1997 some people who opposed the organizers' way of doing things caused a confrontation that led to complications at the meeting after the parade. The direct cause of the problem was a declaration that the organizers wanted to have adopted at a meeting after the parade. People who were opposed to having such a declaration written by only one person (that is, Minami) climbed onto the stage during the meeting, which erupted into chaos when they forcibly obstructed the adoption. In the chaos, one of the organizers used discriminatory language toward a lesbian of the opposition, which further deepened the divide.

Although smaller parades organized by Minami did continue until 1999, there are few who know about them, even among gay men, as they did not attract many participants and involved fewer than a hundred people.[6] Hence, until 2000 the Tokyo parades were to all extents lost. However, in the meantime a parade had begun in Sapporo in 1996—the Sapporo Rainbow March (Sapporo reinbō māchi)[7]—and (apart from 2000) has continued until today, thus demonstrating the need for the existence of events like this. It is no exaggeration to say that the revival of the parade in Tokyo in 2000 could not have happened without the continuance of the parade in Sapporo.

In 2000, the Tokyo Lesbian and Gay Parade was organized in a wholly different manner from the earlier events. I proposed this parade and functioned as the head of the executive committee. However, I personally feel strongly that behind me becoming the head of the executive committee lay "the flow of times."

A BACKGROUND OF HIV ACTIVITIES

Of the three lesbian and gay parades that were organized in Tokyo from 1994 to 1996, I only participated in the second one. At the time, I somehow did not feel strongly about the importance of the parades and I believe that interest among gays in general was low at that time, compared to the revival of the parade in 2000. The number of participants in the second parade in 1995, in which I participated, was said to be about two thousand, but according to the parade staff, the people who actually did the counting, the actual number of participants was more like five to six hundred. When the parade was revived in 2000, the actual number of participants was about two thousand. This means that three to four times more people participated in 2000 than in the earlier parades. Moreover, it was I, who in 1996 had not felt very strongly about the need for a parade, who put my name forward as the organizer of the 2000 event. What were the factors that led to my change of heart and such an increase in the number of participants?

At the time, I was greatly interested in the question of how to handle HIV education activities for gay men since, unlike now, there were very few people involved in such campaigns and extremely little funding. Despite this, however, HIV transmission was definitely spreading very quickly among gay men. In this situation, I was motivated to do something by a feeling of unease, and in 1997 I planned a HIV education campaign with a group named Place Tokyo: Gay Friends for AIDS. This was a combination of a workshop to think about safer sex and an entertainment event.

We were thinking about setting up an HIV education event in which we would hold a concert with the participation of a gay choir, a brass band, and drag queens and which would spread educational messages about HIV. We aimed not only to give the audience but also the performers themselves a chance to think about questions concerning HIV. In the end, this event was much more successful than I had expected. The gay men who had gathered felt a strong feeling of togetherness, and I received many messages of thanks from the audience and performers who had participated in the event. There was excitement about having a high level of musical activities conducted by gays, excitement about having fun together with many other gays, and excitement about being on the stage together. Some of the participants even cried.

This event was the culmination of a gradual accumulation of gay group activities that had begun in the early 1990s. The choir, brass band, and drag performance group that participated in this event had begun their activities at the beginning of the decade and by then had already been performing for five to six years. I, too, as the organizer of the event, had begun my HIV activities during the same period and had gained about the same amount of experience. Hence, this event came about when activities that had begun in a variety of venues in the 1990s came together. This event enabled many gays to physically feel the joy of participating in an event with "fellow gay people," and as differing types of groups stood on the same stage, the result was that groups who had had no point of contact until then discovered a connection.

MY RESOLUTION TO TAKE ON THE PARADE

Personally, I was greatly influenced by this event and this influence worked strongly in my decision to raise my hand as head of the organizing committee of the parade in 2000. Part of my motivation was that I felt I had to recognize the positive feelings that had been inspired among the participants of the Gay Friends for AIDS event, and that I, too, had felt uplifted by the gratitude I felt toward the many people who had cooperated to make the event possible. This is what enabled me to reply in the affirmative when someone asked me to organize the parade. So when asked subsequently about my motivation for becoming the head of the organizing committee of the parade, I had to answer, "to return a favor to the community."

However, because I, who originally had not felt very strongly about the need for a parade, decided to take on the parade in order to "return a favor," I felt nothing more than a feeling of duty and responsibility. As a result, I became increasingly agonized as the preparations for the parade progressed. As this agony wore on, my thoughts about the parade changed again.

After I decided to hold the parade and to attach my name as head of the organizing committee, the first thing I did was to assemble an organizing committee. Thereafter, I went around to a great many people who manage gay businesses, "opinion leaders," and others in order to seek their cooperation. At first, a friend who was invited onto the organizing committee and I said to each other, "As it is the first revival, a small scale will do," but while going around and greeting people and while we talked in the organizing committee about what sort of parade it should be, the image of the parade everyone was hoping for became increasingly ambitious and I was in danger of being crushed by insecurity as their expectations exceeded my abilities. Repeatedly bowing in seeking the cooperation of many people and bowing over the failures of my staff and myself, I became wholly exhausted. However, I could not talk about this exhaustion and grumble openly, and of course I could not say that I would quit.

On the day of the parade, having been unable to sleep for two nights, I prepared to leave my house for the last time almost in a state of panic. I was full of insecurities about whether things would end in disaster before the last part of the parade had returned to the site, since from the beginning of the preparations on the site, accidents had followed one after another. However, the parade ended without a big problem and at the post-parade meeting, perhaps because of a feeling of relief, my tears would not stop flowing and I could hardly say a word.

"MEETING" WITH PARTICIPANTS IN THE PARADE

I often hear stories about feelings of satisfaction after a large event has ended successfully. However, in my case this was not so. Feeling completely burned out and maintaining many painful memories from the organization, I kept thinking that I wanted to forget about the parade. Although I was happy to hear about participants' positive experiences, they did not really impact me.

However, these feelings about the parade changed when I became involved in editing the book *Parade* (Sunagawa 2001), in which reports on the parade were gathered. This book began with a proposal from the writer Matsuzawa Kureichi, who had participated in the parade (although he is not gay), that we should leave a record of events. So we collected articles that had been written in relation to the parade, wrote about the history of the parade itself, and held a roundtable talk looking back at the parade and the Tokyo Rainbow Festival. While engaged in this work, I realized again the extent to which gay magazines had supported the parade and how many people had cooperated to make it happen. While writing a history of parades throughout the world, I also realized the spread of this movement and the depth of its meaning. But what more than anything changed my painful memories of the parade were the expressions on the faces of the participants in the pictures that gay magazines offered for inclusion in the book. Here I actually saw the smiling faces of many people. Each one really had a splendid smiling face and I felt like I was meeting participants in the parade for the first time. I felt in the depth of my heart that the parade was a good thing to have done, and the heavy clump of feelings in my heart I had felt toward the parade finally dissolved.

I believe that there is nothing like the smiling faces in the pictures that can demonstrate the meaning the parade had for individual participants. A parade is there in order that LGBT people, who in daily life are treated as if they do not exist, can demonstrate their existence. It is also a device for reforming negative images such as the notion that LGBT people necessarily lead their life in the shade. However, the majority of the participants did not actually have much of this kind of social and political consciousness. But by gathering with many like-minded others and reveling in the joy of walking all together on public streets, they found strength.

WHAT A "GAY COMMUNITY" IS AIMING FOR

The ways of expression and the political nature of this kind of parade are themes that are much discussed among those concerned. The at-times-gorgeous and at-times-quaint drag queens and the half-naked go-go boys by no means constitute the majority of the participants, but they do draw people's attention. There are more than a few people who criticize such expressions as damaging the parade's image. Also, while there are people who say that given Japan's comparatively low level of discrimination, they don't feel comfortable about making a public appeal for rights, there are also others who criticize the low level of political consciousness exhibited in the Tokyo parade.

However, when seeing the bold, happy smiles on the faces of the participants in the pictures of the 2000 parade and while participating in the parades of 2001 (headed by Fukushima Mitsuo) and 2002 (headed by Sekine Shin'ichi), I thought that the Tokyo parade was fine as it was. Among those participating in the parade there will definitely be people who look unfavorably on drag and go-go. There will also be people who dislike political banners being held up. And there will also be people who feel that the political elements are insufficient. However, all these people walk together and feel uplifted by this experience. Furthermore, it is very significant that LGBT people gather together like this, as in Japan these communities are divided. People who do not otherwise experience a feeling of togetherness discover this feeling by gathering and walking together and are thereby given the confidence that they are all right as they are. I believe this to be a force for empowerment that the parade has to offer. I also believe that this is the shape of the "gay community" that is to be aimed for.

In the sense that it shows the way, I feel the parade is important for the "gay community."

NOTES

1. In Japanese, this parade was named *Tōkyō rezubian & gei parēdo 2000*, a transliteration of its English name. To date, all such "pride events" (*puraido ibento*) have been named using borrowed words. It should be noted, however, that most of these Japanese English words existed in Japanese prior to their borrowing by the LGBT community.

2. Sunagawa's *Parēdo* (2001) is the most complete history of the parades and contains numerous personal accounts. Lesbian perspectives on the parade's history can be found in *Aniisu* (2001: 54–57). English-language accounts can be found in Welker (2004: 134–37), and Izumo and Maree (2000: 108–18).

3. The organization's other name is Ugoku Gei to Rezubian no Kai (Group of moving gays and lesbians), which they translate into English as Japan Association for the Lesbian and Gay Movement.

4. See Lunsing (2005b) for a discussion of this case. It is also discussed from a lesbian perspective in chapter 12 of this volume.

5. See Ōtsuka (chapter 15) in this volume.

6. These events included a Dyke March (Daiku māchi) held in 1997. See *Aniisu* (2001: 57).

7. The march was then called the First LesBiGay Pride March in Sapporo (*Dai-ichi rezu-bi-gei puraido māchi in Sapporo*).

19

HOW I BECAME AN FTM
TRANSGENDER GAY

Fujio Takafumi

My life can roughly be divided in three periods—the period from when I was born until I married at twenty-eight, the period when I was married, and the period of transition after my divorce. I would like to write my own story using parts from all periods. There have been times that were governed by ugly feelings but at present they are all precious to me. There are some embarrassing things but I want to write as factually and honestly as possible.

I was born in Tokyo in 1964. It was the year the Tokyo Olympics were held. When I was born a week late, I was a large baby, weighing 8.5 pounds (3900 grams). Mine was a very average family comprised of my father, who was a company worker, my working mother, and my sister, who was two years older than I. When I was little, my motor development skills were not very good, but I was a lively and restless child. At the time, I often played house with my childhood friends. I liked to play house because when I got to play the role of "father" I could use *boku* (I)[1] with dignity. However, if you ask whether I experienced any gender dysphoria during this period, I have to say no. At that point I had not become aware of

Translated by Wim Lunsing.

this feeling at all. I only became aware of myself as a male after I turned twenty years old.

From my elementary school years, I didn't think anything about whether the children I liked were male or female. I was most likely to think of my own accord that all people were like me. Maybe I didn't understand the concept of sex difference well. In later years, after reading *The Bisexual Option* (Klein [1993] 1997) and wondering whether I should have been troubled about sex difference, I worried why I hadn't been troubled by this when I was younger. But in the end I did not understand why it should have bothered me. Even now, I don't really understand why people are troubled about it.

Let me return to my story. When I was twenty, I had my first relationship as well as sex with a young woman. I had already considerable experience with young men—I did it all the time with whatever men I could get my hands on. This girl said that she was lesbian. The first sex with her made me consider the fact that I had no penis. (When I was a child, I believed that when I grew older, a penis would sprout from my body, but while growing up I ran wild and had forgotten all about this.) After I had sex with her for the first time, I appealed to her for support in my attempts to become more masculine. I grew to love her gradually and continued to penetrate her with my nonexistent penis. After a little over a year, the relationship went awry, and we decided to split up. The cause was that she sought a woman in me and I gave up trying to persuade her otherwise.

Right after that, I abandoned the idea of becoming a man and decided to live as a woman. I found a suitable man at the place I was working and we decided to marry. With a desperate feeling, I moved in with him, and we got married. In the beginning I worked but after a number of months I quit my job and became a no-good housewife who kept sleeping apathetically during the day. After a while I became pregnant and went to the hospital at first, but I was just dozing off all the time and could do nothing at all. After a couple of months I finally went back to the hospital since it was clear that I had developed preeclampsia and needed to go on a special diet until I reached the thirty-eighth week, and in the end I gave birth by cesarean. After giving birth the feeling of responsibility for the baby weighed heavily on me for the first time and it was very painful for me. This pain was brought on by the question of whether it was alright for a warped person like me to raise a child.

Raising my oldest daughter went pretty badly. If I had been living in the United States at the time, perhaps I would have even been arrested for child abuse.[2] I believed I would be able to return to being a normal woman by experiencing pregnancy and giving birth, but after about half a year had passed, I felt that that possibility was nearly zero. I often took out my stress on my daughter. I no sooner wished that she had never been born than I felt how much I loved her. These dramatic swings in my feelings toward her not only robbed me of my emotional strength, but also of my physical strength and my ability to think clearly and make rational judgments.

However, I wasn't the only one who suffered during this period. Although I only learned about it afterward, my husband also hated to come home during that period to face a messed-up house in which he had to confront the face of his messed-up wife and the sound of his screaming child. He was apparently rather worried that the child might be dead when he got home. After we divorced he told me that he was at a loss about whom to talk with about how to find a way out of this situation. I have to write that to my husband's credit he did not simply stand idly by. He dealt with the child's crying in the night and on weekends he took care of her from morning till night.

I got pregnant with my first daughter based on the thought that I didn't want my DNA to end with me and the hope that this would somehow make me into a normal woman. But the second time I got pregnant it was because I thought that when I finally divorced my husband and we were living separately, I didn't want to leave my eldest daughter alone. I got pregnant by having sex once and this time went regularly to the hospital and once again I ended up giving birth by cesarean to a girl. With this I indeed felt that I had fulfilled all my duties.

From that point, the word "divorce" began to enter our conversations. It was due in no small part to the fact that the first surgery for sexual reassignment had just been carried out at the hospital at Saitama Medical School. This was before my second daughter's first birthday, in

October 1998. I think that my husband had given up waiting for things to get better. After the announcement from the Saitama Medical School there were special reports on daytime television shows about the topic. From these I learned the term "gender identity disorder" (*sei dōitsusei shōgai*), but I couldn't face such reports head on, as I felt that I couldn't be one of those freaks (*hentai*). I was like, "What do you expect me to do with this small child here in my arms!" (Nobody expected me to do anything—*ha ha*.)

Shortly thereafter I bought a computer so it became possible for me to use the Internet. It took considerable courage to look at sites related to gender identity disorder. However, once I began to look I could not stop, so I read and read voraciously. At the time there were many personal sites where people published their individual histories. I continued to read from one to the other and couldn't help thinking, "I have to give in" (*sigh*), as there were so many of these personal histories that had things in common with my own. My uncertainty over just what I was—which I had been carrying around with me for the longest time—melted away all at once. In one breath I went from a feeling of anxiety to a feeling of bliss.

From then on things started happening quickly. It was decided that my husband would take the children, and he was busy with the formalities of getting them to elementary school and day school. I was busy looking for an apartment and work. In March 2003 the divorce was finalized. Soon after New Year's, I set up a self-help group for transgender people with children and their families, began to inject hormones, met my current partner, and in the spring I had my breast-removal surgery and changed my name to something that sounds male. These were the steps in my gender transition process. In 2005 I finally found a job as a regular company employee. I praise myself for having come this far. Although I was originally a grasshopper—like in Aesop's "The Ant and the Grasshopper"—I was able to get this far by the one point of lucky faith (in a sense, maybe this is a miracle). Although I had been through gender transition, in the end I became no more than a man-loving *okama* (queen), and I'm still selfish, indecisive, and difficult, as well as a show-off. Even though more than twenty years have passed, I still like *yaoi* (there was a time when I seriously worried that I had begun to think that I was a man because I had been reading too much *yaoi*—*ha ha*)[3] and

I'm still besotted by David Bowie, Johnny Thunders, and Marc Almond. Pornographic magazines and S/M are necessary for me. And I'm still no better at housework. But I love myself, including these most unseemly parts—accepting these parts of me—I expect to keep on living.

I am reaching the end of my story and would like to write something about the self-help group. The group I set up is aimed at transgender people with children and their families, and this appears to be the first time in Japan for such a specialized group. When I checked with a number of old activists, none of them had heard of such a group before. I believe this was probably influenced by the style of activism up to that point. The community in Japan—particularly in Tokyo—had an extreme bias toward seeing transsexuality as being inborn and a strong tendency to exclude others. This is because there is a history of using this as an argument in appeals for changing a person's legal sex on personal registration documents (*koseki*) as well as in appeals for the protection of human rights. It was only after the special treatment law for people with gender identity disorder was adopted that those other than "typical" transsexuals let themselves be heard. It is a phenomenon of people who do not agree with the conditions of the special treatment law all together raising their voices. Coincidentally, shortly after setting up the group, there were reports on the creation of a special treatment law for transsexuals and the exclusion of people with children,[4] but I have no specific intention to engage in activism about this issue. Changing my personal registration details is not one of my life's goals; rather, opportunities to effectively support other people rank higher because I support a middle way! Without changing one's personal registration, the middle solution of changing only the details on one's resident card and insurance card makes it possible to help those who have not had sex-reassignment surgery. After the scheduled review of the law to take place three years after its initial passage, I want to engage in activities for the middle way as much as the situation allows.

Finally, I wish to thank all the people who have been involved in my life. I pray for health and happiness for all: my parents and sister who made efforts to accept me, my former husband who has supported my transgender process, my two children who were born, my partner who currently supports me, my friend S who always advises me, T who is in charge of deputy representatives in the group, K who warmheartedly let me consult him, M and I who gave me the opportunity to write this short history, and my many other friends and acquaintances.

NOTES

1. Japanese has a range of pronouns designating the first-person speaker (i.e., "I"). *Boku* is normally used by male children or adult men in informal situations.

2. The United States has more interventionist policies regarding the (mis)treatment of children than does Japan.

3. *Yaoi* is a genre of girls' manga dedicated to often highly sexualized love stories between beautiful boys. It has often been argued that the androgynous nature of many of the characters has facilitated female readers' identification with the "male" characters, as well as offering a means of escape from rigid social constrictions on gender and romance. See Welker (in press).

4. This became law in 2003. That is, those who have had sex-reassignment surgery are able to legally change their sex provided they are not married at the time and do not have children.

20

MY LIFE AS A "WOMAN"

Mitsuhashi Junko

On the afternoon of 16 August 2004, all dressed up in kimono, I changed trains at Tokyo's Shinagawa Station and boarded the *shinkansen* (bullet train) super-express bound for Kyoto. Soon after checking into my favorite hotel located in a traditional area called Gion, I went along to a party to which I had been invited. At the party I was able to experience a beautiful traditional summer event in Kyoto known as *gozan-no-okuribi*.[1] The next day, I attended an academic conference organized by Professor Inoue Shōichi, who is a professor at the International Research Center for Japanese Studies (Kokusai Nihon Bunka Kenkyū Sentā), and presented my work as a social historian there.

One afternoon a week later, I again dressed up in elegant kimono and headed to the Kabukiza theater, meeting up with two female friends on the way at Ginza Station in downtown Tokyo. The performance of the day was the famous horror story *Tōkaidō Yotsuya kaidan* (The ghosts of Yotsuya) and I was really pleased by the performance of the prominent Kabuki actor Nakamura Kankuro, who played one female role and two male roles in a really outstanding manner.

Translated by Katsuhiko Suganuma.

So you see, I do have a lot of fun in my free time when I am not caught up with my work as a researcher. Having heard this much about my lifestyle, readers might visualize me as an active female researcher who appreciates the beauty of traditional Japanese culture. In fact, my name—Mitsuhashi Junko—is a typical Japanese woman's name, and I do perform most of my social activities as a woman. Most of my academic activities, such as being a visiting scholar at the Institute of Social Science at Chūō University and an associate researcher at the International Research Center for Japanese Studies, are undertaken as a woman named Mitsuhashi Junko. Also, most of my researcher friends and female friends who I met through my interest in kimono only know me as a "woman." However, I was born and raised a man, and even today I am a biological male with my own family. In short, I am a part-time male-to-female (MtF) transgender.

In this short essay, I would like to tell you the story of how I became one of the most active MtF transgenders in contemporary Japan, and how I have styled myself as a "woman" in terms of my figure, in my social gender, and in my relationships with others.

BEFORE THE RISE OF "JUNKO"

I was born in 1955 as the first son of a relatively wealthy family. My family lived in a suburb about fifty miles (80 km) northwest of central Tokyo. Despite the fact that I was loved by my parents and did well in school, by the time I was eighteen and in my senior year of high school, I started to feel a little out of place. I realized that there was a difference between me and my male friends when we talked about women at school. While most of my male friends regarded women as objects of sexual desire, those kinds of feelings were absent in me. But at that time the odd feeling was rather obscure, and I was unsure exactly what it meant.

I was twenty-one years old and in college when I finally figured out what the obscure feeling really was. I still vividly remember that moment. One day I encountered a good looking and extremely stylish lady walking along the platform of Shibuya Station. As I watched her, I wondered if I could ever be that beautiful. But I soon shut down the desire I felt for the woman's graceful demeanor by forcibly reminding myself: "What on earth are you thinking?"

Despite all my efforts at self-denial, the same feeling of desire has subsequently returned to me many times. Since I was not able to hold my anxieties about my secret desires in check, I often searched through psychology manuals at the library where I came across the theory that even in men's psyches there is some sort of "mania" for femininity. I thought that in my case this "mania" was stronger than average and that it was not a good thing and so I needed to do something about it. Since that moment, I lived for about ten years trying to stow away my secret desire to become a woman, instead working hard at being an ordinary man. Yet, despite my efforts, my desire and longing to become a woman was getting stronger and stronger each and every day. These desires continued to construct a feminine self inside me.

There was one woman who I had gotten along with really well since college. She was beautiful and witty and we had a lot in common, and the best thing was she never expected too much masculinity from me—she was my ideal woman. I always thought that she and I could make a life together. When we finally got married, I made up my mind about one thing. I said to myself that I will terminate the woman inside of me and be an ordinary man. Yet at the same time, I thought that it would be a sad thing if I killed the woman in me before I had given her the chance to exist in this world even once. So, in the fall of 1985, at age thirty, I bought a wig, cosmetics, a set of underwear, and a purple women's dress via mail order. Then I put them on thinking this was going to be a one-time thing in my life. At that moment, I discovered in the mirror a woman who looked exactly like my mom had in her youth. That was the moment when the woman who had been growing inside me was born in reality. "Welcome. . . ." sang the woman in the mirror through her rouged lips. I named that self "Junko," and took a picture of myself using the automatic timer of my camera. A few days later, I put all those women's accoutrements away, mumbling to myself "farewell, Junko. . . ."

FIVE YEARS OF STRUGGLE: A TIME OF CROSS-DRESSING AT HOME

Despite my determination, it was extremely difficult for me to shut away the woman in me once I had allowed her to emerge. As a result, for the next five years I repeated my lonely cross-dressing habit once a month at home or in hotel rooms when I traveled. No matter how hard I tried to be an ordinary man, I had never been able to eliminate the existence of Junko. Despite being tortured by my own guilty conscience and self-hatred, I could not stop cross-dressing from time to time. When I recollect those days now, it was perhaps the hardest time in my life. A wooden face with no smile—those pictures that I took by myself during those days really tell of my confusion and agony. Junko never smiled.

Yet in those days, I started to contribute letters and pictures to the correspondence column of an amateur cross-dressing magazine called *Queen* (*Kuiin*). My first contribution as Junko appeared in volume 37, in August 1986. Since then, through the magazine I started to exchange letters with other people who shared the common hobby of cross-dressing. Among many contacts I made, one person with the transgender name Murata Takami, who later on actually became a "woman," influenced me as a cross-dresser the most.

GAINING CONFIDENCE AS A CROSS-DRESSER

In 1990, my life had started to change. Princess Takami enthusiastically recommended that I join a cross-dressing club in Kanda, Tokyo, called Elizabeth Club (Erizabesu Kaikan). Organized by the same association that published the magazine *Queen*, the Elizabeth Club was the largest amateur cross-dressing club in Japan, and Takami, who had made the transition from private to public cross-dresser before me, was already a big star in the club.

I was indecisive. I knew Elizabeth Club was an attractive place for many cross-dressers. It was absolutely an ideal place to be. Yet that was why I was so anxious; I feared that once I stepped into the world, I would never be able to disassociate myself from it. However, by then I was too tired of lying to myself. I could not psychologically continue to struggle alone. In the end, I decided to allow myself to live as the woman Junko.

On 14 August 1990, invited by Princess Takami, I passed through the entrance of the Elizabeth Club for the first time. I was thirty-five years old. I vividly remember that when I went through to the makeup room the lady at the front desk said to me, "Girls with big hips like yours will have good luck in this world."

The Elizabeth Club was the first fee-paying cross-dressing club in Japan and had opened in 1979. When I started going there, it was located on the fourth floor in a five-story building about seven to eight minutes walking distance from Akihabara Station. Inside, there was a shop for cross-dressing goods, lockers to keep them, a makeup room, a lounge space, and a photo studio, and most of the staff members were women. If you signed up for membership, you usually needed to pay about 4,000 yen (US $40) each time you visited.

After becoming a frequent visitor to the club, I became a little uncomfortable about how I looked. Not only Princess Takami, but every senior member of the club looked better than I did, I mean more like a woman than me. I was not sure if I could live up to this high-class cross-dressing society. One day, one woman who was a good confidante at that time stared fixedly at me and said, "Junko, you are a great talent—one among thousands. You can trust me on this, because I've seen many cross-dressed men, and I know who has talent. So just be confident. . . ." Her words really meant a lot to me. In December 1990, six months after I first entered the Elizabeth Club's society, I was awarded the prize for best newcomer (for the division of cross-dressers in their thirties) at the club's Christmas contest. From that moment on, I felt that the complex I had about my looks started to disappear, and a happy Junko came into being. Finally I became a "woman" with a smile.

After the contest, I actively and enthusiastically tried my best to learn many new techniques to become a beautiful cross-dresser. There was a range of criteria judged necessary to be a woman, such as skill in makeup, a sense of fashion, deportment, and the use of vocabulary. So many times I bought magazines about fashion models and tried to be like them by checking myself in the mirror. By repeating those practices, I was able to win a prize as Junko at the national cross-dressing photo contest organized by *Queen*, which was held every summer.

One summer day in 1990, I was awarded the second prize at the national cross-dressing photo contest. I came in first among competitors who were over thirty-five. The next year, at the same contest,

I received the most votes in all divisions and was awarded both the special prize, which was considered an equivalent of the grand prize, and the prize for photo technique. That year's grand prize was awarded to Princess Takami, the very woman who led me to this world. When I stood next to her on the stage of the award ceremony, I could not stop the tears in my eyes. After that, for the next year and a half, she and I regularly appeared on TV being interviewed about the Elizabeth Club and engaged in a lot of social activities as top stars of the club.

It was the summer of 1993 when I finally won a triple crown at the contest—the special prize, the second prize, and the prize for photo technique. Even though I missed out on the grand prize by a very close margin, I was the first competitor in history to win three prizes in one contest. Even today, ten years after my historical achievement, nobody has won the special prize two times in row. The prize is distinctive because to win means that you must receive the most votes from readers of *Queen* magazine. When I won the triple crown I was thirty-eight. Finally I was flowering as a late-blossoming cross-dresser. With my arms overflowing with flowers at the award ceremony, I felt a satisfying sense of fulfillment.

After this I became more confident as a "woman" to some extent, and I gradually started to feel that I wanted to experience the outside world. At the Elizabeth Club we were not allowed to go outside while cross-dressed. We did so only when we went to the club's outside events accompanied by the female staff. You also needed to pay expensive fees to participate in these events. Although I understood that we could secure a free space for cross-dressers only by disassociating ourselves from mainstream society, I felt dissatisfied by the fact that my social status as a "woman" could only be established in a segregated environment. I was literally a bird in a cage.

Without warning in August 1994 I was banned from the Elizabeth Club. On the same day, they also banned Princess Takami.[2] We were banned without being given any explanation. It seems that the club did not appreciate our cross-dressing activities (cross-dressing in public, and on TV) outside the club. In the four years I was a member of the Elizabeth Club, I had learned professional skills for cross-dressing and established my self-esteem as a "woman." Although my relationship with the club broke off in an unfortunate manner, maybe it was a call to move on to something new.

THE CROSS-DRESSING WORLD IN SHINJUKU'S CLUB FAKE LADY

In Autumn 1994, I transferred my playground for cross-dressing to the biggest cross-dressing community in Japan, the Shinjuku entertainment area of Tokyo. To be precise, it was two years earlier that I had first stepped into the cross-dressing world of the area. Guided by Princess Takami, I went to a bar in Shinjuku san-chōme (adjacent to Ni-chōme)[3] called Lisa (named after the mama/owner of the bar, Ayukawa Lisa) where everybody was so convivial and fun, completely different from the Elizabeth Club. In September 1993, I visited one cross-dressers' bar called June (Nakamura Kaoru owned the club), which was located at the center of the cross-dressing town in Shinjuku called Hanazono, in Go-chōme, and there I saw what a full cross-dressing world was like at the time.

The cross-dressing community in Shinjuku has a history of about forty years—dating from the mid-1960s. The community consists of about ten cross-dressers' bars scattered from Kabuki-chō, the biggest red-light district in Japan, to the internationally renowned gay town in Shinjuku ni-chōme. Most of the staff members of those bars are professional cross-dressers' and the guests are usually either amateur cross-dressers or non-cross-dressing men who seek out cross-dressers. Therefore, the bars function as a "place of encounter" for amateur cross-dressers and their would-be lovers.

It is standard within the community that both amateur cross-dressers and their male lovers conduct their relationships according to a hetero-sexual pattern; to be precise, there is a sense of "quasi-heterosexual" love (despite the fact that biologically both partners are men, they are attracted to each other both psychologically and socially as if they were a man and a woman). In this sense, the culture of cross-dressing bars is different from that of the gay town, Shinjuku ni-chōme, where male-identified gay men seek out relations with each other.

Day by day, I was drawn into the cross-dressing world in Shinjuku, and I thought that I would try out a plan of mine there. What I wanted to do was not to hold cross-dressing events produced by profit-oriented cross-dressing clubs, but to have an event organized by our own hands, the hands of cross-dressers themselves. So, in April 1995, along with my sisters from the Elizabeth Club—Akimoto Sayaka, Okano Kana, and Mitsurugi Chiko—I organized a one-night bar-style cross-dressing party called Fake Lady, reserving the whole of the cross-dressers' bar Vivian (owned by Bian Satsuki) in Shinjuku san-chōme. Such a party that was independently organized by cross-dressers themselves was rare at that time, so it was well attended and got a good response. The success of this event has now become legendary among the cross-dressing community in Shinjuku.

In October of the same year, I started the online Club Fake Lady (CFL) via a computer network called EON. The club's slogan was "cross-dressing activities with conviviality, brightness, and fun," and I organized many events such as trips to hot springs, New Year's parties, picnics under the cherry blossoms, summer evening cruises, dinner parties, etc., in order to facilitate communication among cross-dressers. Some of these events were filmed (directed by Ogawa Ruru) and screened as the grand-prix award-winning movie *We Are Transgenders* (1998) at the Seventh Tokyo International Lesbian and Gay Film Festival. The film was also screened abroad.

PRETTY "WOMAN" IN NEON: CROSS-DRESSED HOSTESS IN SHINJUKU'S KABUKI-CHŌ

Since the summer of 1995, after becoming well-known in the cross-dressing world due to the success of the Fake Lady event, I started to hang out at the legendary cross-dressers' bar June (which had moved to Kuyakusho-dōri in Shinjuku's Kabuki-chō in May 1994). Gradually, I began to support Nakayama Maiko, the cross-dressed hostess who worked every Friday at the bar. Soon after, I became an "assistant hostess" on Friday nights (of course it was unpaid work).

Those days, I was teaching at the university every Friday. Right after I finished the fifth-period class (which ended at 5:30), I rushed back to my private office (also my dressing room) and untied my necktie while throwing aside my shirt. Although I didn't have time for dinner, I never forgot to put on perfect makeup, turning myself into a "woman."

Transferring from the Tokyū Tōyoko Line to the JR Yamanote Line, I barely made it to June before 9 p.m. Then I worked all night until the bar closed at 5:00 in the morning.

I was already forty years old when I started to help out at June. However, at the bar I told everyone that I was actually about ten to twelve years younger. Although not everybody believed what I said, most of the male guests seemed to assume that I was somewhere around the age of thirty-two or thirty-three. Thanks to my glamorous look and witty conversation, and my repertoire of over a hundred female songs from the sixties and the seventies, I was treated well by many male guests. To be treated as an attractive "woman" by those guests brought me new confidence in my identity as a "woman."

By spending a night or two a week in Shinjuku, I was coming to be socially recognized as a pretty "woman" in neon lights who had mastered the techniques of cross-dressing and who had fully recognized a sense of community. Those days were times when I felt extremely lively and fulfilled. My time of helping out at June as an assistant hostess from the summer of 1995 to the end of 1998—those years were part of my youth so to speak. I had previously been a man who had known nothing of the world outside his office, but I had opened my eyes to many different aspects of life, including the underground world, and I had learned about ways of thinking and behavior unknown to most men. Later, those experiences were put into words in my academic article, "The Transgender World in Contemporary Japan—Looking at the Cross-Dressing Community in Shinjuku, Tokyo."[4]

NIGHTS WITH MEN—MY BLOSSOMING SEXUALITY

Why don't we put the clock back a little? Since the Elizabeth Club strictly prohibited non–cross-dressing men from entering, there was almost no possibility for sexual relations between cross-dressers and ordinary men to take place there. Having been sexually a late bloomer by nature, I even said to everybody that I was a "man hater." On 25 September 1992, I experienced a man for the first time in my life. I finally lost my virginity at the late age of thirty-seven. I met the man Y through correspondence in the magazine *Queen*. He was a thirty-year-old businessman working at a major company. I made love with him at a hotel in Shinjuku. The reason why I did such a thing all of a sudden was that I had been coldly informed by one female staff member of the Elizabeth Club that "you don't have much sexiness about you because you've never slept with men." I was upset and made love to the guy mostly to soothe my bruised ego and to get rid of the sense of shame.

It was terribly painful that first time. Yet, probably due to the fact that Y was good at it, or that I had talent for it by nature, I felt enough sexual pleasure to enjoy being *ukemi* (sexually passive) in sex with him for a second time. My relationship with Y, having sex once a month, lasted for about two years. Thinking about him again now, I still feel he was a really nice partner to have as my first lover.

After 1994, having realized my sexual desires and gained the freedom to go out on the streets of Shinjuku while cross-dressed, my sexuality was in full bloom. I had no problem at all picking up guys to play with. On every Wednesday night, which was the day when I could set aside time for myself, soon after I started walking slowly down the streets in Shinjuku, I would be picked up and asked out by numerous guys, "Do you have time right now, girl?" "Hey sexy, do you want to have fun with me tonight?" and so on. There were so many requests that I sometimes became sick of turning them down.

This may sound a little too self-confident, yet with my attractive demeanor; five feet, six inches (168 cm) tall with two-and-a-half-inch (6 cm) heels; a glamorous body (unlike ordinary Japanese women's posture—especially given my long legs with lacy tights voluptuously sticking out from teasing short skirts); and my killer fashion sense, no wonder countless men were drawn to me. Tons of guys who tried to pick me up were either men who knew that I was a cross-dressing man, or those who thought that I was a foreign woman (it seemed that I did not look like a Japanese woman at all to them). Not only Japanese guys, but many foreigners enticed me to go out with them. I am not sure why, but somehow I was popular especially among Muslim men from countries such as Iran, Turkey, Pakistan, Morocco, and Azerbaijan. One morning before sunrise, I had a tough time dealing with one Australian guy who enthusiastically begged me to go home with him to meet his mother and marry him.

When I picked guys up on the street who were my type, I always asked them outright, "Is it OK with you that I am biologically male?" in order to avoid creating any fuss. Usually, two-thirds of them were freaked out and ran off right after I told them that, but the rest were, although surprised, open to who I was and said, "Will you still go out with me?" How I spent the night with them pretty much depended on my mood. While sometimes we just ended up having a chat over coffee or dinner, occasionally I also rushed with them by taxi into a love hotel in Kabuki-chō.

Relations with most of those guys were just one- or two-night stands. But I also dated some men for longer, as "sex friends" so to speak; men who could not resist my fine white skin that contrasted so beautifully with my black underwear, my small but hypersensitive nipples, and the shape of my buttocks. Some even said "you really look like a woman on your back!" and my well-controlled anal ability was praised by one playboy who was proudly pursuing the sexual practice of *senningiri* (scoring a thousand partners). I was number 836.

The young owner of a lumber business astutely stimulated all the erogenous zones of my body and made me realize the way to sexually enjoy my body as a "woman." My relation with him lasted almost two years. Another guy, O, who had the hobby of *chōkyō* (bondage and discipline training), exposed my talent for masochism within a nine-month relationship, and I became a full-fledged *mazo-musume* (masochistic princess).

By the time I finally put an end to my season of sexual heat I had dated about sixty men over three years, and the total number of times I had sexual intercourse was 120. Thinking back to those days now, I think I probably had much more "fun" than most women, and I gave the men the same in return. I am thankful to all those guys who helped me be a "woman" through all those lecherous nights. Essentially I felt great pleasure at being treated as a "woman" by those heterosexual men. In other words, I was excited and happy to realize that I could make heterosexual men feel sexually satisfied as a "woman." However, I never felt love—I never fell for any of those guys, not even once. To me, all those heterosexual men were just there to give me sexual pleasure as a "woman," or to function as a sort of mirror to reflect back my status as an "attractive woman."

RESOLUTION TO LIVE AS A "WOMAN"

Due to the fact that part of me, as a "man," had a job as an academic writer, I took charge of the recommended reading section of the magazine *Queen*, and, as "Mitsuhashi Junko," wrote serialized essays and columns for other cross-dressing magazines called *Himawari* (Sunflower) and the commercial cross-dressing magazine *Newhalf Club*.

During those days, I encountered someone who changed my life. In December 1995 I met the gay writer Fushimi Noriaki in a roundtable discussion about designing gender. I was so impressed by his attitude, which encouraged actively speaking out about the social situation of sexual minorities from their own perspectives, that I was determined to speak out myself about my own experience living as both a man and a "woman." My debut as a spokesperson for transgender issues began when the discussion I had participated in was published in a psychology magazine called *Imago* (Fushimi and Mitsuhashi 1996). This discussion addressed the need for transgender to be acknowledged as a legitimate sexual minority category.

After this publication, gradually I started to be contacted by some event organizers and publishers. In February 1998, I was invited as a lecturer for a seminar, "Transcending Gender—Transgression by Cross-dressing," organized by Kinokuniya bookstore in Shinjuku. In May of the same year, I participated in a large-scale cultural forum titled "The 20th Japanese Culture Design Conference 98 in Akita" as a lecturer along with other prominent writers and cultural artists and scholars. And my article "Thinking 'Gender'—from a Perspective of Transgender" was published in the series *Women and Psychology* and received positive responses from various readers. As for activities in universities, I gave lectures as a special speaker in many colleges, beginning with Keiō University in the winter of 1995, then several other schools such as Osaka, Waseda and Chūō universities.

Due to these activities, the world that I lived in quickly changed from nighttime to daytime. I could not be a "woman" at night anymore, but through my daytime activities, I came to know many excellent scholars, writers, and artists and learned a lot from them. Among those people, there was a woman named Matsumoto Yuko, who influenced me significantly, and who I had first met in the autumn of

1997. Having exquisite talent as a writer on the themes of love and gender, alongside her physical beauty and sense of fashion, she was my ideal woman. Furthermore, she was the first female friend who accepted me as her female friend. Her life path, as a woman of wit and beauty, was absolutely a role model for me. I decided that even though I did not have her talent or wit, I would try to live my life as I really am, and I finally put an end to my period as a sex-crazed "lecherous woman."

A RESEARCHER OF TRANSGENDER

It was one night in 1998 that Nakayama Maiko, my senior in cross-dressing society, said to me, "Somebody has to write about and record our cross-dressing culture, otherwise nobody will know that we existed. You are the person who can do this as a legitimate historian." The more I thought about it, I became determined that it was my destiny to record, analyze, and write about the cross-dressing world and the cross-dressers who had lived in this world.

From February 1999, I initiated my sociohistorical research on transgender by establishing the Research Institute for the Social History of Japanese Transgender in Post-War Japan (Sengo Nihon "Toransujendā" Shakai Rekishi Kenkyūkai) in conjunction with Yajima Masami (a professor at Chūō University) and Sugiura Ikuko (a lecturer at Chūō University). One of my papers at the institute was published in a bulletin entitled "Social History of Transgender in Post-War Japan" (2000) by Yajima's research center. The article, "A Sketch of the Historical Transformation of Japanese Transgender in the Postwar Period," was the first article that looked at the general history of Japanese transgender categories and became a pioneering work in the study of social history of Japanese transgender.[5]

In October 1999, I was invited to the 72nd symposium of the Japanese Sociology Association, which was entitled "Questioning the Identity of Mr. Normal," where I presented my paper "The Illusion of 'Mr. Normal' within the 'Cross-dressing Community.'" I was so delighted by the fact that I was able to participate in the conference since it is acknowledged as the most prestigious conference for Japanese sociology academics. At the same time, I realized that Japanese researchers into sexual minorities, especially transgenders, were very behind. I thought that if sociologists would not do it, then I had to do by myself.

On 1 April 2000, I was appointed as a part-time lecturer in sociology in the Faculty of Literature at Chūō University. Even though it was a part-time job, I had never thought that the day would come when I would get a job in the daytime world as a "woman." I was simply delighted. In my lecture series "Studies of Contemporary Society 5," which began in September with the theme "Thinking 'Gender'—from a Transgender Perspective," I taught about the theory of sexual identification, theory of gender image, and the social history of transgender, in front of roughly one hundred students each session. In order to respond to the expectations of Professor Yajima, I put my best efforts into those classes. And, as the first transgender lecturer at a university, I was discussed in the media, including TV and magazines.

That six-month period of teaching was one of the most enjoyable times in my life, which I will never forget, although it was also a time when my personal life was completely preoccupied by the preparation for classes and interviews with the media. Although the university administration seemed unhappy about the fuss that I caused, I was fortunate enough to know that some students really appreciated my lectures since they left comments such as, "Your lecture was the most exciting and productive of all my four years in college." I put some of these great teaching experiences at the university into words in my article "A Half-Year Period as a Transgender University Lecturer—'Practice' for the Social Acceptance of Sexual Minorities."[6]

In addition, in September 2000, I joined the Kansai Association for Sexual Desire Research (Kansai Seiyoku Kenkyūkai). At that time, the representative of the institute was Inoue Shōichi (from the International Research Center for Japanese Studies), who is known for his expertise as a social historian of sexuality. After networking with him on this occasion, I came to participate as an associate researcher in a research project called "The Cultural History of Sexual Desire" run by the research center. (The project started in 2003.) And beginning in May 2001, I started to attend the forum entitled "Feminism and Contemporary Theories: Gender Workshop of Image and Representation" at Ochanomizu

University. Encounters with prominent scholars in those fields on all these occasions significantly awakened my academic instinct and were of great benefit to someone like myself, who was a fledging researcher in the social history of sexuality.

RENUNCIATION OF A FEMALE BODY

In the cross-dressing society in Shinjuku it is not uncommon for cross-dressers to take female hormones in order to transform their male bodies into female. And since 1997 the expanded recognition of gender identity disorder as a mental condition and the need for its medical treatment has resulted in more opportunities for transgenders to transform their bodies. I was privileged enough to become an affiliated staff member for a self-support organization for those suffering from gender identity disorder and was able to obtain a great deal of information about the condition. Looking at my friends who were transforming their biological selves to become what they wanted, at one point I also seriously questioned whether I should do the same.

But I did not take this step for several reasons. First, I wanted to prioritize my relationship with a newborn baby of mine (a boy) who was born in 1994. And second, I felt a considerable distaste for the idea that my proud lifestyle as a cross-dresser should be medicalized as some kind of "disability" in need of cure by an institution. Therefore, even now, I have not done anything to transform my body biologically into that of a woman, except for having my beard permanently removed. As a result, I cannot attain my ideal female body. Yet, I have no regrets. In exchange for giving up that dream, I can keep my precious life with my partner and son as a family together.

TO THE WORLD OF WOMEN—WITH KIMONO FRIENDS

In Japan, at a ceremony for people who come of age at twenty, many women wear *furisode*—that is, a specific kind of kimono with beautiful colors and long hanging sleeves. When I wore *furisode* for the first time, I was thirty-six. Since then, I have gotten seriously involved in this traditional Japanese ethnic dress. Almost 90 percent of contemporary Japanese women cannot even dress in kimono unassisted. Neither could I. Every time I wanted to wear one, I had to go to a beauty parlor and pay a fee to get assistance with it.

In November 1999 I was invited by Kotani Mari, who is a well-known critic of science fiction and fantasy, to a course about how to dress in kimono. From this six-month intensive course (in a format of one teacher for every two students), I mastered the skills of how to dress in kimono properly. More importantly, I learned how to dress in kimono on my own and wear one more often. I was so fascinated by the kimono culture that I really got into it. In contemporary Japanese society, women disproportionately dominate kimono culture and customs. Through my interest in kimono, I made so many female friends. Of course, not every one of them accepted me as a cross-dresser who loved kimono. Yet many of them kindly accepted me for the way I was and even gave me some friendly advice and comments about how to wear kimono saying, "Junko, you look really pretty in that kimono," "your way of putting on an *obi* (a belt for kimono) is beautiful, can you tell me how to do mine like yours?"

Those moments brought joy and peace to my heart. Since that autumn day at the age of twenty-one when I realized there was a part of me, a woman, inside my heart, I always wanted to be a woman, wanted to reach that place. I always wanted to be a woman among women. I feel that I finally made the dream come true.

CONCLUSION

At present, I am spending a great deal of time and effort studying the social history of transgender phenomena in Japan. The more I study, the stronger the sense I get that I am a member of a Japanese transgender community whose history dates back more than two thousand years. At the same time, I continue giving lectures and publishing in order to raise Japanese society's awareness of the rights of sexual minorities, especially transgender people.

In December 2003, I was invited to an international symposium, "New Century for Gender," organized by the Center for the Study of Sexualities at Taiwan Central University. There I could gain more international perspectives on my study. Although right now I am not financially well off, I think I need to continue my current activities—something only I can do. When I look at my life path objectively, it can be said that it is the life of a transgender pioneer who initiated the study of Japanese transgender as a researcher.

To me my life has seemed like a dream—a path toward becoming a "woman"; despite many trials, errors, and detours I have also been kindly supported by many people. Through all these experiences, I also realized that there are indeed some social obstacles that transgenders can never surmount. Thinking about my life, it's interesting to know that I have really made it this far. I turned fifty in 2005. I have no idea how long I can go on living from now or how many further obstacles I will encounter. Yet, I am willing to continue walking my obscure but long life path with pride as a transgender in Japan, a nation that contains the story of a transgender hero in its founding myth.[7]

NOTES

1. *Gozan no okuribi* takes place during August as part of the *o-bon* festival, a celebration of ancestors. During this time the spirits of the deceased are thought to visit their living relatives. On 16 August, fires in the shape of Chinese characters (*kanji*) are lit on five separate mountaintops surrounding Kyoto to guide the spirits back to heaven.

2. At present, after altering most of her body to become a woman, she runs a bar in Shinjuku Kabuki-chō called Takami.

3. Ni-chōme is Tokyo's best known gay area. See chapter 15, "True Tales from Ni-chōme," in this volume for a description of the kind of bars to be found there.

4. Originally published in the *Journal of the Annual Report of the Institute of Social Science*, Chūō University, vol. 7, June 2003; reprinted in Yajima (2006).

5. These and other essays by Mitsuhashi have subsequently been gathered together and published in Yajima (2006).

6. Mitsuhashi (2001).

7. This is a reference to the legendary Prince Yamatotakeru, acclaimed for expanding the territory of the Yamato Japanese into the northern part of the main island of Honshu, which he is supposed to have achieved while dressed in women's clothes he had received from his aunt, the priestess of the Ise Shrine.

21

MY LIFE AS A HUSTLER

Akira the Hustler (Hasurā Akira)

I was feeling a bit down as I got into the bath one day, thinking that I only got into this profession because I want to be loved by a lot of people. I am more lonely than even I realize sometimes. But in fact, before it's a question of love or lust, what motivates me is being really needed by someone.

When I was a child, my father was always busy, unable to be at home much. My poor, lonely mother would give me the supermarket advertisements and have me draw pictures on the backs, which were blank. When I'd produce one for her she always seemed so genuinely happy.

Now I make my customers come. The pleasure I derive from the joy on their faces is not much different from the joy I used to get drawing for my mother. My mother also taught me to respect the value of human touch. I could thank her endlessly for how much she's enriched my life, but in fact, I can't say that thanks to her—I'm a hooker with a heart of gold. And this makes me very sad.

Excerpts reproduced with permission from Hasurā Akira, *Baita nikki (A [Male] Whore Diary)* (Tokyo: Isshi Press, 2000). Translated by David d'Heilly.

Being needed, making customers happy, our sex has value. But so does every sexual act.

A seventy-year-old man came to see me. He asked me to lingeringly kiss the nape of his neck. He said that's all he wanted. I asked why. He said that when he was still a teenager, when Japan was embroiled in the Pacific War, all of his friends kept being recruited. He too was up for enlistment. And the one thing that kept him going during the grueling training that they went through to prepare for battle was the kindness of one of his superiors, a boy seven years older than he who had looked after him. Then, one day, this older boy asked him if he could come to his room. When he arrived the older boy said, "Tomorrow I'm being sent to the front. I may never return. I have one last thing to ask of you." He wanted to spend the night together. He hadn't wanted sex (in a narrow sense) as one might imagine. The boy had simply held him in his arms all night long, caressing his neck with his lips. The older boy never did return. And ever since, this old man has kept the memory of this night, and the warmth and touch of this boy's lips on his neck. Even as he grew older, even through his marriage, he had kept coming to boys like me, to relive this memory.

Old man, were my lips warm like his?

In 1997 I attended the International Conference on Prostitution in Los Angeles. I went with a couple of female sex-worker colleagues of mine. Even though it was nominally oriented around Europeans and Americans, there were a lot of representatives there from Asia, too. It was quite the spectacle. So many people in my industry all under one roof! The shock was not unlike the first time I went to a gay nightclub event. I felt liberated.

The thing that I remember most, though, was something that happened at the male sex-worker meeting, as we fielded questions from the audience. One scholar said, "Listening to you talk, it's as though you consider yourselves to be selling more than sex . . . almost as though you were counselors, or healers to your clients. How many among you share this view?" There were representatives from the United States, Cuba, Brazil, South Africa, Spain, Germany, as well as me from Japan. All of us raised our hands.

I want to be involved in creating a world with a safe working environment for sex workers. I want to contribute to a sex industry that people can enjoy without trepidation. I want to feel fulfilled in my job. And I feel that I met a lot of people committed to similar goals at that conference.

There are those continuing this fight while I sleep. We are connected. This is how history is made.

The other day I was just too tired, and I fell asleep in front of a client. I must have slept about an hour. I awoke suddenly and apologized, but my client just looked at me with sweetness in his eyes. "You really do trust me, don't you?" he said. "I guess I do," I thought as I hurried off home. When I got there, I had a bath, then while we were watching TV, my boyfriend fell asleep on my lap. He farted. He had the most angelic look on his face, and I realized the kind of contentment my client must have enjoyed.

APPENDIX

TIMELINE OF QUEER JAPAN[1]

1948   ●   Press reports about a community of transgender male prostitutes working in Tokyo's Ueno Park. Scandal magazines
report on Tokyo's emerging sexual subcultures.

        ●   Among the first modern gay bars, the Brunswick, opens in
the Ginza area of Tokyo.

1949   ●   Sumi Tatsuya publishes the novel *Grove of Male Prostitutes*
about Ueno Park's transgender scene.

        ●   Author Mishima Yukio publishes his pioneering novel about
homosexuality, *Confessions of a Mask.*

1950   ●   *Amatoria*, a popular magazine featuring stories about "perverse desire" is published.

        ●   Tokyo's Hibiya Park emerges as a venue for assignations
between Japanese gay men and members of the U.S. Occupation forces, as discussed in Yukio Mishima's novel *Forbidden Colors.*

        ●   Alfred Kinsey's *Sexual Behavior in the Human Male* is trans-
lated into Japanese and much discussed in the media.

        ●   Yanagi, a bar for male cross-dressers, opens in Tokyo.

1951   ●   Japan's first sex reassignment surgery is carried out on entertainer Nagai Akiko.

- Miwa Akihiro, who is to become Japan's most famous transgender entertainer, starts work at Tokyo's Brunswick gay bar.

1952
- Japan's first gay organization Adonis Kai is founded and begins to publish the privately circulated *Adonis* magazine (until 1962).

1953
- The magazine *Fūzoku zōshi* prints regular letters from readers in its "Sodomia" and "Lesbos" columns.

1954
- The magazine *Fūzoku kagaku* founds FKK, a social group for gay men.
- Successful tour by women's pro-wrestling star Mildred Burke sparks interest in Japan. The women's pro-wrestling circuit supports a small lesbian subculture.

1955
- *Engeki hyōron* (Theatrical review), a privately circulated magazine for male cross-dressers, begins publication.

1956
- The Hollywood movie *Tea and Sympathy* popularizes the term "sister boys" for gay men.

1957
- "Gay boy" Maruyama (later known as Miwa) Akihiro has a hit with his single "Meke meke."
- Sex educator Ōta Tenrei publishes *The Third Sex*, a positive account of male homosexuality written with the cooperation of gay men.

1958
- The popular press begins to talk of a "gay boom" in relation to the sudden popularity of transgender performers.
- Androgynous French actress Jean Seberg, star of *Saint Joan*, becomes an idol figure for Japanese "gay boys."

1959
- Japan's 1958 Anti-Prostitution Law begins to take effect and numerous gay bars begin to spring up in recently vacated red-light districts such as Tokyo's Shinjuku ni-chōme, now home to the largest concentration of gay bars in the world.
- Privately circulated homophile magazine *Dōkō* (Same preference) begins publication in Osaka.

1960

1961
- Alessandro Blasetti's movie *Europe by Night*, featuring French transsexual star Coccinelle, is a big hit.

1962
- Singer Carrousel Maki has her testicles removed as the first step toward sex reassignment.

1963 • French transsexual cabaret Le Carrousel appears at Tokyo nightclub Golden Akasaka, sparking a "blue boy boom" in the media.
 • Fuki Kurabu begins to circulate an intermittent newsletter for male cross-dressers.
1964 • Privately circulated homophile magazine *Bara* (Rose) begins publication.
 • The success of Le Carrousel tour leads to the opening of show bars in cities all over Japan featuring male-to-female transgender entertainers.
 • A few clubs featuring "dandy beauties" (female-to-male cross-dressers) as "hosts" appear in Tokyo.
1965 • Touring members of Le Carrousel die in plane crash.
 • Surgeon who had removed the sex organs of several male prostitutes is prosecuted under Japan's Eugenic Protection Law, leading to the "Blue Boy Trial."
1966
1967 • Interest in clubs featuring "male-dressing" women reaches a peak.
 • *Josō kōyū roku* (Cross-dressing friendship record) magazine is privately distributed via a Tokyo cross-dressers' bar (until 1974).
1968 • Inagaki Taruho publishes *Shōnen'ai no bigaku* (The aesthetics of boy love).
 • Fukusawa Kinji's movie *Black Lizard*, starring Miwa Akihiro as the femme fatale, is a great success.
 • Popular transgender performer Miwa Akihiro's autobiography becomes a best seller.
 • The books *Lesbian Technique* and *Homo Technique* are published and sell well despite being written by a straight man, Akiyami Masami.
1969 • Matsumoto Toshio's movie *Funeral Parade of Roses* is an underground hit and launches the career of gay boy Peter.
 • A Tokyo court rules that Japan's Eugenic Protection Law forbids unnecessary surgery resulting in infertility, making sex-reassignment surgery illegal.
1970 • Novelist Mishima Yukio commits suicide.

1971 • First lesbian social group Wakakusa no Kai (Young grass club) founded; continues for fifteen years.

• Openly gay candidate Tōgō Ken runs for a seat in Japan's House of Councilors—the first of many attempts, none successful.

• *Barazoku*, Japan's first commercial gay magazine, is published (folded in 2004).

1972 • Singer Carrousel Maki undergoes full sex-reassignment surgery in Morocco.

• *Nuida otokotachi* (Stripped guys), Japan's first photo collection of naked men, is published.

1973 • The bar Kikōshi (Young nobleman) is opened in Tokyo's Roppongi entertainment district and is staffed by *onabe* or "butch," male-dressing women.

• Gay magazine *Adonis Boy*, later *Adon*, is published by Minami Teishirō (until 1996).

1974 • Gay magazine *Sabu* published (until 2001).
1975
1976 • *Subarashii onnatachi* (Wonderful women) lesbian zine, published; folds after one issue.

• A counseling room for gay youth is set up in Shinjuku ni-chōme, sponsored by *Barazoku* magazine.

1977 • Minami Teishirō publishes *MLMW* (My Life My Way), Japan's first gay lifestyle magazine; lasts only one year.

• Small gay rights groups are founded in Tokyo and Osaka, including Front Runners and Platonika.

• Gay activist magazine *Platonika* published; lasts for four issues.

1978 • Osugi and Peeko, two openly gay twins, appear regularly on a TBS radio program about fashion and the arts. They go on to have careers in television as popular chat-show guests and panel members.

• Ōtsuka Takashi appears as an openly gay "talent" on the controversial radio talk show *The Snakeman Show* and goes on to found the gay community group Our Work Community.

• Lesbian zines *Za daiku* (The dyke) and *Hikari guruma* (Shining wheel) are published.

- *June*, a magazine featuring comics and other representations of love among beautiful boys for girl readers, is first published.
1979 • Activist magazine *GAY* founded; runs for eight issues.
- Japan Gay Center is founded, publishes newsletter.
- Elizabeth Club, a club for male cross-dressers, opens in Tokyo.
1980 • *Queen*, Japan's first commercial magazine for male cross-dressers, is published (still in print).
- Activist Tōgō Ken publishes the magazine *Za gei* (The gay).
- The press publish rumors that popular singer Sagara Naomi is a lesbian.
- *Allan*, a magazine focused on depictions of beautiful boys, often in love with each other, is published (through 1984). From 1982 to 1984 it runs *Yuri tsūshin* (Lily communication), a personals column for girls and young women seeking romantic relationships with other young women.
1981 • Lesbian magazine *Eve & Eve* is published by Wakakusa no Kai but folds after two issues.
- "Gay boy" Betty introduces a new term for male-to-female transgenders in the entertainment business—*nyūhāfu* (newhalf).
- "Roppongi girl" Matsubara Rumiko wins a beauty competition, is revealed to be a newhalf and becomes an overnight sensation.
1982 • Gay magazine *Samson* published.
- The newsletter *Rezubian tsūshin* (Lesbian communication) commences publication.
- Shinjuku gay bar Matsuri begins holding women-only parties on Monday nights.
1983 • Lesbian disco event "Space Dyke" held in Tokyo
1984 • A branch of the International Lesbian and Gay Association (ILGA) is founded in Japan by Minami Teishirō.
1985 • Ribonne and Mars Bar, Japan's first (non-cross-dressing) lesbian bars, open in Shinjuku.
- First of many "lesbian weekends" is held near Tokyo; attracts sixty participants.

1986 • OCCUR, or the Japan Association for the Lesbian and Gay Movement, is founded in Tokyo.

• Japanese delegation attends the Eighth International Lesbian Information Service (ILIS) Conference in Geneva and helps found the Asian Lesbian Network.

• Lumiere gay bookstore opens in Shinjuku.

• Japan's first candlelight AIDS vigil is held in Shinjuku.

1987 • The first mainstream book by and about lesbians, *Onna wo aisuru onnatachi no monogatari* (Stories of women who love women) is released.

• Lesbian support group Regumi Studio Tokyo is founded, publishes newsletter.

• *Himawari* (Sunflower), a commercial magazine for cross-dressing men, starts publication.

• Himiko, a women-only party, is held monthly at the gay bar New Sazae; about eighty women attend.

1988 • ILGA Japan starts the first AIDS support group.

• Popular lunch-time TV show *It's OK to Laugh* features a regular transgender entertainer segment, popularizing the term "Mr. Lady."

1989 • A branch of ILGA Japan is founded in Sapporo, the capital of Hokkaido, Japan's northern island.

• Kansai yancha Lesbian Power (later renamed Open lesbian power) begins activities at Kyoto's women's festival.

1990 • Japanese delegates attend first Asian Lesbian Network meeting in Thailand.

• EON, a computer bulletin-board system for transgender men, is founded.

• Alis, a "women's disco," runs for two years in Shinjuku, Tokyo.

1991 • The publication of an article entitled "Gay Renaissance" in the women's magazine *CREA* sparks the "gay boom" in which gay people, fashion, and lifestyle are taken up by the mainstream media.

• The first gay and lesbian nights are held separately at popular Tokyo disco Gold.

- Gay rights group OCCUR launches a successful campaign to remove references to sexual perversion from dictionary definitions of homosexuality.
- Lesbians in OCCUR (LIO) open counseling line.
- Fushimi Noriaki publishes *Private Gay Life*, an important landmark in Japanese gay studies.

1992
- Second Asian Lesbian Network gathering is held in Japan; 170 participate.
- First Tokyo International Lesbian and Gay Film Festival attracts an audience of one thousand.
- Kakefuda Hiroko publishes her pioneering book *On Being Lesbian*.
- Ōtsuka Takashi, Ogura Tō, and Fushimi Noriaki edit a gay edition of the popular magazine *Takarajima*.
- OCCUR publishes its *Gay Report* on gay life in Japan.
- Lesbian and bisexual women's magazine *Labrys* begins publication, developing a readership of more than 1,500.
- Osaka University gay group Puapua participates in the university festival.

1993
- Japanese television airs in primetime, *Class Reunion*, the first soap drama centered on gay characters.
- Hands on Hands lesbian and gay information center opens in Shinjuku.
- Second Tokyo International Lesbian and Gay Film Festival attracts an audience of two thousand.
- Osaka-based coalition Gay Front Kansai begins activities.
- Tokyo Gay Deaf Community is founded.
- Hashiguchi Ryōsuke's film about a male hustler, *A Touch of Fever*, is an underground hit.

1994
- Tokyo hosts the first Lesbian and Gay Parade. It attracts one thousand participants.
- Third Tokyo International Lesbian and Gay Film Festival attracts an audience of 2,300.
- Gay magazine *Badi* is published.
- OCCUR succeeds in its legal case against the Tokyo metropolitan government, which had forbidden them access to public youth facilities. The government appeals the ruling.

- Gay Friends for AIDS support group is founded.
- Torai Masae begins publishing *FTM Nippon*, a newsletter for FtM transsexuals.
- Japanese gay organizations are represented at the Tenth International AIDS Congress in Yokohama.
- International Bians United lesbian group founded; holds kiss-ins and other media events in central Tokyo.
- Kyoto University gay groups participate in the university's festival.

1995
- OCCUR succeeds in having homosexuality declassified as a category of mental illness by the Japanese Society of Psychiatry and Neurology.
- The gay magazine *G-Men* is published.
- *Newhalf Club*, a commercial magazine for and about transgender men, starts publication.
- Project P, a sexuality rights group, is founded in Kyoto.
- Gay Front Kansai establishes a group for the disabled.
- Fourth Tokyo International Lesbian and Gay Film Festival attracts an audience of 2,400.
- OCCUR sponsors a queer theory workshop at Tokyo University.
- Community center for lesbian and bisexual women opens in Nagano.
- *Phryné*, the first commercial magazine for women who love women is published but folds after two issues.
- Second Lesbian and Gay Parade in Tokyo attracts 2,500.
- Gay director Hashiguchi Ryōsuke's movie *Like Grains of Sand* is an underground hit.
- Lesbian singer Sasano Michiru publishes her book, *Coming OUT*.
- Osaka's Club Town hosts regular *Rezubian naito* (Lesbian night) events.

1996
- First Sapporo Rainbow March attracts 250 participants.
- Third Lesbian and Gay Parade held in Tokyo is fractured by infighting among different interest groups; attracts 1,250.
- Saitama Medical University applies for a license to begin performing sex-reassignment surgery.

- FtM transsexual Torai Masae publishes a book about his transformation.
- Hijra Nippon, a support group for intersex and transsexual people, is founded.
- Activist Itō Satoru's gay rights group Sukotan Project sponsors school visits to talk about homosexuality and attracts positive notice in the press.
- Men's Net Japan, the popular Internet site, is opened.
- Fifth Tokyo International Lesbian and Gay Film Festival attracts 3,700; also screens in Osaka (700) and Kyoto (1,000).
- *Anise*, a new commercial magazine for women who love women, is published.
- *Queer Studies 96*—a volume of queer theory—is published.

1997
- OCCUR's win in a court case against the Tokyo metropolitan government seeking equal access to public meeting facilities is upheld by court of appeal.
- Sixth Tokyo International Lesbian and Gay Film Festival attracts 4,300; also screens in Osaka and Kyoto.
- Fourth Lesbian and Gay Parade in Tokyo attracts only seventy participants because of previous year's infighting.
- Second Sapporo Rainbow March attracts 250.
- Tokyo holds its first Dyke March with 213 women attending.
- OCCUR edits a lesbian and gay studies edition of influential journal *Gendai shisō* (Contemporary thought).
- Japanese Society of Psychiatry and Neurology publishes its guidelines for sex-change surgery.
- Itō Satoru's gay rights organization Sukotan Projects opens a website.
- Women-only club event Goldfinger opens in Tokyo.

1998
- Japanese hospitals recommence sex-reassignment surgery.
- Seventh Tokyo International Lesbian and Gay Film Festival attracts eight thousand.
- Third Sapporo Rainbow March is held.
- VOICE AIDS event is held in Tokyo.

1999
- Deregulation of the telecommunications industry leads to cheaper Internet access and an explosion of lesbian, gay, and transgender websites.

- Eighth Tokyo International Lesbian and Gay Film Festival attracts six thousand.
- Fourth Sapporo Rainbow March attracts five hundred.
- Gay lifestyle magazine *Fabulous* is launched by Ogura Tō; folds after four issues.
- *Queer Japan*, gay lifestyle and identity journal, is launched; folds after five issues.
- True Travel, an agency specializing in gay clients, opens.
- First national drag queen event, Diva Japan, is held in Osaka.
- Ikeda Kumiko's book *A Teacher's Lesbian Declaration* becomes a hot media topic.

2000
- Tokyo Lesbian and Gay Parade relaunched with two thousand people participating.
- A group of gay bar owners in Shinjuku ni-chōme inaugurates the first Rainbow Festival.
- Transsexual author Asano Chiyo wins prestigious Akutagawa prize.
- SWITCH 2000 AIDS community event is held in Osaka.
- Murder of a gay man in a Tokyo park attracts widespread attention.
- PRIDE 2000 holds a lesbian and gay day at Tokyo Disneyland.
- Homosexuals are included in a Tokyo metropolitan government whitepaper on human rights.
- Ninth Tokyo International Lesbian and Gay Film Festival attracts 7,200.

2001
- Tokyo Lesbian and Gay Parade attracts approximately three thousand.
- Transsexual singer Carrousel Maki is arrested on a drugs charge and detained in a male prison.
- SWITCH 2001 AIDS event is held in Osaka.
- Gay Revolution event is held in Nagoya.
- OCCUR and other organizations petition the Law Minister to recognize sexual orientation in cases of discrimination.
- Tenth Tokyo International Lesbian and Gay Film Festival is held.

- Popular website All about Japan publishes information for and about gay and lesbian Japanese.
- Fifth Sapporo Rainbow March is held.

2002
- Movie *Hush!* directed by Hashiguchi Ryōsuke was released.
- Ishikawa Taiga's book *Boku no kareshi wa doko ni iru?* (Where is my boyfriend?) is released by mainstream publisher Kodansha.
- Speedboat racer Ando Hiromasa reenters competition as a man after sex-reassignment surgery.
- Launch of lesbian sex magazine *Carmilla*.

2003
- Law enabling some postoperative people with gender identity disorder to change sex on official documents enacted.
- Kamikawa Aya becomes the first transsexual to be elected to public office in Japan, winning a seat on a local Tokyo council.
- Miyakonoji in Miyagi Prefecture is the first city in Japan to pass an ordinance forbidding discrimination on the grounds of "sexual orientation" as well as gender.

2004
- The most long-lived commercial gay magazine *Barazoku* (with Daini shobō) ceased publication due to financial difficulty.
- Carrousel Maki officially changed her gender in the record of family register, applying the Exceptional Treatment Act of People with GID passed in 2003.

2005
- The thrice-revived Tokyo Lesbian and Gay Parade was held in August.
- Otsuji Kanako, a member of the prefectural assembly of Osaka, publicly announced that she was a lesbian on the day of the Tokyo Lesbian and Gay Parade, also the release date of her book *Kamingu auto: jibun rashisa wo mitsukeru tabi* (Coming out: a journey in search of my own selfhood).
- *QJr* (Queer Japan returns), edited by Fushimi Noriaki, started publication with Potto shuppan.
- *Carmilla* ceased publication with its final volume 10 at the end of the year.

NOTE

1. This timeline was developed with reference to Kuia Sutadiizu Henshū Iin Kai (1996: 18–35); Fushimi (2002: 302–16); Kadoya (2005: 105–13); and *Aniisu* (2001: 28–78).

BIBLIOGRAPHY

Akatsu Masanobu. (1927). *Seiten* (Bible of sex). Tokyo: Seibundō.

Akita Masami. (2005). *Sei no ryōki modan* (Modern curiosity-seeking about sex). Tokyo: Seikyūsha.

Akiyama Masami. (1970). *Hentaigaku nyūmon* (Introduction to queer studies). Tokyo: Dai ni shobō.

Aoki, Darren. (2006). "Itō Bungaku and the Solidarity of the Rose Tribes [*Barazoku*]: Stirrings of *Homo* Solidarity in Early 1970s Japan." *Intersections*, issue 12. Online: <http://wwwsshe.murdoch.edu.au/intersections/issue12_contents.html>.

Aniisu (Anise). (2001). "Komyuniti no rekishi 1971–2001: nenpyō to intabyū de furikaeru" (Community history 1971–2001: reflecting back with timelines and interviews), *Aniisu* (Summer): 28–78.

Barazoku (Rose tribe). (1976). "Yurizoku no heya" (Lily tribe's room). *Barazoku* 46 (November): 66–70.

Bessatsu takarajima. (1994). *Gei no gakuen tengoku* (Gay campus heaven). Tokyo: Takarajimasha.

———. No. 159. (1992). *Gei no okurimono* (Gay presents). Tokyo: JICC shuppankyoku.

———. No. 146. (1991). *Hentai-san ga iku* (There goes Mr./Ms. Queer). Tokyo: JICC shuppankyoku.

———. No. 64. (1987). *Onna wo ai suru onnatachi no monogatari* (Stories of women who love women). Tokyo: JICC Shuppankyoku.

Bessatsu takarajima EX. (1993). *Gei no omochabako* (Gay toy box). Tokyo: JICC shuppankyoku.

Bessatsu taiyō, ed. (1997). *Hakkinbon* (Banned books). Tokyo: Heibonsha.

Boston Women's Health Book Collective. (1974a). *Onna no karada: sei to ai no shinjitsu* (Women's bodies: the truth about sex and love). Trans. Akiyama Yōko, Kuwahara Kazuyo, and Yamada Mitsuko. Tokyo: Gōdō shuppan.

———. (1974b). "Rezu to yobarete" (They call us lez), pt. 1. Trans. Amano Michimi. *Onna erosu* (Woman eros) no. 2 (April): 86–104.

———. (1974c). "Rezu to yobarete" (They call us lez), pt. 2. Trans. Amano Michimi. *Onna erosu* (Woman eros) no. 3 (September): 80–92.

———. (1973). *Our Bodies, Ourselves: A Book by and for Women.* New York: Simon and Schuster.

Califia, Pat. (1993) [1980]. *Safisutori: Resubian sekushariti no tebiki* (Sapphistry: the book of lesbian sexuality). Trans. Hara Minako. Tokyo: Taiyōsha.

Chalmers, Sharon. (2002). *Emerging Lesbian Voices from Japan.* London: RoutledgeCurzon.

Curran, Beverley, and James Welker. (2005). "From *The Well of Loneliness* to the *akarui rezubian.*" In *Genders, Transgenders, and Sexualities in Japan*, edited by Mark McLelland and Romit Dasgupta. London: Routledge, 65–80.

Dower, John. (2000). *Embracing Defeat: Japan in the Wake of WWII.* New York: W. W. Norton.

Duberman, Martin, Martha Vicinus, and George Chauncey, eds. (1991). *Hidden from History: Reclaiming the Gay and Lesbian Past.* London: Penguin.

Faderman, Lillian. (1996) [1991]. *Resubian no rekishi* (*Odd girls and twilight lovers: a history of lesbian life in twentieth-century America*). Trans. Tomioka Akemi and Hara Minako. Tokyo: Chikuma Shobō.

Fujin minshu kurabu. (2005). "Femin to wa" (Femin is . . .). *Femin.* Online: <http://www.jca.apc.org/femin/femin/femintoha.htm>.

Fukunaga Taeko. (1982). *Rezubian: mō hitotsu no ai no katachi* (Lesbian: another shape of love). Tokyo: Tairiku shobō.

Fukushima Jūrō. (1987). *Zasshi de miru sengoshi* (Postwar history as seen through magazines). Tokyo: Ōtsuki shoten.

Furukawa Makoto. (1994). "The Changing Nature of Sexuality: Three Codes Framing Homosexuality in Modern Japan." Trans. Angus Lockyer. *U.S.-Japan Women's Journal English Supplement*, no. 7, 98–127.

Fushimi Noriaki. (2003). *Hentai (kuia) nyūmon* (An introduction to *hentai* [queer]). Tokyo: Chikuma bunko.

———. (2002). *Gei to iu "keiken"* (The "experience" called *gei*). Tokyo: Potto shuppan.

———. (1998) [1991]. *Puraibē to gei raifu* (Private gay life). Tokyo: Gakuyō bunko.

Fushimi Noriaki and Mitsuhashi Junko. (1996). "Jendā wo dezain suru kuia dai sensō" (The great queer gender design war). *Imago* 7, no. 2 (February): 152–67.

Fushimi Noriaki, Oikawa Kenji, Noguchi Katsuzō, Matsuzawa Kureichi, Kurokawa Noboyuki, and Yamanaka Toshio. (2000). *"Okama" wa sabetsu ka: Shūkan kinyōbi no "sabetsu hyōgen" jiken* (Is *"okama"* discriminatory?: The case of a "discriminatory expression" in *Shūkan kinyōbi*). Tokyo: Potto shuppan.

Frühstrück, Sabine. (2003). *Colonizing Sex: Sexology and Social Control in Modern Japan*. Berkeley: University of California Press.

Gekkō (Luna). (1985). "Ribonnu no yoru: kensō no rezubian bā" (Evening at Ribonne: a lively lesbian bar). *Gekkō* 8 (October): 19–21.

Gottlieb, Nanette. (2006). "Review of *Okama wa sabetsu ka?*" *Intersections*, issue 12. Online: <http://wwwsshe.murdoch.edu. au/intersections/issue12/gotlieb_review.html>.

Hentai shiryō (Perverse documents). (1928). "Lesbiche Liebe" (Lesbian love). *Hentai shiryō* 3, no. 1 (January): 73.

Hirano Hiroaki. (2001). "Dare ga dare wo hajiru no ka" (Who should be ashamed of whom?). *Shūkan kinyōbi* no. 387 (9 November): 49–51.

Hirosawa Yumi. (1987a). "Dandi na Roshia bungakusha Yuasa Yoshiko hōmonki" (A visit with Yuasa Yoshiko, a dandy scholar of Russian literature). *Bessatsu takarajima* no. 64, *Onna wo ai suru onnatachi no monogatari*. Tokyo: JICC shuppankyoku, 67–73.

———. (1987b). "Nihon hatsu no rezubian sākuru—'Wakakusa no Kai' sono jūgonen no rekishi to genzai" ("Wakakusa no Kai": the first fifteen years of Japan's original lesbian organization). *Bessatsu takarajima* no. 64, *Onna wo ai suru onnatachi no monogatari*. Tokyo: JICC shuppankyoku, 111–19.

———. (1986). "Sekai rezubian kaigi ni sanka shite" (Attending a world lesbian meeting). *Fujin kōron* 71, no. 7, (June): 420–27.

Hiruma Yukiko. (2003). "Kindai Nihon ni okeru josei dōseiai no 'hakken'" (The "discovery" of female homosexuality in modern Japan). *Kaihō shakaigaku kenkyū* 17: 9–32.

Hisada Megumi. (1987). "Genki jirushi no rezubian 'Regumi no Gomame' tōjō!" (They've got their happy faces on: the birth of "Regumi no Gomame"). In *Bessatsu takarajima* no. 64, *Onna wo ai suru onnatachi no monogatari*. Tokyo: JICC shuppankyoku, 120–29.

Honda Masako. (1991). "'S'—taainaku, shikamo kongentekina ai no katachi" (The shape of essential yet frivolous love). *Imago* 2, no. 8 (August): 68–73.

Hyakuman nin no yoru. (1963). "Sengo no ryūkōgo" (Popular postwar terms). February, 146–51.

Ihara Saikaku. (1990) [1687]. *The Great Mirror of Male Love*. Trans. Paul Gordon Schalow. Stanford, CA: Stanford University Press.

Iida, Keisuke. (2004). "Human Rights and Sexual Abuse: The Impact of International Human Rights Law on Japan." *Human Rights Quarterly* 26: 428–53.

Ikeda Kumiko. (1999). *Sensei no rezubian sengen: Tsunagaru tame no kamu auto* (A teacher's lesbian declaration: coming out to connect). Kyoto: Kamogawa shuppan.

Ishida Hitoshi. (2006). "Interactive Practices in Shinjuku Ni-chōme's Homosexual Bars." *Intersections*, issue 12. Online: <http://wwwsshe.murdoch.edu.au/intersections/issue12/ishida1.html>.

Ishida Hitoshi, Mark McLelland, and Takanori Murakami. (2005). "The Origins of 'Queer Studies' in Postwar Japan." In *Genders, Transgenders, and Sexualities in Japan*, edited by Mark McLelland and Romit Dasgupta. London: Routledge, 33–48.

Itō Satoru and Yanase, Ryūta. (2000). *Coming Out in Japan*. Trans. Francis Conlan. Melbourne: Trans Pacific Press.

Iwabuchi Hiroko. (1995). "Rezubianizumu no yuragi: Miyamoto Yuriko no 'Ippon no hana.'" (The swaying of lesbianism: Miyamoto Yuriko's 'Ippon no hana'). In *Feminizumu hihyō e no shōtai: kindai josei bungaku wo yomu* (An invitation to feminist criticism: reading modern women's literature), edited by Iwabuchi Hiroko, Kitada Sachie, and Kōra Rumiko. Tokyo: Gakugei shorin, 149–74.

Izumo Marou. (1993). *Manaita no ue no koi* (Love upon the chopping board). Tokyo: Takarajimasha.

Izumo Marou, and Claire Maree. (2000). *Love upon the Chopping Board*. North Melbourne, Australia: Spinifex.

Izumo Marou, Hara Minako, Tsuzura Yoshiko, and Ochiya Kumiko. (1997). "Nihon no rezubian mūvumento" (The Japanese lesbian movement). *Gendai shisō* 25, no. 6 (May): 58–83.

Kabiya Kazuhiko. (1955). "Gei bā no seitai" (Lifestyles in the gay bars). *Amatoria* (July): 38–46.

Kadoya Manabu. (2005). "GAY chronology." In *Queer Japan returns*, vol. 0. Tokyo: Potto shuppan, 105–13.

Kakefuda Hiroko. (1992). *"Rezubian" de aru to iu koto* (On being "lesbian"). Tokyo: Kawade shobō shinsha.

Kinsey, Alfred, Wardell Pomeroy, and Clyde Martin. (1948). *Sexual Behavior in the Human Male*. Philadelphia: Saunders.

Klein, Fritz. (1997) [1993]. *Baisekusharu to iu ikikata* (*The bisexual option*). Trans. Kawano Makimi. Tokyo: Gendai shokan.

Kondō Takashi. (1954). "Danshoku henreki: aru sodomia no shuki" (My career in *danshoku*: notes on sodomy). *Fūzoku kurabu* (May): 143–49.

Kuia Sutadiizu Henshū Iin Kai (eds). (1996). "Kuia hisutorii" (Queer history). In *Queer Studies '96*. Tokyo: Nanatsumori shokan, 18–35.

Kusama Kei. (1987). "Rezubian tanjō monogatari" (A lesbian is born). In *Bessatsu takarajima* no. 64, *Onna wo ai suru onnatachi no monogatari* (Stories of women who love women). Tokyo: JICC Shuppankyoku, 47–53.

Leap, William L., and Tom Boellstorff. (2003). "Introduction: Globalization and 'New' Articulations of Same-Sex Desire." In *Speaking in Queer Tongues: Globalization and Gay Language*, edited by William L. Leap and Tom Boellstorff. Urbana: University of Illinois Press, 1–22.

Leupp, Gary. (1998). "'The Floating World is Wide. . .': Some Suggested Approaches to Researching Female Homosexuality in Tokugawa Japan (1603–1868)." *Thamyris* 5, no. 1: 1–40.

————. (1995). *Male Colors: The Construction of Homosexuality in Tokugawa Japan.* Berkeley: University of California Press.

Lionni, Leo. (1969). *Suimii (Swimmy).* Trans. Tanigawa Shuntarō. Tokyo: Nihon paburishingu.

Louis, Lisa. (1992). *Butterflies of the Night: Mama-sans, Geisha, Strippers, and the Japanese Men They Serve.* New York: Tengu Books.

Lunsing, Wim. (2005a). "The Politics of *okama* and *onabe*: Uses and Abuses of Terminology Regarding Homosexuality and Transgender." In *Genders, Transgenders, and Sexualities in Japan*, edited by Mark McLelland and Romit Dasgupta. London: Routledge, 81–95.

————. (2005b). "LGBT Rights in Japan." *Peace Review* 17, no. 2–3: 143–48.

————. (2001). *Beyond Common Sense: Sexuality and Gender in Contemporary Japan.* London: Kegan Paul.

Mackie, Vera. (2003). *Feminism in Modern Japan: Citizenship, Embodiment, and Sexuality.* Cambridge: Cambridge University Press.

Maree, Claire. (2004). "Same-Sex Partnerships in Japan: Bypasses and Other Alternatives." *Women's Studies* 33: 541–49.

Matsuzawa Goichi. (1997). "Meiji, Taishō, Shōwa, kindai fūzoku shuppan no rekishi" (Meiji, Taisho, Showa, a history of modern sexual-customs publishing). In *Ero no hon* (Erotic book), edited by Wani no ana. Tokyo: Wani no ana, 52–56.

McLelland, Mark. (2006). "A Short History of *Hentai*." *Intersections*, issue 12. Online: <http://wwwsshe.murdoch.edu.au/intersections/issue12/mclelland.html>.

————. (2005). *Queer Japan from the Pacific War to the Internet Age.* Lanham, MD: Rowman & Littlefield.

Miki Sōko, Saeki Yōko, and Mizoguchi Akiyo, eds. (1995.) *Shiryō Nihon ūman ribu shi* (Japan's women's lib history reference). 3 vols. Kyoto: Shōkadō shoten.

Mitsuhashi Junko. (2001). "Toransujendā daigaku kyōshi hantoshikan seiteki mainoriti no shakaiteki ukeirenitsuite no "jikken"" (A half-year period as a transgender university lecturer—'practice" for the social acceptance of sexual minorities). *Chūō hyōron* no. 236 (July).

Miyamoto Yuriko. (1979). *Miyamoto Yuriko zenshū,* vol. 23, *Nikki* 1 (The collected works of Miyamoto Yuriko: Diary 1). Tokyo: Shin Nihon shuppansha.

———. (1969). *Nihon no bungaku 45: Miyamoto Yuriko* (Japanese literature 45: Miyamoto Yuriko). Tokyo: Chūōkōronsha.

Mori Ōgai. (1971) [1909]. *Zenshū* (complete works), vol. 1, *Wita sekusuarisu* (Vita sexualis). Tokyo: Chikuma shobō.

———. (1972). *Vita Sexualis.* Trans. Sanford Goldstein. Tokyo: Charles Tuttle Co.

Morihara Taichi. (1953). "Ware ga guntai jidai no kaiko" (Nostalgia for my time in the army). *Kitan kurabu* (March): 94–97.

Nawa Kaori. (1987). *Rezubian bā no yoru to yoru* (Night in and night out at lesbian bars). In *Bessatsu takarajima* no. 64, *Onna wo ai suru onnatachi no monogatari*. Tokyo: JICC Shuppankyoku, 100–10.

Ochiai Keiko. (2001). "Hyōgen no jiyū to sabetsu no saiseisan" (Freedom of expression and reproduction of discrimination). *Shūkan kinyōbi* 376: 21.

Ōgiya Afu. (1958). *Sodomia banka* (Elegy to homosexuality). Tokyo: Shin'eisha.

Ōgura Yūko. (1987). "Yama ni sumu rezubian no hanashi" (Lesbians living in the mountains). In *Bessatsu takarajima* no. 64, *Onna wo ai suru onnatachi no monogatari*. Tokyo: JICC Shuppankyoku, 56–63.

Oikawa Kenji. (2001). "Densetsu no okama Tōgō Ken: Aiyoku to hangyaku ni moetagiru" (The legendary *okama* Tōgō Ken: burning with sexual desire and revolt). *Shūkan kinyōbi* no. 367 (15 June): 34–39.

Ōta Tenrei. (1981) [1957]. *Daisan no sei: sei wa hōkai suru no ka?* (The third sex: is sex breaking down?). Rev. ed. Tokyo: Ningen no kagakusha.

Ōtsuka Takashi. (1995). *Ni-chōme kara uroko: Shinjuku geisutoriito zakkichō* (Ni-chōme rediscovered: notes from Shinjuku's gay street). Tokyo: Shōeisha.

Pflugfelder, Gregory M. (1999). *Cartographies of Desire: Male-Male Sexuality in Japanese Discourse, 1600–1950*. Berkeley: University of California Press.

Queer Japan. (2000). "Hentai suru sarariiman" (Salarymen doing queer), special feature. Vol. 2 (April).

Reichert, Jim. (2006). *In the Company of Men: Representations of Male-Male Sexuality in Meiji Literature*. Stanford: Stanford University Press.

Robertson, Jennifer. (1998). *Takarazuka: Sexual Politics and Popular Culture in Modern Japan*. Berkeley: University of California Press.

———. (1999). "Dying to Tell: Sexuality and Suicide in Imperial Japan." *Signs: Journal of Women in Culture and Society* 25, no. 1 (Autumn): 1–35.

Roden, Donald. (1990). "Taisho Culture and the Problem of Gender Ambivalence." In *Japanese Intellectuals during the Inter-War Years*, edited by J. Thomas Rimer. Princeton, NJ: Princeton University Press, 37–55.

Saijō Michio, Ōgiya Afu, Ueshima Tsugi, Miwa Yōko, and Kawakami Seiko. (1955). "Zadankai: josei no homo makari tōru" (Roundtable: female homos here we go). *Fūzoku kagaku* (March): 148–57.

Sansaki Namiki. (1954). "Miniya karapa: Sodomii no kazekaoru" (*Minyak Kelapa*: A fragrant breeze of homosexuality). *Fūzoku kagaku* (May): 152–59.

Sasano Michiru. (1995). *Coming OUT!* Tokyo: Gentōsha.

Sataka Shin. (2001). "Koritsu—'koritsu wa osorenai ga rentai wo motomeru'" (Isolation: "not afraid of isolation, but seeking coalition"). *Shūkan kinyōbi* no. 376: 22.

Sawabe Hitomi (1996) [1990]. *Yuriko, dasuvidāniya: Yuasa Yoshiko no seishun* (Yuriko, *do svidanya*: Yuasa Yoshiko's youth). Tokyo: Gakuyō shobō.

Sei ishiki chōsa gurūpu. (1998). *Sanbyakujū nin no sei ishiki: Iseiaisha dewa nai onnatachi no ankēto chōsa* (The sexual consciousness of 310 people: a survey of women who are not heterosexual). Tokyo: Nanatsumori shokan.

Shiba Fumiko. (1997). "Nemurenu yoru no tame ni" (For sleepless nights). *Aniisu* (Anise) no. 4 (Summer): 110–11.

————. (1993). "Shōwa rokujū [sic] nendai rezubian būmu" (Lesbian boom in the 1960s). In *Tanbi shōsetsu, gei bungaku bukkugaido*, edited by Kakinuma Eiko and Kurihara Chiyo. Tokyo: Byakuya shobō, 290–291.

Shibata Tomo. (1999). "Japan's Wartime Mass Rape Camps and Continuing Sexual Human-Rights Violations." *U.S.-Japan Women's Journal English Supplement* no. 16: 48–86.

Shimokawa Kōshi. (1995). "Hentai no sōgō depāto *Kitan kurabu* kara *SM serekuto* ga ubugoe wo ageru made" (From *Kitan kurabu*, perversity's general department store, to *SM serekuto*'s first cry). In *Bessatsu takarajima* no. 240, *Sei media no 50-nen* (50 years of sex media). Tokyo: Takarajimasha, 48–55.

Standish, Isolde. (2000). *Myth and Masculinity in the Japanese Cinema: Toward a Political Reading of the "Tragic Hero."* Richmond, Surrey: Curzon.

Suganuma, Katsuhiko. (2006). "Festival of Sexual Minorities in Japan: A Revival of the Tokyo Lesbian & Gay Parade in 2005." *Intersections*, issue 12: <http://wwwsshe.murdoch.edu.au/intersections/issue12/katsuhiko.html>.

Summerhawk, Barbara, Cheiron McMahill, and Darren McDonald (eds). (1998). *Queer Japan: Personal Stories of Japanese Lesbians, Gays, Bisexuals, and Transsexuals*. Norwich, VT: New Victoria.

Sumi Tatsuya. (1949). *Dansho no mori* (Grove of male prostitutes). Tokyo: Hibiya shuppan.

Sunagawa Hideki, ed. (2001). *Parēdo: Tōkyō rezubian & gei par ē do 2000 kiroku* (Parade: a record of the Tokyo Lesbian & Gay Parade 2000). Tokyo: Potto shuppan.

Suzuki Michiko. (1983). "Rezubian no kai wo shusai shite jūnen" (Running a lesbian society for ten years). *Fujin kōron* 68, no. 1 (January): 340–44.

Takemura Tamio. (2004). "Aka-sen" (Red line). In *Sei no yōgoshū* (A guide to sex terminology), edited by Inoue Shōichi, Saitō Hikaru, Nagai Yoshikazu, and Furukawa Makoto. Tokyo: Kōdansha, 302–8.

Tamanoi, Mariko Asano. (1999). "Japanese Nationalism and the Female Body: A Critical Reassessment of the Discourse of Social Reformers on Factory Women." In *Women and Class in Japanese History*, edited by Hitomi Tonomura, Anne Walthall, and Wakita Haruko. Ann Arbor, MI: Center for Japanese Studies, 275–98.

Toyama Hitomi. (1999). *MISS dandi: otoko toshite ikiru joseitachi* (Miss dandy: women living as men). Tokyo: Shinchōsha.

Tsuruga Minako. (1995). "'Regumi Sutajio Tōkyō' de no hachi nenkan." (Eight years of "Regumi Studio Tokyo"). *Imago* 6, no. 12 (November): 46–51.

Ujiya Tomiyoshi, Kabiya Kazuhiko, Fujii Seiji, Sugita Hitoshi, Yamamoto Tatsuo, and Yoshimura Yutaka. (1953). "Nanshoku no yorokobi to nayami wo kataru: sodomia dai zadankai" (Grand *sodomia* conference: a discussion of the joys and agonies of homosexuality). *Fūzoku zōshi* (December): 165–78.

Warner, Michael. (1999). *The Trouble with Normal: Sex, Politics, and the Ethics of Queer Life*. New York: Free Press.

Watanabe, Tsuneo and Jun'ichi Iwata. (1989). *The Love of the Samurai: A Thousand Years of Japanese Homosexuality*, Trans. D. R. Roberts. London: GMP.

Welker, James. (2004). "Telling Her Story: Narrating a Japanese Lesbian Community." *Japanstudien* 16: 119–44.

———. (In press). "Lilies of the Margin: Beautiful Boys and Queer Female Identities in Japan." In *AsiaPacifiQueer: Rethinking Gender and Sexuality in the Asia-Pacifi*c, edited by Peter Jackson, Fran Martin, Mark McLelland, and Audrey Yue. Urbana: University of Illinois Press.

Yajima Masami, ed. (2006). *Sengo Nippon josō, dōseiai no kenkyū* (Postwar Japan cross-dressing, homosexuality research). Chūō daigaku shakaikagaku kenkyūjō kenkyū sōsho no. 16. Tokyo: Chūō daigaku shuppanbu.

———. (1999). *Josei dōseiaisha no raifu hisutorii* (Life histories of female homosexuals). Tokyo: Gakubunsha.

Yasuda Tokutarō. (1935). "Dōseiai no rekishikan" (A historical perspective on same-sex love). *Chūō kōron* (March): 146–52.

Yuasa Yoshiko, ed. (1978). *Yuriko no tegami* (Letters from Yuriko). Tokyo: Chikuma shobō.

INDEX

Page numbers in parentheses refer to the original context of endnotes not otherwise referenced in the entry.

ABOUT THE TRANSLATORS

Micah Auerback is a Ph.D. candidate in the Department of Religion at Princeton University. Along with his dissertation research in the history of Japanese Buddhism in the nineteenth and twentieth centuries, he also maintains an enduring interest in queer studies, and the more broadly conceived study of gender and sexuality, in and of Japan and Korea.

David d'Heilly is a writer, filmmaker, curator, and translator based in Tokyo and New York.

Takashi Fujita is a professional translator from Japanese to English. He lives in Sydney.

Joseph Hawkins has been the president of the board of directors of ONE National Gay and Lesbian Archives for the past three years. ONE Archives houses the largest collection of LGBT materials in the world and is the oldest such organization in the United States. Hawkins also teaches both in the Anthropology Department and in the Gender Studies Program at the University of Southern California in Los Angeles. He is currently writing an ethnography of his research on queer community in Japan, editing a film about ritual and *hadaka matsuri*, or naked festivals in Japan, and writing an accompanying study guide.

Todd A. Henry is assistant professor of history at Colorado State University. His teaching and research focus on the intersection of modern Japanese and Korean history, urban history, and the history of gender and sexuality. He is the author of "Sanitizing Empire: Japanese Articulations of Korean Otherness and the Construction of Early Colonial Seoul, 1905–19," *Journal of Asian Studies* 64, no. 3.

Wim Lunsing received his M.A. in Japanese studies from Leiden University, 1988, and his Ph.D. in anthropology from Oxford Brookes University, 1995. He has taught at Oxford Brookes and Copenhagen universities and was a research student at Kyoto Seika University (1991–1993) and a research fellow at Tokyo University (1996, 2001–2002). He is the author of *Beyond Common Sense: Sexuality and Gender in Contemporary Japan* (2001) and numerous papers on sexuality, gender, and research methods and ethics in Japan.

Mark McLelland lectures in sociology in the School of Social Sciences, Media, and Communication at the University of Wollongong. He is author of *Male Homosexuality in Modern Japan* (2000) and *Queer Japan from the Pacific War to the Internet Age* (2005), and the coeditor of *Japanese Cybercultures* (2003), *Genders, Transgenders, and Sexualities in Japan* (2005), and *AsiaPacifiQueer: Rethinking Sexuality and Gender in the Asia-Pacific* (forthcoming).

Katsuhiko Suganuma is a Ph.D. candidate in the Department of English with Cultural Studies at the University of Melbourne. His areas of research focus on contemporary Japanese sexuality politics, queer globalization, and postcolonial feminism. Some of his essays have appeared in *Intersections: Gender, History & Culture in the Asian Context*. He is currently working on his Ph.D. thesis, tentatively titled "The Politics of Global Desires: Intercultural Homo-Eroticism in Post-War Japan."

James Welker is currently working on a doctorate in the Department of East Asian Languages and Cultures at the University of Illinois at Urbana–Champaign. His publications include "Telling Her Story: Narrating a Japanese Lesbian Community," *Japanstudien* 16 (2004);

"From *The Well of Loneliness* to the *akarui rezubian*: Western Translations and Japanese Lesbian Identities," (with Beverley Curran) in *Genders, Transgenders, and Sexualities in Japan* (2005); "Beautiful, Borrowed, and Bent: Boys' Love as Girls' Love in *Shōjo* Manga" in *Signs* 31:3 (Spring 2006); and "Lilies of the Margin: Beautiful Boys and Queer Female Identities in Japan," in *AsiaPacifiQueer: Rethinking Gender and Sexuality in the Asia-Pacific* (forthcoming).

STUDIES OF MODERN JAPAN

Series Editor: Edward R. Beauchamp, University of Hawaii

Studies of Modern Japan is a multidisciplinary series that consists primarily of original studies on a broad spectrum of topics dealing with Japan since the Meiji restoration of 1868. Additionally, the series aims to bring back into print classic works that shed new light on contemporary Japan. In all cases, the goal is to publish the best scholarship available, by both established and rising scholars in the field, in order to better understand Japan and the Japanese during the modern period and into the future.

Editorial Advisory Board

William K. Cummings, George Washington University
Sin'ichi Kitaoka, Tokyo University
Sharon Minichiello, University of Hawaii
Masato Miyachi, Tokyo University
T. J. Pempel, University of California, Berkeley
Merry White, Boston University

Titles in the Series

Jews in the Japanese Mind: The History and Uses of a Cultural Stereotype, by David G. Goodman and Masanori Miyazawa

Chōshū in the Meiji Restoration, by Albert M. Craig

Japan and the Security of Asia, by Louis D. Hayes

The Web of Power: Japanese and German Development Cooperation Policy, by Kozo Kato

Unhappy Soldier: Hino Ashihei and Japanese World War II Literature, by David M. Rosenfeld

In the Shadow of the Miracle: The Japanese Economy since the End of High-Speed Growth, by Arthur J. Alexander

Spanning Japan's Modern Century: The Memoirs of Hugh Borton, by Hugh Borton

Agony of Choice: Matsuoka Yosuke and the Rise and Fall of the Japanese Empire, 1880–1946, by David J. Lu

A Yankee in Hokkaido: The Life of William Smith Clark, by John M. Maki

Roadblocks on the Information Highway: The IT Revolution in Japanese Education, edited by Jane M. Bachnik

Limits to Power: Asymmetric Dependence and Japanese Foreign Aid Policy, by Akitoshi Miyashita

Constructing Opportunity: American Women Educators in Early Meiji Japan, by Elizabeth Eder

The Return of the Amami Islands: The Reversion Movement and U.S.–Japan Relations, by Robert D. Eldridge

Life and Resources in America, by Mori Arinori; edited, annotated, and introduced by John E. Van Sant

Japan and Germany under the U.S. Occupation: A Comparative Analysis of the Post-War Education Reform, by Masako Shibata

Japan in a Dynamic Asia: Coping with the New Security Challenges, edited by Yoichiro Sato and Satu Limaye

Modern Japanese Theatre and Performance, edited by David Jortner, Keiko McDonald, and Kevin J. Wetmore Jr.

Murakami Haruki: The Simulacrum in Contemporary Japanese Culture, by Michael Seats

Queer Voices from Japan: First Person Narratives from Japan's Sexual Minorities, edited by Mark McLelland, Katsuhiko Suganuma, and James Welker